The Complete Book of

LONDON

Discover Britain's Capital City

*An ageing but indomitable
Churchill has kept an eye on
Big Ben and the Houses of
Parliament since being unveiled in
1973.
The clock tower housing the
13½-ton bell called Big Ben stands
at the north end of the New Palace
of Westminster, and a light shining
above the clock at night indicates
that Parliament is still in session.*

The Complete Book of

LONDON

Discover Britain's Capital City

◆ ◆ ◆

◆ ◆ ◆

AA

Published by The Automobile Association,
Fanum House, Basingstoke, Hampshire RG21 2EA

Editorial consultant: Richard Cavendish
Writers: LONDON AREA BY AREA: Paul Atterbury, Felix Barker,
Rosemary Burton, Russell Chamberlin and Bob Smythe;
INTRODUCTION, SPECIAL FEATURES, LONDON'S RIVER and
A LONDON DIRECTORY: Richard Cavendish
Special thanks are due to the London Tourist Board and Convention
Bureau for their help with the preparation of this publication.
Editor: Edwina Johnson

Typesetting by Microset Graphics Ltd.
Colour reproduction by Scantrans PTE Ltd., Singapore
Printed by Resopal Printers, Portugal

Published by The Automobile Association, Fanum House,
Basingstoke, Hampshire RG21 2EA

A CIP catalogue record of this book is available from the British
Library.

ISBN 0 7495 0395 5 (hardback)
ISBN 0 7495 0400 5 (softback)

Contents

Introduction

The Household Cavalry plays a key role in London's ceremonies.

Rich in history, heritage and character, London is one of the world's most rewarding cities to visit. Perhaps its most attractive characteristic is its remarkable variety. The city changes in atmosphere and style not merely from one district to another, but sometimes from one street to the next. The delights it offers to the eye and ear are varied, subtle and intense. In fine weather there are streets to walk, parks and gardens to linger in, the river to enjoy, pageantry to thrill to. In the wet or the cold there is the greatest concentration of historic and cultural attractions in the kingdom. Whether you are busy exploring history or art, shopping, or just sitting and watching the world go by, London has something to offer every season and mood.

London is the capital of the United Kingdom. Well within living memory it was the capital of an empire on which the sun never set and which encompassed a quarter of the entire population of the earth. This imperial past is the background to much of the splendour of the city's heritage today. It is also a factor in the city's cosmopolitan character. London has always attracted immigrants, from the rest of the country and the rest of the world. Today, one Londoner in every three was born somewhere else. The result is a rich mixture of traditions, customs and ways.

The city stands on the River Thames, about 40 miles (64km) inland from the North Sea as the crow flies, or 50 miles (80km) as the river runs. The river, providing easy access to the rest of the world, is the fundamental geographical reason for London's existence, and for most of its history the city has flourished as a great trading port.

Three Londons

There are three Londons, one inside the other. Sprawling out on either side of the Thames is the vast conurbation of Greater London, which covers more than 600sq miles (1,554 sq km). Within the roughly oval shape of Greater London, like a juicy nut inside its shell, is the central London area, of about 100sq miles (259sq km). Over to the eastern side of central London is the City of London, which is tiny — a little over 1sq mile (2.5sq km) in extent — where it all began.

Much of London has been built from local clay, which for centuries provided the city's bricks. The Thames flows from west to east, with many twistings and turnings, and divides London into northern and southern halves. The northern half is much the more important of the two. It contains most of the historic buildings: the Tower of London, the royal palaces, the Houses of Parliament. It also contains most of the theatres, the smartest shopping streets and the most prestigious office and residential areas.

This northern sector itself divides roughly into three: the West End, the City and the East End. The West End is the smart quarter of London in which to live, shop or be entertained. This is the elegant world of Mayfair, of Harrods and theatreland, of Soho and also the best restaurants and hotels.

The City is London's financial centre and the oldest quarter of London — centuries old when Mayfair was still covered in open fields and corn still grew in Chelsea. Once the most thickly inhabited area, it is now almost a ghost town at evenings and weekends. The resident population is only about 5,000, but 500,000 commute in every weekday to work in banks, insurance companies and offices. Some of the leading visitor attractions are in the City, including the Tower of London and St Paul's Cathedral.

The East End, to which the prevailing winds always bore London's smoke and grime, is traditionally the area of docklands and the poor working-class. The home of cockneys and rhyming slang, it used to be the polar opposite of the West End. The East End, however, was the area most severely damaged in the Second World War. After it, many families moved away to new towns outside London, and by 1960 the population was less than half what it had been at the beginning of the century. Much of the East End has been rebuilt and parts of the old docklands have been dramatically redeveloped with modern office blocks, yachting marinas and expensive housing.

London has grown and developed naturally over the years. It was never planned in a sweeping, overall way, in the manner of Paris, for example. Hence London's winding streets and small secretive alleyways and courtyards. Some areas of the West End were planned by developers in the 18th and 19th centuries, laid out in a tidy pattern of squares, crescents and terraces, but even there the stroller will find plenty of back streets and many charming mews. Almost one-third of London's total area is open space and it is easy to dodge out of a busy main street and find refuge for a while in a park or secluded square. In its main streets and quiet squares London is full of history and interest.

About This Book

The Complete Book of London has four main sections. On the following pages you will find chapters on the many different aspects of London, ranging from its history, royal connections and pageantry, to its hidden and curious side.

The next part is a guide to London's most popular tourist attractions, arranged by area. Each attraction is described in detail, with full information about opening times, where relevant. Locator maps and travel details are provided to help you find your way. Each attraction gives the name of its nearest tube station or stations, and an atlas reference. This locates the attraction either on the Central London street atlas, or on the Greater London conurbation atlas, both at the end of the book.

Atlas references are of two types; some consist of both a page and grid number, such as that given for the National Gallery, 172 B1. This refers to page 172, square B1 on the Central London street atlas. Other attractions have atlas references giving a page number only, such as The Queen's House, Greenwich. Its reference is 186, which means that it can be found on page 186, in the Greater London conurbation atlas.

The area by area guide to London's tourist attractions begins in Central London and then moves further afield, to Hampstead, Kew and other districts on London's perimeters. It ends with a description of all the major sights along the historic Thames, in an imaginary boat trip from Battersea Reach to Tower Bridge.

The third part of this book is a directory, giving practical information about travelling in London, shops and markets, pubs, entertainment and places to eat.

Finally, there are atlases of Central and Greater London and a theatreland map, to help you put the book to full practical use.

It could take most of a lifetime to get to know London really well. Best start now!

London's Past

◆ ◆ ◆

The Roman temple of Mithras, dedicated to the god of light, was used until at least AD350 (see also page 108).

The remains of the earliest town of London lie 20ft (6m) or more beneath today's street level, buried under the building layers, rubbish and clutter of 20 centuries. Extensive construction work during London's development boom in the 1980s led to many exciting discoveries, among them the remains of Shakespeare's original 'wooden O' — the Globe theatre on Bankside — and another Elizabethan theatre, the Rose. One excavation at Bucklersbury in the City revealed debris from the Blitz of 1941. Deeper down was charred evidence of the Great Fire of 1666. Deeper down still was a Roman jeweller's shop, where a tradesman made luxury items for his customers almost 2,000 years ago, when London was first born.

It was the Romans who created London and gave it its name — *Londinium* — soon after their successful invasion of England in AD43. At that time there were small British settlements along the Thames here and there, with others dotted about inland, but if there was a pre-Roman village on London's site, archaeologists have not yet found evidence of it.

The site of what would become the City of London was chosen with a sharp Roman eye to strategic and practical advantage, at the highest point to which ships from the Continent could navigate up the Thames with the tide. The river had been the main highway between Britain and the Continent since far back in prehistoric times. On the northern bank were two low hills, flanked by marshes and woods, with the River Fleet on the west running down to the Thames.

This was a readily defensible position. The two hills, tightly packed with buildings today, are Ludgate Hill and Cornhill. Between them ran the Walbrook stream, through beds of chickweed and watercress. Centuries later, both the Fleet and the Walbrook are buried underground.

The Romans built quays and warehouses on the river, which was considerably wider then than it is today. A bridge was constructed a few yards downstream from the present London Bridge. Traces of it have been found just to the south of the Monument. Roads radiated out to the rest of the Roman province of Britain from London, which developed into a lively, cosmopolitan commercial centre. When Queen Boudicca (Boadicea) of the Iceni and her tribesmen rose in revolt they sacked and burned the fledgling town, but it was quickly rebuilt.

Contrary to the usual Roman style, streets were not laid out in a neat grid pattern, but wandered about irregularly, as they have done ever since. There was a forum, or civic centre, where Leadenhall Market stands today, and the governor of Roman Britain had a grand palace a little to the north of Cannon Street station. Wild animal fights and gladiatorial combats thrilled a bloodthirsty audience at the amphitheatre, close to today's Guildhall. The town had a fort, bath-houses and temples.

In about AD200 a substantial wall was built around the landward side of the town. It was about 2 miles (3.2km) long. Its ends reached as far as the river, one where the Tower of London is now, the other close to today's Blackfriars Bridge. Sections of it can be admired in the Museum of London's grounds.

English and Danes

Harried by Picts, Irish and Saxons, Britain ceased to be part of the Roman Empire early in the 5th century AD. By the year 600 the whole of the eastern side of England was in the hands of various groups of Saxons (the original English). They established a new town of their own, called *Lundenwic*, outside the Roman town of *Londinium*. It stood to the west of the Fleet, along the Roman road which is now the Strand. Like *Londinium* before it, *Lundenwic* became a busy commercial centre, which drew merchants from abroad.

Missionaries from Rome, sent to convert the pagan Saxons to Christianity, arrived in Kent in 597. In 604 a bishop of London was appointed and a little wooden church was built on Ludgate Hill, dedicated to the Apostle Paul. It took many years to convert the Londoners, who were determined

*Both sides of a penny minted in King Alfred's reign. The letters of **Londonia** can be seen on the reverse.*

pagans, but St Paul's was to become the premier church of the City of London. St Paul is seen holding a sword in one hand and the banner of England in the other on the common seal of the City to this day, and his sword also appears in the first quarter of the City's coat-of-arms, a red cross on a white ground.

What was happening inside the Roman town meanwhile is not clear. It may have been abandoned altogether, for the Saxons disliked regimented Roman towns, whose gods were not their gods. Or a few people may still have lived in it.

In the 9th century the prosperous Saxon town was repeatedly raided and plundered by Vikings, who sailed up the Thames in hundreds of serpent-prowed longships to loot and burn. A Danish host spent the winter of 871-2 encamped in London. Alfred the Great rallied the English, subdued the Danes and, in 886, founded a fortified town inside the old Roman wall, along the bank of the Thames. It was as not as large as its Roman predecessor, and St Paul's was outside it, to the west. The Saxon town of *Lundenwic* was now abandoned — to be remembered as Aldwych, 'old town' — and London was reborn.

Edward The Confessor

Alfred's son and grandson were recognised as rulers of all England. London was not their capital, but it was an important town and they probably had a palace inside the Roman wall. The townspeople used to meet

Edward the Confessor's coffin is carried to Westminster Abbey, in this detail from the Bayeux Tapestry.

regularly on the open ground outside St Paul's to discuss the town's affairs. By the 11th century London was a leading exporter of wool to the Continent and was trading profitably with Scandinavia and Ireland.

The city had now to stand off renewed Danish attacks until Cnut (Canute), the Danish King, was accepted as ruler of England in 1016. London's solid wealth is indicated by the heavy taxes he imposed on it.

In 1042 the crown returned to an English king in the person of Edward the Confessor. A devout Christian, he built a new abbey church for the Benedictine monastery on Thorney Island, among marshes where the River Tyburn flowed into the Thames. This was 1½ miles (2.4km) west of London and separated from it by open country. The abbey was consecrated in 1065 and today we know it as Westminster Abbey. Next to the abbey the king built himself a palace. The effect was to create two Londons — the commercial centre inside the Roman wall, and the royal centre at Westminster. When Edward died at the beginning of the fateful year 1066, he was buried in his new church and his grave became a centre of pilgrimage.

The Medieval City

On Christmas Day 1066 William of Normandy was crowned king of the English in Westminster Abbey, as all his crowned successors have been. To keep London in subjection the new king built castles. The two on the western side — Baynard's Castle and the Montfichet Tower — have not survived, but the Conqueror's intimidating stronghold, the Tower of London, stands beside the

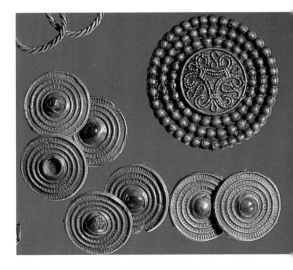

Pewter jewellery from 11th-century London.

river at London's south-eastern corner to this day.

The White Tower, at the heart of the Tower of London, stands 90ft (27m) high and its walls are 15ft (4.5m) thick at the base. In later centuries outer walls and towers were built round it. It was used as a state prison for political offenders.

The royal centre remained at Westminster, which in the Middle Ages became a regular meeting place of Parliament. London itself meanwhile developed rapidly as a crowded, clamorous, dirty and lively trading city. The richer merchants lived in stone mansions, but most of the houses were hovels of wood and mud, roofed with thatch. They were easily rebuilt after frequent fires. Pigs rooted in the garbage in the streets, and the privies drained into the Thames, from which the citizens drew their drinking water. Devasting epidemics broke out, the

worst being one of bubonic plague, or the 'Black Death', in the 14th century.

Craftsmen and traders tended to collect together; hence street names like Ironmonger Lane and Bread Street. The spires of more than a hundred churches climbed to the sky above the stink and hubbub. Suburbs grew up in Southwark and along the road to Westminster, where important noblemen and prelates built houses. Londoners liked to go hunting and hawking in the country outside the city wall. There were riotous football games on Shrove Tuesday, and regattas on the Thames at Easter. At dead of winter the citizens would go skating on the frozen marshes outside Moorgate.

St Paul's Cathedral was severely damaged by fire in 1087 and again in 1136, and rebuilt. Old St Paul's was even bigger than the present church. It was possibly the biggest church in the world in its day, with the tallest spire in Christendom, a wooden steeple 450ft (137m) high. The nave, or 'Paul's Walk', was used for business meetings and all kinds of secular purposes. Beer barrels were trundled through it, horses were led along it and pickpockets and prostitutes swarmed over it.

As the Middle Ages wore on, the London merchant guilds used their wealth to buy a growing degree of self-government from kings who were always needing money. There was a mayor of London by the 1190s and the running of the city was increasingly placed in the hands of aldermen, leading citizens who met in a building on the site of today's Guildhall.

Tudor London

The 16th century saw an astonishing growth in London's population, which by the end of it was above the 200,000 mark. The city was spilling over its walls like a pot boiling over, and it had become home to one in every 20 people living in England.

Parliament now regularly met at Westminster. The Lords used a room in the royal palace called the White Chamber, but the Commons had to meet in Westminster Abbey, in the chapter house or the refectory. When the Chapel of St Stephen went out of use in 1547, however, the Commons started to meet there. The original arrangement of the chapel has determined the physical layout of the Commons ever since. The Speaker's chair was placed where the altar had stood. Members bowed to it, as to an altar, and they sat facing each other in opposing rows, in the choir stalls. (The

chapel burned down, along with most of the Royal Palace of Westminster, in a catastrophic fire in 1834, after which the present Houses of Parliament were built.)

The Dissolution of the Monasteries meant that large tracts of Westminster Abbey's land in what is now the West End became available for building development. Along the Strand, now built up all the way between London and Westminster, stood town houses of great nobles, with gardens running down to the Thames. Over on the Southwark bank was an area of bawdy

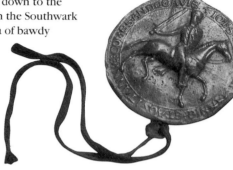

This charter was issued in 1215 by King John, with the royal seal attached. It gave Londoners the right to choose their own mayor every year.

houses and theatres, Shakespeare's Globe among them. In the City itself, meanwhile, merchants were handling 90 per cent of England's entire foreign trade, with cargoes going to and from America, Africa, the Mediterranean and the East. London businessmen organised the Muscovy Company in 1550 to trade with Russia. The Levant Company had its agents in the eastern Mediterranean. The East India Company was formed in 1600. And already foreign tourists were coming to London to see the Tower, Westminster Abbey and the palaces of Whitehall, Greenwich and Hampton Court.

'Bring Out Your Dead!'

By the 17th century London had become a single unit as the political, administrative and commercial capital of England. In the early hours of 5 November 1605 a Roman Catholic soldier of fortune named Guy Fawkes was found lurking in a cellar underneath the House of Lords, in close proximity to 36 barrels of gunpowder and a length of slow-match. Fireworks still arch into the sky on Guy Fawkes' Night (5 November) each year, commemorating his frustrated attempt to blow up Parliament and King James I.

During the Civil War the City of London supported Parliament, and its opposition to Charles I was a potent factor in his defeat. The king paid with his head, in Whitehall. At the

The Tower of London is seen on this plate, issued in praise of Queen Elizabeth I.

Restoration of the Monarchy in 1660, Charles II rode in triumph through a bedecked and rejoicing London. Two dramatic events soon followed — the Great Plague and the Great Fire.

The epidemic of bubonic plague in 1664-5 probably killed 100,000 people in London, or about one in every three living there. Over 8,000 died in one week when the plague was at its peak. Those who could, took their families out of town. A cross was roughly daubed on the doors of houses where plague struck. Carts rumbled through empty streets to the shout 'Bring out your dead!', carrying corpses to plague pits, where they were thrown into mass graves and covered with quicklime.

Disaster struck again in 1666, when a fire in a baker's shop in Pudding Lane turned into a raging holocaust, which in four days destroyed four-fifths of the City. Old St Paul's was burned down, as were dozens of other churches and 13,000 houses.

Plans to rebuild were swiftly afoot. Sir Christopher Wren designed a new St Paul's and a host of City churches in sumptuous splendour, but his scheme for an orderly new street plan with squares and avenues was not accepted. The City was reconstructed on the same higgledy-piggledy lines as before, but in brick instead of wood. Normal business was resumed and when a group of London merchants combined to form the Bank of England in 1694 the City's pre-eminence as a financial centre was assured.

Gin Lane

Georgian London was not only England's largest city and principal port, but the centre of all political, social, artistic, commercial and financial affairs of the country. All the talents were drawn to it. Dr Samuel Johnson ruled the roost among literary men; Sir Joshua Reynolds presided over the new Royal Academy; and the music of George Frederick Handel echoed from opera houses. Handsome squares and terraces were laid out in Mayfair and Bloomsbury in the measured, harmonious Classical style. The metropolis was expanding fast, and pleasant villages in London's country-side like Chelsea and Kensington were soon being swallowed up in the advancing sprawl.

London was an affluent and civilised city of coffee-houses, sedan chairs and luxury shops, with huge signs hanging over the streets and wares lavishly displayed in bow windows. At the same time it was crude, dangerous and filthy. Open sewers ran noxiously through the streets. The River Fleet was a stinking

*Above: Hogarth's famous **Gin Lane**. Below: **London's Burning**. The Great Fire was painted by a Dutch eye-witness.*

John Nash's stately Regent Street, as it was in the middle of the 19th century.

ditch crammed with refuse and the bloated carcasses of dogs and cats. The air was fouled further by the smoke of coal fires. Gin-drinking reached epidemic proportions and drunks sprawled, dead to the world, in alleyways. Hogarth pilloried 18th-century London life in prints like *Gin Lane* and *The Rake's Progress*.

The Infernal Wen

The 19th century would see an expansion of what the journalist William Cobbett called 'the Infernal Wen' on a scale dwarfing its previous history. In a major exercise in town planning early in the century, the architect John Nash designed Regent Street as a grand boulevard, running

north to Regent's Park with its graceful terraces. On the way he created both Piccadilly Circus and Oxford Circus. At the same time London's docks were extending busily downriver, and new bridges were being built over the Thames.

The stately precincts of Belgravia were laid out for the rich and aristocratic by the builder Thomas Cubitt. Multitudes of the poor, meanwhile, were crammed into appalling slums or 'rookeries', brought vividly to life in the novels of Charles Dickens. He described a London of fogs, grime, disease, crime and grinding poverty, which has lived on to haunt the imagination ever since.

Many of the poor had already been

gravitating to the East End in the 17th century. Now the expansion of the docks created a demand for casual labour and the population grew to meet it. Conditions were so abominable that in Bethnal Green in 1840 the average age of death was 16; a figure primarily reflecting the appalling rate of infant mortality.

Improvements were in store, however, brought about by vigorous Victorian reformers, and aided by the arrival of the railways in the 1840s. For the first time cheap transport was available, which enabled ordinary workers in London to live some distance from the centre. Villages like Hampstead and Highgate were engulfed as 'the Wen' spread further still, while the population of the centre began to decline and office blocks began to take the place of houses.

London became a safer place as streets were lit by gas and the Metropolitan Police and the London Fire Brigade were formed. The world's first underground railway opened in 1863, with steam trains puffing sootily between Paddington and Farringdon Street. The 1860s also saw the creation of a huge main drainage system for London by Sir Joseph Bazalgette. He was chief engineer of the Metropolitan

Off to the country: King's Cross Station, painted by George Earl in 1893. Well-to-do passengers are shown leaving London for grouse shooting in the country in August.

Board of Works, formed in 1855 as the first local authority for all London. It was replaced by the London County Council in 1889.

Victorian London was the world's largest city, the capital of the world's foremost industrial nation and the centre from which the biggest empire in history was ruled. Its power, wealth and bounding self-confidence are reflected in many of today's familiar landmarks, from the National Gallery and the Houses of Parliament to Nelson's Column, the Royal Albert Hall and Tower Bridge.

'London Can Take It'

The population of Inner London went on rising to a peak of 4.8 million in 1921, from which it then began to fall. Greater London's population peaked at close to 9 million in 1939. In the early days of the twentieth century the coming of the motor car drove hansom cabs and horse buses off the streets.

The First World War caused comparatively little physical damage to London, which at the time seemed serious enough. Enemy planes and zeppelins dropped almost 1,000 bombs on the city, killing 524 people and wounding 1,264 more. The Second

World War was a very different story. On 7 September 1940 hundreds of German bombers attacked London's docks, and the teeming streets of the East End took a pounding which cost 2,000 casualties that night. The Blitz went on through the winter and 20,000 people were killed. The slogan was 'London can take it', and London did. Underground stations were used as shelters. Meanwhile, the Guildhall was reduced to a shell and in one night 28 incendiary bombs fell on St Paul's.

After the war came a dreary period of austerity. The Festival of Britain was planned to raise the nation's spirits, and took place on what is now the site of the South Bank Arts Centre, in 1951. In 1956 the Clean Air Act made London the first smokeless zone in Britain and banished the old, impenetrable 'pea-souper' fogs. By the end of the decade a new age of affluence was dawning, with youth culture, pop music and permissiveness ushering in the 'Swinging London' of the 1960s. Up to this time London was still Britain's biggest port, but a sharp decline set in during the 1960s. A campaign to clean up the Thames started to bring fish and birds back to the river. With the city

A German Heinkel, seen above the Isle of Dogs during the London Blitz.

sinking at the rate of 12in (30cm) or so a century, new flood barriers had to be constructed in the 1970s.

Meanwhile, an alliance of property developers, town planners and architects created some of the ugliest and most uncomfortable buildings ever to mar London's skyline. Despite their work, London has come through it all with its spirit intact, as it has survived the changes and chances of every century before.

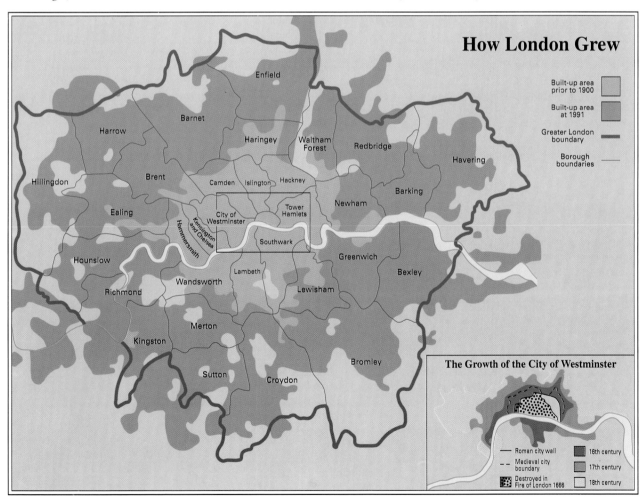

London's People

◆ ◆ ◆

London has drawn its inhabitants from virtually every corner of the globe. A glance through London's phone books will reveal the diversity of the city's population and give at least a rough idea of the relative balance of different national groups. With alphabetical entries running from Aaab-Richards to Zzaman, there are more than 16 pages of Smiths and close to four pages of Patels. Generations of foreign immigrants have contributed to the richness of London life.

All through its history London's population has been recruited as much or more by immigration as by natural increase. The bulk of this immigration has always been from other parts of England, as people have moved to London to better their lot. From the beginning, however, the city had a strongly cosmopolitan character, and the citizens of Roman London came from all over the Roman world: from Italy, France, Spain, North Africa and the Danube. Greek merchants played an important role in London's trade, while the slaves and small tradesmen and craftsmen were mostly Britons.

When Alfred the Great refounded London in the 9th century, he moved Saxon settlers in. Danes settled in the city, too, and the church of St Clement Danes in the Strand, outside the Roman wall, may have been founded for them.

The Norman Conquest brought with it an influx of Norman settlers and merchants. By 1130 there was a Jewish colony in London, centred on the street now called Old Jewry, not far from the Guildhall, where there was a synagogue. Jews had to live in constant fear of hostility and persecution. In an anti-semitic outbreak in 1262 the Jewry was looted and more than 500 people were murdered. In 1290 Edward I banished the Jews, and they did not return until the 17th century.

In medieval London colonies of foreign merchants lived in the city, including Germans, Gascons and Flemings. Financiers from northern Italy took over as bankers when the Jews departed. Dutch and Flemish craftsmen came to the city, and at the same time there was substantial migration there from the rest of England. Most of the City apprentices, for example, came from outside its boundaries.

Huguenots and Hats

From the 16th century onwards, Protestants fleeing religious persecution in France came to England. Many of them were skilled craftsmen. Nicknamed Huguenots, they settled in Soho, the Spitalfields district, Chelsea and Paddington. When Carnaby Street (later famous for its pop boutiques) was first laid out in the 1680s, many of the first inhabitants were Huguenots. Soho Huguenots took over a chapel originally built for Greek Christians who had settled in London (hence the name Greek Street). Long afterwards they built the French Protestant Church in Soho Square, designed by Sir Aston Webb and completed in 1893.

Other Huguenot refugees made homes for themselves in villages outside London, to the south-west. Along the banks of the River Wandle in Merton, and at Colliers Wood, they set up in the calico business. Ironically, Huguenot hatters living in Wandsworth in the 18th century almost cornered the market making red hats for cardinals in Rome.

The first substantial wave of Scottish immigration followed the accession of James I (James VI of Scotland) to the English throne in 1603. London has been a magnet to able and ambitious Scots ever since. A few Spanish and Portuguese Jews came to London in Charles I's time, fleeing the terrors of the Spanish Inquisition, and under the Commonwealth it was officially agreed that there should be no legal barrier to Jewish immigration into England. The handsome Spanish and Portuguese Synagogue in Heneage Lane, EC3, opened in 1701.

Bards and Baptists

In the 18th century Soho was described as so French in character that a visitor could easily think himself in France. Immigration to London from Wales, Scotland and Ireland was on the increase. In 1737 a Welsh charity school was opened in Clerkenwell Green for the children of poor Welsh families (it became the Marx Memorial Library in 1933). Welsh exiles in London took a leading part in the revival of the Welsh language and the burgeoning of Welsh nationalism, and staged the first Bardic ceremony on Primrose Hill in 1792.

Irish immigration rose dramatically in the 1840s, years of crippling famine in Ireland. A steady flow has continued ever since and there are sizeable Irish colonies today in Kilburn, Camden Town and Brent.

Italians, Germans and Swiss moved into Soho, many of them to work in the restaurants. The Saffron Hill area north of Holborn became an Italian preserve, with its own Roman Catholic church. The German Hospital in Ritson Road, E8, was opened in 1845 for poor German settlers. Elderly German doctors there placidly continued treating patients all through the First World War, but in the Second all the German staff were interned.

The London Scottish, Welsh and Irish rugby clubs date from between 1878 and 1898. The handsome Welsh Baptist Church in Eastcastle Street, W1, with its grand Corinthian pillars, was opened in 1889 to provide services in Welsh.

From East and West

From the 1880s until the outbreak of the First World War in 1914 thousands of Jewish families came to London, fleeing persecution in Russia and Eastern Europe. They homed in at first on the Whitechapel area and

London's Jewish community has had a chequered history.

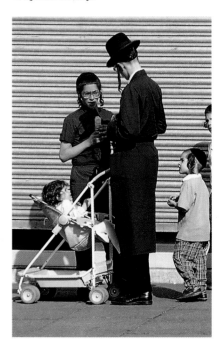

Spitalfields, but as they established themselves their children tended to move away to more comfortable suburbs, such as Golders Green. The Stamford Hill area in North London is home today to many Orthodox Jews, whose menfolk can be seen in broad-brimmed hats and long black coats.

The London docks area, meanwhile, attracted Lascars and Chinese seamen off ships in the port. A Chinese community had grown up in Limehouse by 1900, inspiring lurid tales of opium dens and sinister Chinamen by writers such as Sax Rohmer. Soho later replaced Limehouse as London's Chinatown.

Every generation of immigrants has left its stamp on London's character. After the Second World War the Earl's Court area virtually became an extension of Australia. Large numbers of immigrants arrived from the West Indies, Pakistan and Bangladesh, Uganda

First organised in the 1960s and held on August Bank Holiday, Notting Hill Carnival is Europe's biggest of its kind.

and Cyprus, a development partly sparked off in the 1950s by London Transport's decision to recruit labour in the Caribbean. The annual Notting Hill Carnival and the mosque in Regent's Park are just two of the additions to the London scene made by yet another wave of incomers.

Royal London

◆ ◆ ◆

Royal pageantry: the iron gates and stately pillars of Buckingham Palace make a regal setting for the Foot Guards in their splendour of scarlet.

The history of London is bound up with the annals of kings and queens. Royal palaces grace Westminster and Kensington. The principal parks are royal property and the crown estate owns 300,000 acres (121,500ha) of London land, while much of London's pageantry is royal. From the royal tombs in Westminster Abbey to the Serpentine in Hyde Park and the Household Cavalry jingling down The Mall, royalty makes its mark on London life.

For more than 400 years the principal royal residence in London was the Palace of Westminster. It was begun originally by Edward the Confessor, in about 1050, as a residence from which he could keep a close eye on the construction of Westminster Abbey. William the Conqueror and his successors also lived in the palace. The Conqueror's son, William Rufus, built Westminster Hall, which is still standing. For many centuries it was crowded with lawyers, judges, jurors and witnesses, as the place where the law courts met. Charles I was tried and condemned in the hall in 1649, and it was here that coronation banquets were held on the accession of each monarch until King George IV's time. On such occasions the royal champion would ride dramatically into the hall in full armour, his horse's hooves ringing on the stone floor, and throw down a mailed gauntlet to challenge to mortal combat anyone rash enough to dispute the new sovereign's right to the throne. There is no record of anyone ever venturing to pick up the gauntlet.

Tombs and a Zoo

Westminster Abbey is packed with royal associations and memories. Every coronation since 1066 has been celebrated in this great church, and the abbey's portrait of Richard II is the earliest contemporary likeness of an English king to have survived.

Many of England's kings and queens are buried in the abbey, from Edward the Confessor, its founder, to George II, who died in 1760 and was the last monarch to be interred there. Buried with Queen Anne are her 17 children, all of whom died in infancy. Also here are the bones of the Princes in the Tower, believed to be the pitiful remains of the boy-king Edward V and his younger brother Richard, who are thought to have been murdered in the Tower in 1483.

On a happier note, in 1947 Queen Elizabeth II, then Princess Elizabeth, married Lieutenant Philip Mountbatten here in a ceremony of glittering splendour before a congregation of 2,500 people. Crowds 50 deep lined The Mall and Whitehall as the princess drove to the abbey in the Irish State Coach. Later, Princess Margaret and Princess Anne were both married in the abbey, but Prince Charles chose St Paul's for his wedding to Princess Diana in 1981.

The Tower of London was used as a royal residence until the early 17th century, and it is still officially a royal palace. Henry VI was murdered in the Wakefield Tower in 1471, while saying his prayers. Two of Henry VIII's wives, Anne Boleyn and Catherine Howard, were beheaded in the Tower and Traitor's Gate yawned threateningly for Anne Boleyn's daughter, the young Princess Elizabeth, in 1554.

The Tower was also the home of the royal menagerie. This collection of wild animals was housed there until the 19th century, when it was transferred to Regent's Park Zoo. Members of the public were let in to see the animals when they were at the Tower. In 1609 there were lions and leopards, a jackal, mountain cats and a few moth-eaten eagles and owls living there.

Tudors and Stuarts

The medieval kings of England had country residences within easy reach of London. Edward II and Edward III both spent time pleasurably at Eltham Palace, not far from Greenwich, which was substantially enlarged in the 15th century. Greenwich Palace, known as Placentia, 'the pleasant place', was a favourite home of the Tudors. Henry

In its warmth of red brick, Hampton Court (above) is one of the royal palaces which bears the imprint of Henry VIII, seen here in a masterly portrait by Holbein.

VIII was born there in 1491, and so was his daughter Elizabeth, in 1533. Here, too, Henry signed Anne Boleyn's death warrant. Greenwich was Elizabeth I's main summer residence; she in her turn signed the death warrant of her cousin Mary, Queen of Scots, while staying here. Greenwich was also the scene of Sir Walter Raleigh's gallant gesture in putting his cloak down on a puddle to let Elizabeth walk dryshod. James I gave Greenwich Palace to his queen, Anne of Denmark, and Inigo Jones designed the Queen's House for her, which still survives in Greenwich Park.

The Tudor gatehouse still stands in Old Palace Yard, off Richmond Green, but little is left of Richmond Palace, the old Royal Palace of Sheen, where Edward III died in 1377. Henry VII was particularly fond of it. He rebuilt it after a fire in 1499 and renamed it Richmond Palace. Henry died in the palace in 1509, and the area has been known as Richmond ever since.

Henry VIII, who spent much of his boyhood at Richmond, was a redoubtable builder of palaces. When fire swept through the old wooden buildings of the Royal Palace of Westminster in 1512, he built Bridewell Palace at Blackfriars instead (where Unilever House is now). When Cardinal Wolsey fell from favour in 1529, however, the king took the opportunity to possess himself of the cardinal's opulent houses of Hampton Court and York Place. He made both of them even bigger and more splendid than before, and rechristened the latter the Palace of Whitehall. It stood on the river bank north of the present Houses of Parliament, and with its gardens and orchards, its real tennis court and its tiltyard for jousting, it became the principal Tudor and Stuart residence in London, a rambling warren of more than 2,000 rooms.

Henry also acquired the site of the leper hospital of St James in 1531 and built a comfortable brick manor house there. St James's Palace, with its original gatehouse, still stands at the foot of St James's Street, guarded by sentries. In 1538 Henry built Nonsuch Palace in Sutton as a hunting seat and a place for entertaining foreign visitors. It stood where Nonsuch Park is now, but nothing is left of the house.

The only substantial surviving part of Whitehall Palace is the Banqueting House, designed for James I by Inigo Jones and completed in 1622. On 30 January 1649 Charles I stepped out through one of its windows onto the scaffold erected for his beheading. Oliver Cromwell subsequently occupied Whitehall Palace as Lord Protector, and died there. After the Restoration in 1660 Charles II moved in, with his mistresses. It was from Whitehall Palace that James II stole away from London for the last time in 1688. Ten years later the palace burned to the ground after a serving-woman left clothes drying too close to the fire.

No attempt was made to rebuild it. The new king, William III, suffered from asthma and disliked riverside locations. He had taken over Nottingham House in Kensington (now Kensington Palace), and Sir Christopher Wren and Nicholas Hawksmoor were appointed to rebuild it and lay out the grounds. (Wren was also employed to build new state apartments at Hampton Court.) Rotten Row in Hyde Park was originally the *route du roi*, William III's private road to Kensington Palace, along which he liked to ride. It was lit by lamps at night to discourage highwaymen.

Queen Anne spent much time at Kensington Palace, where she died in 1714 of an apoplexy brought on by over-eating. She had also been fond of St James's Palace and her successors, the first two Georges, enjoyed both places. George II and his queen would go strolling in The Mall, joined by crowds of Londoners. After the destruction of the Palace of Whitehall, St James's became the official London residence of the sovereign.

Rustic Idylls

While the future George II was Prince of Wales, he and his wife, the German princess Caroline of Ansbach, lived in Richmond, where the charming terrace known as Maids of Honour Row was built for her ladies-in-waiting. Queen Caroline, as she became in 1727, was an enthusiastic landscape gardener. She

had the Serpentine created in Hyde Park, by damming the Westbourne stream, and the royal family kept two yachts on the newly made lake. At Kensington she had the grounds improved and the Round Pond, which has delighted generations of children and model boat enthusiasts, was constructed at her request.

King George II and Queen Caroline were the last royals to live at Hampton Court. They had another, much smaller and more intimate home in Kew. Here the queen leased the small, 17th-century Dutch House, now known as Kew Palace and the smallest of England's royal palaces. It was Queen Caroline's daughter-in-law, Augusta, Princess of Wales, who first laid out the botanical gardens at Kew. This was the beginning of Kew Gardens as we know them.

George III succeeded his grandfather in 1760 after the latter's death at Kensington Palace, in his privy. The new king abandoned Kensington and bought Buckingham House (now known as Buckingham Palace) as his principal London home; 14 of his 15 children were born there. In the summer he and Queen Charlotte liked to enjoy rural simplicity at Kew, where the older children were taught the rudiments of gardening and agriculture — not subjects in which they grew up to take a marked interest. The queen

Kensington Palace became a favourite royal residence from the late-17th century until the reign of George III in the 18th.

enjoyed giving tea parties in the royal cottage which still stands in Kew Gardens. It was at Kew in 1765 that George III suffered the first bout of the madness that would eventually engulf him.

'Above the Shop'

George IV was born in St James's Palace and spent his childhood at Buckingham House and Kew. He was married in St James's Palace, spending his wedding night in a drunken stupor lying in the fireplace. He became Regent for his father in 1811 and commissioned his favourite architect, John Nash, to create Regent Street and Regent's Park. He employed Nash to turn Buckingham House into Buckingham Palace at colossal expense, but died before the work was finished. He was succeeded by his brother, William IV, who had been living at Clarence House in St James's (which Nash had also rebuilt for him).

Queen Victoria was born and grew up at Kensington Palace, where her bedroom, with her toys and dolls' house, can still be seen. The dolls were the little girl's substitutes for the friends she was denied, but she enjoyed

It was Queen Victoria who made Buckingham Palace the main royal home in London.

riding her donkey in Kensington Gardens. It was at Kensington, in her dressing-gown at six o'clock in the morning, that the 18-year-old princess was told of her accession to the throne.

The new queen promptly moved into Buckingham Palace, where she held her first levee and had her hand kissed nearly 3,000 times (as she noted excitedly in her diary). Although the drains were defective, the toilets stank and many of the 1,000 windows would not open, Victoria loved Buckingham Palace and since her reign the 600-room house has been the royal family's main London home. George V was not especially fond of it, and once confided to a courtier that he would be quite happy to pull it down, sell off the grounds and use the money to rebuild Kensington Palace. In Buckingham Palace he remained, however, rising punctually at seven o'clock every morning, sitting down to breakfast at nine, filling his day with meetings and taking a brisk walk in the garden after lunch.

During the Second World War, King George VI and Queen Elizabeth refused to flee abroad and remained in Buckingham Palace. It was bombed in the Blitz, to the relief of the queen, who said she could now 'look the East End in the face'. The royal visits to bombed-out Londoners helped to keep morale high, and on 13 May 1945 an enormous crowd gathered in front of the palace to celebrate the end of the war in Europe and to cheer the Royal Family, who appeared on the balcony. Similar royal appearances are made at coronations, royal weddings and other notable occasions.

KINGS AND QUEENS FROM 1485 TO THE PRESENT

DYNASTIES	REIGNS	PERIODS
Tudors		
Henry VII	1485-1509	Tudor 1485-1603
Henry VIII	1509-1547	
Edward VI	1547-1553	
Mary I ('Bloody Mary')	1553-1558	
Elizabeth I	1558-1603	Elizabethan 1558-1603
Stuarts		
James I	1603-1625	Jacobean 1603-1625
(James VI of Scotland)		
Charles I	1625-1649	Carolean 1625-1685
The Commonwealth	1649-1660	
Charles II	1660-1685	
James II	1685-1688	Jacobean 1685-1688
William III (of Orange)	1688-1702	William-and-Mary 1688-1702
(and Mary II, 1688-1694)		
Anne	1702-1714	Queen Anne 1702-1714
Hanoverians		
George I	1714-1727	Georgian 1714-1811
George II	1727-1760	
George III	1760-1820	
George IV	1820-1830	Regency 1811-1837
William IV	1830-1837	
Victoria	1837-1901	Victorian 1837-1901
Edward VII	1901-1910	Edwardian 1901-1910
House of Windsor		
George V	1910-1936	
Edward VIII	1936	
George VI	1936-1952	
Elizabeth II	1952-	

St James's Palace has not been used extensively as a royal home since the early 19th century, though Queen Victoria was married there. Marlborough House and Clarence House, in St James's, have both been used by royalty. Edward VII lived at Marlborough House as Prince of Wales. Queen Alexandra spent her widowhood there, as did Queen Mary, King George V's widow. She died there in 1953.

Prince Charles and Princess Diana, and other royals, have apartments at Kensington Palace. The main focus of interest, however, remains Buckingham Palace, where the royal family live 'above the shop', as Prince Philip remarked; for most of the rooms are offices for staff. Royal garden parties are held in the grounds and the Changing of the Guard is one of the capital's most popular tourist attractions.

The Royal Family appear on the balcony of Buckingham Palace on state occasions.

Pageantry and Tradition

◆ ◆ ◆

The most glamorous and spectacular pageantry in London surrounds royal coronations and weddings, but every year brings a host of lively regular events. They range from set-piece historic spectacles like Trooping the Colour and the State Opening of Parliament to much smaller, traditional, and sometimes eccentric observances. With its major festivals and sporting events as well, London has no shortage of occasions to attract visitors.

London's most impressive annual military parade is the Trooping the Colour (it is not correct to call it the Trooping *of* the Colour), which is staged on Horse Guards Parade in June to mark the sovereign's official birthday. It has taken place regularly since 1805, the days of King George III, and goes back ultimately to the military custom of parading, or 'trooping', the regimental standard past the soldiers, so that they would recognise it as a rallying point in the confusion of battle.

The five regiments of Foot Guards — Grenadier, Coldstream, Scots, Irish and Welsh Guards, in order of seniority — take it in turn to provide the colour and the escort. There are massed bands and the Household Cavalry also takes part, with a mounted band. More than 1,400 soldiers, 400 bandsmen and 200 horses are involved in arcane and elaborate drill, as long lines of guardsmen stamp and wheel, slow march and quick march. The cavalry parades past the Queen in splendid array — plumes tossing, breast-plates gleaming, bits and bridles jingling.

Trooping the Colour on Horse Guards Parade is London's most glittering military event.

There is a ballot for tickets, which are as rare as snow in August, but you can see the glitter of it all along the route, from Buckingham Palace down The Mall to Horse Guards Parade, and back again.

The Life Guards parade in scarlet tunics and white-plumed helmets. The regiment's history goes back to the 17th century.

On Guard

It is perfectly acceptable to talk about the Changing *of* the Guard at Buckingham Palace, a particularly powerful magnet to tourists, who turn up in busloads. The ritual again involves the Foot Guards, though other units are sometimes invited to take a turn. The purpose of the ceremony, at 11.30am daily from April to the middle of August, and on alternate days from the middle of August until April, is to replace the previous day's sentries, both here and at St James's Palace. A regimental band plays while the new guard is posted. A ceremonial guard-changing (called Mounting the Guard) also takes place every day at Horse Guards in Whitehall, where the sentries, seated motionless on their patient horses, are another popular visitor attraction.

On ceremonial occasions the Foot Guards wear scarlet tunics and towering black bearskins, but they have different coloured bearskin plumes: white for the Grenadiers, red for the Coldstream, blue for the Irish, green and white for the Welsh, no plume for the Scots. The regiments also have different collar and shoulder badges.

The Household Cavalry consists of two regiments. The Life Guards wear scarlet tunics, with white plumes in their headdress, while the Blues and Royals have blue tunics and red plumes. Their mounted bands are led by skewbald horses carrying magnificent drums of solid silver, with trumpeters on grey horses and bandsmen resplendent in scarlet and gold. All seven guards regiments have extremely distinguished fighting records.

Parliament and Yeomen

The Foot Guards and the Household Cavalry escort the Queen to the State Opening of Parliament every year (in November, usually). The Queen drives from Buckingham Palace by way of The Mall and Whitehall to Parliament Square in the Irish State Coach. The cellars of the Houses of Parliament are searched beforehand by the Yeomen of the Guard, a ritual that has been performed ever since the alarming discovery of Guy Fawkes and his explosives in 1605. The royal procession to the House of Lords includes the Heralds and Pursuivants in their gorgeous panoply, the Earl Marshal (the Duke of Norfolk), who is in charge of state ceremonials, and other dignitaries. The members of the House of Commons are summoned to attend by the Gentleman Usher of the Black Rod, whose invitation is accepted only after the door of the Commons' chamber has been slammed in his face as a mark of the Commons' independence. The members proceed unhasting to the Lords, where the Queen reads her speech from the throne, setting out the government's programme for the coming session.

The Irish State Coach, made in Dublin in the 1850s, was bought by Queen Victoria specially for this ceremony. The older Gold State Coach was built for George III and is always used in coronations. George V bought the Glass State Coach in 1910 and it is often used for royal weddings. The state coaches can normally be admired at the Royal Mews in Buckingham Palace Road.

The Yeomen of the Guard are the world's oldest surviving royal bodyguard, formed by Henry VII in 1485. They wear a scarlet Tudor uniform, embroidered with royal emblems in gold. The other royal bodyguard seen on ceremonial occasions is the Honourable Corps of Gentlemen at Arms, founded by Henry VIII in 1509. They dress in skirted red coats and helmets with white plumes, and carry ceremonial battle-axes. They keep their helmets on at all times, even in church. Both bodyguards are recruited from retired members of the armed forces.

The Yeomen of the Guard are a separate body from the Yeomen Warders ('Beefeaters') of the Tower of London, who wear similar Tudor uniform. They carry out the 700-year-old Ceremony of the Keys every night, when the gates of the fortress are formally locked.

Wreaths for Remembrance

On the last Sunday in January each year the execution of Charles I is commemorated with services at the Banqueting House in Whitehall and in Trafalgar Square, where a wreath is laid at the king's statue. Clowns in full make-up and costume attend the service at Holy Trinity Church, Dalston, E8, in February when a wreath is laid at the memorial to Joseph Grimaldi, the

Clowns at their annual church service.

father of modern clowning. The statue of Charles II at Chelsea Hospital is decked with oak leaves for Oak Apple Day on 29 May.

A moving occasion is the annual laying of wreaths of poppies at the Cenotaph in Whitehall on Remembrance Sunday in memory of those who fell in the two World Wars. The ceremony is attended by the Queen and other members of the Royal Family, leading politicians and service and ex-service personnel, with massed bands. On the first stroke of 11 o'clock from Big Ben, a single gun is fired to mark the beginning of the two-minute silence. Then a second gun is fired and bugles sound the *Last Post*.

Guarded by bemedalled pikemen, this 18th-century golden coach is a highlight of the annual Lord Mayor's Show.

the Queen is greeted by the Lord Mayor, who presents the hilt of the Pearl Sword, said to have been given to the City by Queen Elizabeth I, in acknowledgement of royal overlordship of the City. The Queen touches the hilt and the Lord Mayor then carries the sword before her.

Sermons and Swans

Besides these grand occasions, there are all sorts of lesser ceremonies, left over from days gone by and still warmly cherished. One of the most eccentric of them is the Lion Sermon, which is preached in the City Church of St Katharine Cree in October, according to the will of a 17th-century Lord Mayor, Sir John Gayer. This wealthy merchant had a miraculous escape from a lion while travelling in the East and left money to the poor, on condition that a sermon on his escape be delivered every year, as it still is.

Each April the Lord Mayor places a fresh quill in the hand of the statue of John Stow in the Church of St Andrew Undershaft. Stow was a London tailor and author of the notable *Survey of London* of 1598. July sees the Master and brethren of the Vintners' Company tread delicately on foot from their livery hall in Upper Thames Street to the Church of St James, Garlickhythe, each carrying a nosegay against disagreeable odours. Ahead of them goes a porter in top hat and white smock, wielding a besom with which he sweeps the road so that the august procession does not tread in anything unpleasant.

In this procession are the company's barge-master and swan-markers, who take part in the annual custom of swan upping on the Thames. Many of Britain's swans are royal birds and belong to the Queen, but some are owned by the Vintners and some by the Dyers. The cygnets belonging to the two livery companies are marked on the beak every summer by the royal swan-keeper and the companies' swan-markers, who set off up river from Sunbury in traditional costume.

Another odd relic of the past is the Blessing of the Throats in the Roman Catholic Church of St Etheldreda in Ely Place, on St Blaise's Day in February. A special service is held, at which sufferers from throat afflictions are blessed by a priest and touched with two unlit candles, held in the shape of a

City Pageantry

The most spectacular annual event in the City is the Lord Mayor's Show in November. A new Lord Mayor is chosen every year and in the Middle Ages he had to present himself to the king for approval, in what became a stately progress. For centuries he travelled to Westminster by river, attended by City livery companies in their elegant barges. Nowadays he rides to the Royal Courts of Justice in the Strand in his sumptuous golden coach, made in the 18th century, drawn by six massive Shire horses and horribly

uncomfortable. (At other times it can be seen in the Museum of London.) The Lord Mayor is escorted by pikemen and musketeers of the Honourable Artillery Company in their 17th-century uniforms, and preceded by floats and bands. The theme for the floats is chosen each year by the new Lord Mayor himself. The route of the procession is from the Guildhall, past Mansion House and St Paul's and along Fleet Street.

Ceremony also attends visits to the City by the sovereign, who halts at the site of Temple Bar in Fleet Street. There

In traditional costume, the swan uppers carry out the annual census of swan families on the Thames.

cross. There is a grimmer note to the Tyburn Walk in April, when a silent procession makes its way on foot from the Old Bailey to Bayswater Road in memory of Roman Catholics executed for their religion at Tyburn in the 16th and 17th centuries. The procession follows the route that the condemned took on their way from Newgate Prison to the gallows.

Easter Bonnets and Veteran Cars
'Oranges and lemons say the bells of St Clement's' in March, at a special children's service at St Clement Danes in the Strand. Easter sees a 2 mile (3.2km) procession of floats and bands wind its way through Battersea Park with majorettes, clowns and Easter bonnets in the Easter Parade; while the Harness Horse Parade in Regent's Park brings out equines in their best finery, from Shetland ponies to lumbering dray horses.

The Notting Hill Carnival erupts on August Bank Holiday. It began modestly in 1965 and soon grew into a lively celebration of Caribbean culture with steel bands, limbo dancers and stalls selling West Indian delicacies. Dripping with cascades of pearl buttons, Pearly

Kings and Queens attend the Costermongers' Harvest Festival at St Martin-in-the-Fields. In November, cars of astonishing antiquity are burnished till their gaskets squeak in order to set off from Hyde Park Corner and toot and stagger their way to Brighton in the Veteran Car Run. The event goes back to 1896, when it ceased to be

Cockney finery: Pearly Kings and Queens in costumes covered with pearl buttons.

necessary for horseless carriages to be preceded on the highway by a man waving a red flag.

Arts and Sport
Numerous arts festivals illuminate the London scene. In the summer the City of London Festival concentrates on music and dance, with concerts and recitals in St Paul's, the Barbican Centre and other City venues. Down river a little earlier in the year, the Greenwich Festival presents music from classical to reggae, with plenty of other lively events. At the Royal Albert Hall the Promenade Concerts fill the summer evenings with glowing sound and the 'Last Night of the Proms' is celebrated with spirited singing of *Rule Britannia* and *Land of Hope and Glory*.

At Earl's Court the Boat Show and the Ideal Home Exhibition liven up the early months of the year. So do the Chinese New Year fire-crackers and lion-dancers in Soho. The calendar's major sporting events run from the Boat Race, the London Marathon and the FA Cup Final, to Wimbledon and the Horse of the Year Show. Christmas lights sparkle in Regent Street and carols are sung round the Norwegian Christmas tree in Trafalgar Square in December. The annual Christmas Day Swimming Race in the Serpentine brings the year to a shivering close.

The Famous and the Infamous

◆ ◆ ◆

London has been a magnet to ability and ambition for centuries. Men and women with careers to make in politics and business, the professions, the arts, the stage and every walk of life have come to London to make them. Refugees from other countries have sheltered or settled in London. The capital's roll of fame naturally also has its shady side.

One of the pleasures of strolling in London is to spot the blue plaques which mark houses where famous people were born, lived or died. The first plaque was put up in 1867 at 24 Holles Street, W1, where Lord Byron was born in 1788. Today, some streets fairly bristle with plaques. Former residents of South Street in Mayfair, for example, include the 18th-century statesman Charles James Fox, Lord Lucan, Commander of the British Cavalry division at the Charge of the Light Brigade in 1854, the great 19th-century medical reformer Florence Nightingale, and the Victorian courtesan Catherine Walters, familiarly known as 'Skittles'.

Accidents of proximity produce all sorts of contrasts and associations. Beatrix Potter's childhood home was in Bolton Gardens, SW5. This is just off The Boltons, whose past residents have included Douglas Fairbanks Junior and the 19th-century singer Jenny Lind, otherwise known as 'the Swedish nightingale'. Dame Agatha Christie lived for many years unobtrusively round the corner, at Christie Cottage in Creswell Place. Sir Winston Churchill's last home was at 27/28 Hyde Park Gate, SW7. The sculptor Sir Jacob Epstein lived for years a few doors away, at No. 18, while the novelist Virginia Woolf was born at No. 22.

Artists in Residence

Many artists have been drawn to London, to paint the city or to live and work in it. Canaletto came from Venice in 1746 and spent much of the next 10 years in London, staying at 41 Beak Street, Soho, and painting London views. In 1870 the French Impressionist, Camille Pissarro, fled to South London from the Franco-Prussian War. He stayed at 65 Palace Road, Norwood, and painted local scenes. Vincent Van Gogh stayed at 87 Hackford Road, Lambeth in 1873, while working for an art dealer. Here he fell hopelessly in love with his landlady's daughter.

This view of Westminster Bridge is by Antonio Canaletto, the Venetian painter who lodged in Soho.

John Constable, who came to London from Suffolk, lived in Charlotte Street, W1, but loved the country air of Hampstead. He would rent a cottage there in summer, and it was here that he painted some of his best-known works. From 1827 he had a house in Well Walk, Hampstead, and he is buried in St John's churchyard.

Dante Gabriel Rossetti had rooms at 17 Red Lion Square, WC1 in 1851, later occupied by two of his friends in the Pre-Raphaelite Brotherhood, Edward Burne-Jones and William Morris. The firm of Morris and Co started at No. 8. Morris later moved to Kelmscott House in Upper Mall, beside the river in Hammersmith.

The 'Fitzrovia' area, near Fitzroy Square, W1, became a rival to Chelsea as an artists' quarter after the foundation of the Slade School of Art in Gower Street in 1871. Practically every leading British artist of the period studied there. Augustus John had a studio at 8 Fitzroy Street, and Matthew Smith had one at No. 2.

Walter Sickert, who loved to paint what he called 'the most wonderful and complex city in the world', occupied a studio at 10 Glebe Place, Chelsea, in 1890, but later moved to Camden Town, where he lived at 6 Mornington Crescent. He held meetings in his Fitzroy Street studio of what became known as the Camden Town Group, whose members painted scenes of working-class London life.

The Bloomsbury Group of writers and artists moved to this same part of London. Lytton Strachey lived at 42 Gordon Square. Duncan Grant and Vanessa Bell had a studio at 8 Fitzroy Street from 1920 to 1940, while Virginia Woolf and her husband Leonard occupied 52 Tavistock Square (Charles Dickens had lived in this square in the 1850s). John Maynard Keynes was based for 30 years at 46 Gordon Square.

Hampstead had a lively artists' colony in the 1930s. Barbara Hepworth worked at 7 Mall Studios with her husband, Ben Nicholson. Henry Moore lived at 11a Parkhill Road, and Paul Nash at 3 Eldon Grove. When the German school of architecture, art and design known as Bauhaus was closed by the Nazis in 1933, two of its most influential members, Walter Gropius and László Moholy-Nagy, came to Hampstead.

Cutting Edge

Like all large cities, London has always had a flourishing underworld. Guided walks today follow in the bloody footsteps of Jack the Ripper, who murdered and mutilated prostitutes in Whitechapel in 1888, and wrote mocking notes to the police. He was never caught and his identity is still unknown. A reconstruction of the grimy, cobbled East End streets through which the killer stalked can be seen at Madame Tussaud's, along with displays about other London murderers.

Among the most repulsive of these was the necrophiliac, John Reginald Haliday Christie, tenant of 10 Rillington Place in the Notting Hill district. He murdered at least eight women at this address. He walled some of their bodies up in the house, and buried others in the garden. He was hung in Brixton Prison in 1953. The name of Rillington Place was changed and the street has since been demolished.

The Attentions of Jack Ketch

In earlier centuries executions were staged in public, theoretically as a deterrent. Certainly they attracted large crowds. From the 14th century to the 18th the main place of execution was the gallows at Tyburn (Marble Arch).

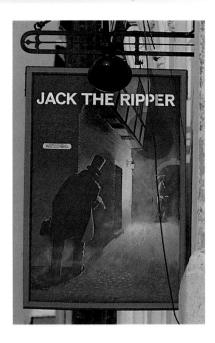

This pub in Spitalfields is named after London's most celebrated villain.

The condemned prisoner was driven here from Newgate Prison and along Oxford Street, in a cart. At the gallows the executioner fastened a noose round the wretch's neck and tied the other end of the rope to the gibbet. He then whipped up the horse and the cart pulled away, leaving the neck to snap and the body to swing.

In 1714 it was estimated that 200,000 people gathered to see the famous highwayman Jack Sheppard 'turned off at Tyburn Tree'. A hero to the watching throng, he had escaped from Newgate twice, even though he was in handcuffs and chained to the floor the second time. In 1760 another capacity crowd saw Earl Ferrers dispatched on a silken rope, the privilege of his rank.

In 1783 executions were moved to Newgate Prison itself. They were staged in Old Bailey, in front of the prison, and the gallows here was fitted with a drop. Public execution was abolished in 1868, and the prison was eventually knocked down in 1902, to be replaced by the Central Criminal Court.

The hangmen worked for the City of London and were paid at piece rates. They were called, generically, Jack Ketch, after the man who bungled the execution of the Duke of Monmouth in 1685. Five blows with the axe failed to sever the unfortunate Monmouth's head and Ketch had to finish the job with a knife.

In the 16th century victims were burned at the stake at Smithfield for their religion. A man named John Forest was roasted alive in a cage there in 1538. More than 200 Protestants were burned at Smithfield between 1553 and 1558, during the reign of 'Bloody Mary'. Not all Smithfield's victims were martyrs, though. A cook was boiled alive there in 1530 for poisoning soup.

Punishments were brutal even during the 18th century, when pirates were hanged in chains at Execution Dock in Wapping at low tide, and left to dangle through three high tides. The notorious Captain Kidd breathed his last there in 1701.

The 18th-century novelist Henry Fielding saw the seamy side of London life as a magistrate at Bow Street. His brother, the blind Sir John Fielding, served there, too. It was said that he could recognise 3,000 thieves by their voices. The Fieldings were reformers who founded the Bow Street Runners, a group of professional thief-takers who were the precursors of the Metropolitan Police.

The Literary Life

The archetypal London man of letters was Dr Samuel Johnson, whose house at 17 Gough Square, off Fleet Street, is now a museum. Nearby is the famous Ye Olde Cheshire Cheese tavern, where he and his cronies dined and drank in the 18th century. A massive figure, Johnson was clumsy, slovenly, afflicted by nervous twitchings and grimacings, and prey to black depressions, but he was a magical talker. He came to London from Lichfield in Staffordshire in 1737, when he was 28, and the city was his home for the rest of his life. His was the famous dictum: 'When a man is tired of London, he is tired of life, for there is in London all that life can afford.'

The writer most closely identified with London is Charles Dickens, whose novels contain vivid descriptions of life in the Victorian city. Brought up in Chatham in Kent, he came to London as a young man. After working as a clerk in a Lincoln's Inn solicitor's office, and becoming, briefly, a shorthand writer at the Law Courts, he was employed at a parliamentary reporter. These experiences left him with a lasting distaste for both the Law and Parliament. He was married in St Luke's, Chelsea in 1836 and that year scored his first big literary success with *The Pickwick Papers*. Few of the houses that he lived in have survived.

Charity and Education

The condition of the London poor, which so horrified Dickens, inspired Victorian social reformers to vigorous action. Among them was Dr Barnardo,

who came from Ireland as a young man in 1866 to study at the London Hospital in Whitechapel Road, E1. He was so shocked by what he saw in the East End that he founded the first Barnardo homes for destitute children.

'General' William Booth also came to London in the 1860s, with his wife Catherine, to carry out Christian missionary work in the East End. They founded the Salvation Army in 1878, which aroused violent hostility at the time, but has since become an immensely respected, world-wide institution. Booth died in 1912 and is buried in Abney Park Cemetery in Stoke Newington.

London's clubs, hospitals and schools have all been nurseries of talent over the centuries. Past members of the exclusive White's Club for gentlemen in St James's have included three kings and innumerable prime ministers. William Harvey, the discoverer of the circulation of the blood, was chief physician at St Bartholomew's Hospital in the 17th century, and Marie Stopes, the birth-control pioneer, taught at University College in the 20th. Meanwhile, former pupils of Westminster School include Sir Christopher Wren and John Dryden. Among those of St Paul's School are John Milton, Samuel Pepys and Lord Montgomery of Alamein. The villainous Judge Jeffreys was at both.

From Abroad

Foreign celebrities abound in London's annals. Benjamin Franklin lived at 36 Villiers Street, WC2, in the 1750s and 1760s. Wolfgang Amadeus Mozart wrote his first symphony in London in 1764, at 180 Ebury Street, SW1. He was eight years old at the time, and Haydn gave him lessons in the garden. Karl Marx began writing *Das Kapital* at 28 Dean Street, Soho, in the 1850s.

The great Russian ballerina Anna Pavlova ended her days at Ivy House, North End Way, Hampstead, in 1931. Sigmund Freud died at 20 Maresfield Gardens, NW3 (now a museum to his memory) in 1939. Mahatma Gandhi used to stay at the Hyde Park Hotel in Knightsbridge, where a goat was specially milked for him every day, and Rudolf Valentino, the Hollywood heart-throb, used to stay there in the 1920s. Even the former North Vietnamese President Ho Chi Minh once worked in London, at the (now demolished) Carlton Hotel in the Haymarket. The heroes and villains of tomorrow are living today in London's streets and squares.

Inigo Jones

THE MAKERS OF LONDON

Inigo Jones

Architect and town planner, who introduced the Renaissance Classical style into England. Born in London, 1573, son of a Smithfield clothworker. Travelled in Italy, France and Denmark, where he was employed by Christian IV. Designed costumes, stage décor and effects for masques at the English royal court. Appointed principal architect to James I, 1615. Designed the Queen's House at Greenwich, the Banqueting House in Whitehall for masques and feasts, and Queen's Chapel in St James's. Laid out Covent Garden for the Earl of Bedford, which set the pattern for future London formal squares and streets. Died in London in 1652. Buried in St Benet's Church, Paul's Wharf.

Sir Christopher Wren

Architect and astronomer. Born at East Knoyle, Wiltshire, 1632. Brought up at Windsor, where his father was Dean. Educated at Westminster School and Wadham College, Oxford. Savilian Professor of Astronomy at Oxford, 1661. A founder member of the Royal Society. Principal architect to Charles II, James II, and William III. Rebuilt St Paul's Cathedral and 55 other London churches after the Great Fire of 1666. Designed Royal Hospital, Chelsea. Substantial work at Kensington Palace, Hampton Court and Greenwich Hospital. Died in his chair after dinner at his house in St James's Street, aged 90, in 1723. Buried in St Paul's Cathedral. ('Reader, if you seek his monument, look around you.')

Sir Christopher Wren

Earl of Burlington

Sir Joseph Bazalgette

Nicholas Hawksmoor

Architect. Born in Nottinghamshire, 1661. Started work in London for Wren at the age of 18 and became his principal assistant at St Paul's. Also worked with Wren on the City churches, Royal Hospital Chelsea, Kensington Palace and Greenwich Hospital. From 1723 chief architect to Westminster Abbey, where he designed the western towers. His principal London creations are churches: St Mary Woolnoth in the City; St George's, Bloomsbury; St George in the East, Shadwell; St Anne's, Limehouse; Christ Church, Spitalfields; and St Alphege's, Greenwich. Died at his Millbank home in 1736.

Earl of Burlington

Richard Boyle, third Earl of Burlington, wealthy connoisseur, patron and a leading influence on the adoption of the Palladian Classical style of architecture in England. Born in London, 1694. Travelled extensively in Italy. An enthusiastic admirer of Inigo Jones, he commissioned Colen Campbell to rebuild his London mansion, Burlington House in Piccadilly (now the home of the Royal Academy of Arts). He also employed William Kent there and in the building of Chiswick House, the Palladian villa and art gallery which he designed himself. Died in London in 1753, aged 59.

John Nash

Architect and town planner. Born in London, 1752. Built up a successful practice as a country-house architect in partnership with Humphry Repton, the landscape designer. Favourite architect of the Prince Regent (later King George IV), for whom he built the Royal Pavilion in Brighton. In London he designed Regent's Park and its elegant terraces as a pioneer garden city, and created Regent Street as a magnificent avenue, leading north to the park from The Mall. Piccadilly Circus,

Thomas Cubitt

Oxford Circus and All Souls Langham Place, were all part of this noble conception. Nash also designed Marble Arch, the portico of the Haymarket theatre and Royal Opera House Arcade, off Haymarket. His work at Buckingham Palace was fiercely criticised for its cost. Died in 1835 at Cowes.

Thomas Cubitt

Builder. Born at Buxton, Norfolk, 1788. A carpenter, he set up in business for himself in Holborn, 1811. Founded the first large building contracting firm of the modern type and built some of London's most attractive squares, terraces and houses. His greatest achievement was the planning and creation of Belgravia, organised around four major squares (Belgrave, Eaton, Chester and Lowndes Squares). He also developed Pimlico and much of Bloomsbury, including Tavistock Square and Gordon Square, and Cubitt Town on the Isle of Dogs for dock workers. His

standards of workmanship were extremely high, and his houses have lasted better than many built since his day. His younger brother, Lewis Cubitt (architect of King's Cross Station) often worked with him. Died a millionaire in 1855, at his house near Dorking in Surrey, aged 67.

Sir Joseph Bazalgette

Engineer. Of French descent, born at Enfield, Middlesex, 1819, son of a naval officer. Set up in business as an engineer in Westminster, 1842. From 1855, chief engineer to the Metropolitan Board of Works. Responsible in the 1860s and 1870s for a dramatic improvement in public health by constructing a vast main drainage system, which involved more than 83 miles (133.5km) of sewers, draining an area of over 100 square miles (259 square km) and coping with an average of 420 million gallons of rainwater and sewage per day. He constructed the Victoria Embankment, the Albert Embankment, Chelsea Embankment, Northumberland Avenue, Battersea Bridge and Putney Bridge. Knighted 1874. Died in 1891 aged 71, at his home in Wimbledon Park.

Sir Aston Webb

Successful Edwardian architect. Born in London 1849, son of an artist. Set up in practice, 1873. His main creations in London include Admiralty Arch; the surroundings of the Queen Victoria Memorial; the eastern façade of Buckingham Palace; the main block of the Victoria and Albert Museum and, also in South Kensington, the Imperial College of Science and Technology. He also restored St Bartholomew the Great, Smithfield. Outside London, his principal works included the University of Birmingham and Christ's Hospital School, Sussex. Knighted 1904. President of the Royal Academy, 1919-24. Died in London in 1930, aged 81.

London's
Legends and Ghosts

• • •

Tradition has it that London was founded by Trojan exiles, and that Britain will fall if the ravens ever leave the Tower. London is also said to be the world's most haunted capital city. Many of its buildings are stalked by spectral figures from its turbulent past.

According to the legendary history of Britain, written in the 12th century by Geoffrey of Monmouth and accepted for centuries as genuine history, the first ruler of Britain was a Trojan prince named Brutus, who led a band of settlers to this island in the northern seas after the Fall of Troy. The island was called Albion, and was inhabited only by giants, whom the Trojans slaughtered. One giant, Gogmagog, wrestled with a Trojan champion named Corineus, who hurled the brute into the sea.

The giants were now exterminated and the legendary history goes on to say that the island took its new name, Britain, from Brutus, who founded a capital on the Thames called New Troy. According to Geoffrey of Monmouth's fictitious history, a later king, Lud, rebuilt the wall of the city and changed its name to *Caer Lud* ('Lud's Town' in Welsh), which afterwards became London. He is said to be buried near Lud Gate and has given his name to the King Lud pub, at Ludgate Circus. Statues of Lud and his two sons stood on Lud Gate in the Middle Ages, and when the gate was demolished in 1760 the battered figures were placed in the church porch of St Dunstan-in-the-West, Fleet Street, where they can be seen today.

Gog and the land of Magog are mentioned in the Old Testament as enemies of God and God's people. Geoffrey of Monmouth describes two fictitious giants, Gog and Magog. Figures of them were kept in the Guildhall in the Middle Ages. They were carried about in guild processions and they welcomed Queen Elizabeth I to the City in 1558. The originals were burned in the Great Fire of London and in 1708 new figures replaced them. These were made of fir wood and were 14½ft (4.4m) high. They were destroyed in the Blitz, and replaced. The replicas can be seen today in the Guildhall. The two giants who strike the hour with clubs on the clock of St Dunstan's, Fleet Street, also represent Gog and Magog.

Ravens in the Tower

Another superhuman figure linked with London is Bran the Blessed, who appears as king of Britain in the *Mabinogion*, a collection of early Welsh stories. Here Bran is described as a giant, the size of a mountain. In a battle against the Irish he was mortally wounded, thrust through the foot with a poisoned spear. He told his warriors to cut off his head, take it to London and bury it in the White Hill with his face towards France. This was duly done. The severed head talked and was good company on the way to London. It became one of the Three Fortunate Concealments, protecting Britain from any plague coming across the sea. Another Welsh tradition says that because King Arthur later rashly dug up Bran's head, the Saxon plague was able to overwhelm the Britons.

The name Bran means 'raven'. He was probably a Celtic god and the story recalls the veneration which the Celts, who were head-hunters, paid to the human head. The White Hill described in the *Mabinogion* is Tower Hill, and the legend is no doubt the origin of the idea that as long as ravens are kept at the Tower, Britain will be safe from disaster.

One of London's most frequently observed ghosts is a young man dressed in grey, who is seen in the upper circle of the Theatre Royal in Drury Lane.

To stop the birds from flying away today, the wings of the Tower ravens are clipped. They are looked after by the Yeoman Ravenmaster and have their own burial-ground in the moat. There is something distinctly sinister about the birds. They croak hoarsely and move with a predatory, hopping gait.

Stone of Destiny

There is a story that Queen Boudicca (Boadicea) lies buried under Platform 10 at King's Cross Station; alternatively she was buried on Primrose Hill, or under a mound near Parliament Hill, Hampstead Heath. Legendary tales have also grown up about some London churches. St Paul's is said to stand on the site of a pagan temple to the Roman goddess Diana, while St Peter himself is supposed to have come from heaven in the 7th century to dedicate his church on Thorney Island (subsequently rebuilt by Edward the Confessor as Westminster Abbey).

In the base of the Coronation Chair in Westminster Abbey is the Stone of Scone. This slab of sandstone was the coronation throne of the kings of Scots. It had once been in Ireland, where it was called the *Lia Fail*, or Stone of Destiny, and used to crown Irish kings at Tara. Irish legend said that the stone could test the new king's right to accede, as it would scream when the rightful ruler sat on it. The stone was taken to Scotland for the coronation of an Irish king there, and was used at Scone in Perthshire until 1297, when the English King Edward I carried it off. According to tradition, the stone was used as a pillow by Jacob when he dreamed of angels ascending and descending a ladder in the sky in the book of Genesis.

'Turn Again, Whittington'

The story of Dick Whittington was in circulation by the 17th century or earlier. It tells of a poor boy who came to London to make his fortune and found work in the kitchen of a rich merchant's house. He saved up a penny and bought a cat to kill the kitchen mice. It was his only friend. Lonely and dispirited, he ran away. When he

The Whittington Stone, complete with cat, marks the spot where the future Lord Mayor is said to have heard the bells.

reached Highgate Hill, he sat down on a stone to rest, and heard Bow bells ringing. They seemed to be saying 'Turn again, Whittington, Lord Mayor of London'. He turned back and in due course did indeed become Lord Mayor.

The bells of St Mary le Bow, Cheapside, are the Bow bells within sound of which all true cockneys are born. How they became associated with the legend of Dick Whittington, nobody knows. A Sir Richard Whittington did indeed live in London in the 15th century. He was four times Lord Mayor of London, but he came from a well-to-do Gloucestershire family and was never a poor country lad. It has been suggested that the 'cat' in the legend was a type of boat that he used in his business. In 1409 Whittington paid for the rebuilding of the Church of St Michael Paternoster Royal, in College Hill, EC4. During repair work carried out there after the Second World War, a mummified cat was found under the roof. It was promptly called Whittington's cat. A cat is carved on the Whittington Stone, near the foot of Highgate Hill, the spot where Whittington is supposed to have heard the prophetic bells.

The Demon Barber

The black side of legendary London is represented by Sweeney Todd, 'the demon barber of Fleet Street'. He is said to have murdered unsuspecting patrons by dropping them out of his barber's chair, through a trap-door and into the cellar, where he finished them off with his razor. The bodies were supposed to have ended up in the tasty meat pies sold by his neighbour, Mrs Lovatt of Bell Yard. This gruesome tale is almost certainly entirely fictitious, but Sweeney has left his name, through cockney rhyming slang, to Scotland Yard's flying squad.

The Bloody Tower

'With 'er 'ead tucked underneath 'er arm,' the music hall song says, 'she walks the Bloody Tower.' When a prisoner was beheaded on Tower Hill, the body was carried back to the Tower, with the head placed neatly beneath the arm.

The Tower is the most haunted building in London, which in view of its long history of violence, torture and apprehension is hardly surprising. A headless figure in white has been seen more than once gliding silently towards Tower Green, where Anne Boleyn's pretty neck was sliced through with a sword in 1536. Her ghost has also been seen in a room in the Martin Tower and elsewhere in the fortress. The shade of Sir Walter Raleigh, imprisoned in the Bloody Tower for almost 13 years, walks the ramparts by moonlight.

Prisoners brought to the Tower along the Thames entered by Traitor's Gate. The Tower is London's most haunted building.

Margaret, Countess of Salisbury, was beheaded on Tower Green in 1541. It is said that on the anniversary of her death her ghost has been seen running screaming in terror round the spot where the block stood. The spirit of poor Lady Jane Grey, executed in 1554 at the tender age of 16, also haunts the Tower, and a throng of phantoms crowds the Tower's Chapel of St Peter ad Vincula, where many of the executioner's victims are buried.

The Man in Grey

Several London theatres are haunted. At the Theatre Royal in Drury Lane many observers have reported seeing a handsome young man in grey, with either a white wig or powdered hair, a three-cornered hat, riding boots and a sword. There seems to be nothing frightening about him, and in fact his appearances are regarded as a good omen. He appears at any time between 10.00am and 6.00pm ('haunting to rule,' as it has been said) in the fourth row of the upper circle. He walks across to the far gangway and vanishes into the wall.

In 1840 workmen making alterations to the theatre broke down part of the side wall and found behind it the skeleton of a man with a 17th-century dagger between his ribs. No one knows who he was or how he came to die, but the skeleton was found at the point in the wall where the ghost always vanishes.

Another haunted playhouse is the Adelphi in the Strand, where in 1897 the actor-manager William Terriss was stabbed to death by a jealous professional rival, who was sent to Broadmoor and died there 40 years afterwards. Ever since the murder the theatre has been prey to uncanny knocks and rapping noises, and mysterious footsteps. People have reported uneasy feelings of being watched, or sudden sensations of cold.

Curiously enough, Covent Garden tube station, not far away, has also been plagued with uncanny footsteps and heavy sighs. A ghostly figure has been seen late at night in the tunnels, or starting up the spiral staircase, but somehow he never reaches the top. A man who worked at the station and had seen the figure was shown a photograph of William Terriss. He identified it instantly as the ghost.

Sleight of Hand
Some pubs are haunted, too. Probably the best-known is the Grenadier in Old Barracks Yard, off Wilton Road, SW1. It was formerly called the Guardsman. It is said that the Duke of Wellington sometimes played cards with his officers here, and that gambling for high stakes was common. A young Guards officer who was caught cheating was badly beaten up, and then either fell or was pushed down the stairs into the cellar, where he died. There have been many sightings here of

a mysterious figure, of a shadow where no shadow should have been. There are also reports of lights going on and off by themselves, taps turning on and off, knocking noises and objects being unaccountably moved. There are also curious 'atmospheres' that build up to a peak in September — the month of the young officer's death — and then fade away again. Dogs show a marked dislike of the cellar.

She-Wolf and Holy Maid
The unquiet spectre of Queen Isabella, 'the she-wolf of France,' wife of Edward II, is one of a number of ghosts said to haunt quiet Greyfriars Churchyard in Newgate Street, EC4. Isabella helped to

depose and murder her husband, and she was buried here in 1358. The graveyard is beside Christ Church, ruined in the Blitz, which was originally the principal London church of the Franciscans. Two other queens of England lie buried here, the widows of Henry III and Edward I. So does Elizabeth Barton, 'the Holy Maid of Kent', who was hanged at Tyburn in 1534 for preaching against Henry VIII. She, too, has been seen in the churchyard, a wild figure in a grey habit.

In the haunted gallery at Hampton Court the terrible despairing screams of Catherine Howard have been heard, condemned to death and desperately pleading for her life with her adamant husband, Henry VIII. The new Langham Hotel in Portland Place has a non-paying guest, in the form of the cloaked ghost of a German who committed suicide there early this century. The Grey Lady, a ghost in an old-fashioned nurse's uniform, is seen from time to time in the corridors of St Thomas's Hospital. Even a place as open and airy as Wimbledon Common is haunted, so it is said, by the spirit of an 18th-century highwayman who gallops across it by night. London's past, so it seems, still has its ghostly echoes.

The convivial Grenadier pub (left and below) is said to be haunted by the ghost of a young Guards officer.

Hidden and Curious London

◆ ◆ ◆

Underneath London, unseen by most eyes, lies a labyrinth. The ground is honey-combed with tunnels, sewers, subways, subterranean car parks, church crypts, water mains, and thousands of miles of pipes, wires and cables. Above ground, too, there are engaging oddities and stray reminders of the forgotten past.

A recent major addition to London's hidden labyrinth is an underground tunnel 50 miles (80.4km) long. Its purpose is to ease demand on existing water mains, some of which date back to the 19th century.

Centuries before that, Londoners drew their water from wells and rivers — the Thames and its tributaries, such as the Walbrook and the Fleet. The tributaries still run, but for the most part out of sight. Roofed over by streets and buildings, they flow underground through pipes and culverts, before draining into the Thames.

Lost Rivers

Driving or walking down King's Cross Road and Farringdon Street today, from King's Cross station to Ludgate Circus, few people are aware that unseen beneath them is the River Fleet. Also known as the Holbourne, it gives its name to Fleet Street and the Holborn district. Once a fresh and bubbling stream, but in the 18th century a repulsive ditch choked with filth and offal, it rises in the ponds on Hampstead Heath and makes its subterranean way beneath Camden Town and King's Cross to the Thames near Blackfriars Bridge. The river valley can be seen easily today where it is crossed by Holborn Viaduct.

A line of watermills used to stand where Farringdon Street is now, some

Above: hunting treasures in the sewers. Below: the opening of the pneumatic mail despatch tube in Holborn, 1865.

of them commemorated in the name of Turnmill Street, close to Farringdon tube station. All the filth of the Smithfield butchers and tanners turned the river red before it flowed stickily under Holborn Bridge and past the coal wharf, where Seacoal Lane is today.

Further to the west, the Tyburn rises on Haverstock Hill and runs south past Primrose Hill and across the Grand Union Canal in an iron pipe, to supply the water for the boating lake in Regent's Park. Then it goes under Baker Street and Marylebone Lane, whose winding route follows the stream's course, beneath Oxford Street, Berkeley Square, Piccadilly and Green Park, to divide into two branches to reach the Thames. Between the branches is Thorney Island, the site of Westminster Abbey.

Further west still, the Westbourne, also called Bayswater Brook, rises on Hampstead Heath. It lends it name to the Westbourne Park district and Bayswater. After surfacing cheerfully in Hyde Park as the Serpentine, it disappears to cross the District Line tube tracks at Sloane Square in a massive iron pipe. From here it runs beneath the grounds of Royal Hospital, Chelsea, to the Thames.

Some of London's streams have not only disappeared from sight, but have vanished completely. No one knows where the Langbourne has gone, though in the 16th century it was described as 'a great stream' which broke out of the ground in Fenchurch Street in the City and ran along Lombard Street to the Thames. Also lost is the Cranbourne, which used to flow from Leicester Square to the Thames. It may have been an illicit sewer, built by the first developer of Soho.

A Basilica of Waste

All the rivers and streams in London turned into sewers as time went by. They were mostly covered over by the 19th century, when 'toshers' used to brave their murky depths, armed with sticks against rats, and waded through them to hunt for valuables. The toshers made an adequate living underground and attributed their robust health to the powerful odours they encountered in their work.

Even in the mid-19th century there were still some open sewers, however. One of them was at Jacob's Island in Bermondsey, on the Neckinger stream, where Jacob Street is today. This is where Bill Sykes meets his death in *Oliver Twist*. Charles Dickens considered it 'the filthiest, the strangest, the most extraordinary of the many localities that are hidden in London', with its crumbling, tiny-roomed, broken-windowed houses linked by wooden galleries above the stinking mud. A

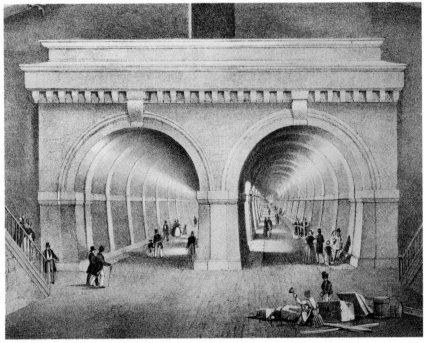

Workmen were drowned when the river broke into the Brunels' new Thames Tunnel (top), but work went on and the completed tunnel (above) was opened by Queen Victoria. It is now used by tube trains.

newspaper in 1849 called it 'the Venice of drains' and 'the very capital of Cholera'.

Victorian consciences were shocked. A new main drainage system was soon constructed in the area by the great Sir Joseph Bazalgette, whose magnificent brick-lined sewers are still in use. A particularly grand example is the one running from Hammersmith to Cheyne Walk and then inside Chelsea and Victoria Embankments to Tower Hill. From here it leads on, under Whitechapel and Bow, to the stupendous Abbey Mills Pumping Station in West Ham. This building was designed by Bazalgette in Venetian Gothic, a Byzantine basilica of waste. Since then the system has been improved, of course, and a handsome new pumping station was opened in 1988 on the Isle of Dogs.

A Maze of Tunnels

More than 20 tunnels burrow beneath the Thames, downstream of Hammersmith Bridge. A brick tunnel was constructed between Wapping and Rotherhithe in the face of appalling danger in 1843, by Sir Marc Brunel and his son, Isambard Kingdom Brunel. It was opened by Queen Victoria, and now carries tube trains. Another Victorian tunnel ran from Tower Hill, under the river to Vine Lane, off Tooley Street. A notorious haunt of prostitutes and muggers, it became redundant when Tower Bridge opened in 1894, and today it carries water mains. There is still an inconspicuous entrance to it on Tower Hill.

Also beneath the Thames is the Waterloo to City underground railway, unaffectionately known as 'the Drain', which opened in 1898. The original Blackwall Tunnel (now the northbound part of the tunnel), was the first road tunnel under the river. It was another product of the 1890s and in its day the largest underwater tunnel in the world.

The most travelled tunnels in London, naturally, are those which carry tube trains. The city's deepest underground station is Hampstead, which is 192ft (58m) below ground level. The Post Office has its own electric underground railway line between Whitechapel and Paddington, by way of the big sorting office at Mount Pleasant, off Farringdon Street. Work on the tunnel began in 1913, and the Elgin Marbles were stored in it for safety during the First World War.

Towards the northern end of Kingsway, in the middle of the road, can be seen the exit of an abandoned tram tunnel, built in 1908 as part of a subterranean tram network which got no further. Another oddity is the complex of tunnels known as the Camden Catacombs, which are situated under the Roundhouse and beneath the main railway line into Euston station. Used for storage now, the tunnels were first built as stables for the horses employed in shunting goods wagons in the 19th century.

Under and In the Street

Besides tunnels, untold miles of telephone and electricity wires snake their way beneath London's streets, along with gas pipes and water pipes. These can be anything from 2in (5cm) to 5ft (1.5m) in diameter. The pleasure of strolling about London can be enhanced by paying attention to manhole covers, inspection plates and coalhole covers set in the pavements, with their varied designs, dates and the names of vanished gas and water companies.

Also of interest, seen on the walls of buildings, are fire marks, property marks and parish boundary markers. Fire marks were put up by insurance companies to identify properties entitled to their fire-fighting services. A property mark shows the badge of the institution to which a building belonged, and parish boundary markers the badge of the parish. In Carey Street, WC2, behind the Law Courts, two inconspicuous stones carry the badges of St Clement Danes and St Dunstan in the West.

London street furniture is a study in itself. The paraphernalia of lamp posts, signs, traffic lights, pillarboxes, bollards, railings, seats and benches, bus shelters, parking meters, rubbish bins, sand and grit containers is so familiar that most of it passes unnoticed, but it is eloquent

Some of London's delightful street furniture: a camel supports a bench on the Victoria Embankment (above), while the lamp standard (right) is a credit to Westminster Bridge.

of social history and changing fashions. Incidentally, the classic red telephone boxes designed by Sir Giles Gilbert Scott between the First and Second World Wars, which used to be an elegant ingredient of the London street scene, are now a rare sight, as many of them have been destroyed by British Telecom.

Some of London's handsome old gas lamps can still be seen, now converted to electricity; the last gas lamps still lit by hand every evening were in the Temple area in 1986. One or two old communal water pumps have survived. There is a cast-iron beauty with two spouts in Bedford Row, WC1 (which also boasts three old-style phone boxes and an Edward VII double pillarbox). Another is nearby in Queen Square, WC1. The water from Aldgate Pump in the City, at the junction of Leadenhall Street and Fenchurch Street, used to have a curious taste. It was eventually discovered that the water ran through a cemetery.

Drinking fountains and horse-troughs were products of the Victorian drive to improve public sanitation, backed by the powerful temperance movement. Some of them are wonderfully ornate and impressive. The Buxton Memorial Fountain in Victoria Tower Gardens next to the Houses of Parliament is sheltered by a medieval church spire, covered with enamelled plates. It was

designed in the 1860s by S S Teulon in honour of the emancipation of slaves in the United States of America. The fountain originally stood in Great George Street nearby, and was moved here in 1957.

Fountains often double as memorials. The grand fountain in Catherine Street, WC2, set in the wall of the Theatre Royal, Drury Lane, honours the Victorian impresario Sir Augustus Harris. It has a fine bronze bust of him by Sir Thomas Brock. In the

Essays in the macabre: the mummified body of Jeremy Bentham (left) sits in its cabinet in University College, while stone skulls greet visitors to the church Dickens christened 'St Ghastly Grim'.

Victoria Embankment Gardens next to Temple station is a delightful fountain in memory of a temperance campaigner, Lady Henry Somerset. A bronze figure of a girl holds an alms dish and the inscription reads, 'I was thirsty and ye gave me a drink'. The figure is a replica of the original, which was stolen in 1970.

Near the Marlborough Gate entrance to Kensington Gardens, from Bayswater Road, two bears wrestle on a drinking fountain erected in 1939. Close by, a shrubbery at Victoria Gate shelters the diminutive tombstones of hundreds of dogs, cats, birds and monkeys, buried lovingly in the pets' cemetery.

In the Midst of Death

Tunnels and pipes are not the only things hidden in the ground beneath Londoners' feet. There are also the bones of generations of Londoners who went before. Every now and again, excavations for a new building take a macabre turn when an unsuspected burial ground or a plague pit is broken into. This happened when the Royal Lancaster Hotel on Bayswater Road was built in the 1960s. There is a tradition that the Piccadilly Line takes a sharp bend west of Knightsbridge station to avoid a plague pit. The same story is told of the curve in the Central Line between Bank and Liverpool Street.

The pressure of the dead on city space mounted over the centuries to become overwhelming. By the early 19th century the state of inner London churchyards and burial grounds was disgusting and insanitary. Hence the creation of the great Victorian necropolises further out, at Brompton and Kensal Green, and at Hampstead and Highgate. They are fascinating places to visit today, with their imposing vaults and tombs, their serried rows of gravestones, sorrowing angels, mourning cherubs, broken obelisks and poetic inscriptions.

The best-known of them is Highgate Cemetery in Swain's Lane, N6, with its brutal monument to Karl Marx. The author George Borrow and Emmeline Pankhurst, the Suffragette leader, repose in Brompton Cemetery, Old Brompton Road, SW10. Kensal Green Cemetery in Harrow Road, W10, is the final resting-place of Isambard Kingdom Brunel, William Makepeace Thackeray and Anthony Trollope. It is also that of James Miranda Barry, an Inspector-General of the Army Medical Department who, upon dying in 1865, was discovered to general incredulity to have been a woman.

London churchyards make reflective visiting, too. The Church of St Olave, Hart Street, EC3, still has a 17th-century graveyard gate, liberally adorned with skulls and bones. They caused Charles Dickens to rechristen the church St Ghastly Grim (the gateway is in Seething Lane). Mother Goose was buried here in 1586, as was Samuel Pepys in 1703.

The most bizarre object in London is surely the mummified body of the philosopher Jeremy Bentham, one of the founders of University College London, in Gower Street. When he died in 1832 his body was embalmed, as he had wished, seated in a glass case in the college entrance hall, dressed in his customary clothes, and arranged holding his cane. The head that can be seen today is a replacement, however. The original was used as a football by the students too often for its own good.

Green London

◆ ◆ ◆

In London's early centuries the citizens had open space and country amusements to hand immediately outside the city wall. They went wildfowling in the Lambeth marshes, for instance, or hunting otters in Moorfields, north of Moorgate. As the town grew and ate up the surrounding countryside, however, there came a need for parks and gardens.

The principal London parks were royal ground — and still are — and originated in Henry VIII's zeal for hunting. Three major parks in central London lie in a line from west to east, a broad ribbon of green stretching from Kensington to Whitehall: Hyde Park, Green Park and St James's Park. The first to be enclosed was St James's Park, which was nearest to the Royal Palace of Whitehall. In the 16th century it was a muddy field where the pigs of the local leper hospital grunted and wallowed.

After expelling the lepers and building St James's Palace, Henry VIII had the land drained and used it for rearing deer. Formal gardens were constructed for James I, with a menagerie which included two crocodiles. Charles II had the park laid out in the formal French style. He liked to walk his spaniels and his mistresses there. Ordinary citizens were allowed to stroll in the park, too, and in time it became uncomfortable for royalty to use it.

It was also Charles II who had Green Park laid out, as an extension of St James's Park. Both parks have traditionally been looked after by the same staff.

Daffodils in Spring

Hyde Park, with Kensington Gardens, is much bigger than St James's Park, extending to over 600 acres (243ha). In the Middle Ages the land was part of the manor of Hyde and belonged to Westminster Abbey. It was wild countryside then, watered by the Westbourne stream (which has now disappeared underground), and grazed by deer, boar and wild cattle. At the Dissolution of the Monasteries the land was sequestered by Henry VIII, who used it for hunting deer and preserved hare, pheasant and partridges here. Elizabeth I enjoyed hunting here, too; deer were hunted in Hyde Park as late as the 1780s.

The area was opened to the public in the 17th century and Charles II had a circular drive built, called The Ring. All of fashionable London liked to see and be seen there, either on horseback or in elegant equipages. At night the park was infested by highwaymen and robbers, and it was a popular place for duels.

In 1851 the Crystal Palace was constructed in Hyde Park to house the Great Exhibition. A stupendous glasshouse, 2,000ft (610m) long and 400ft (122m) wide, it stood between Rotten Row and the southern edge of the park. In the 1860s Hyde Park was improved with water gardens, fountains and statues, and flowers were planted for the first time. Today the daffodils nodding in the spring breezes on the banks beside Park Lane make one of the pleasantest sights in London.

On a sunny summer day as many as 50,000 people use the park, starting with early morning joggers and intrepid swimmers in the Serpentine, followed by those who walk across it on their way to work, dog-walkers, nannies and others. Besides strolling and swimming, activities include boating, riding, cycling, football, tennis and bowls, band concerts, sailing model boats on the Round Pond, and listening to the oratory at Speakers' Corner. The park is also used for mass meetings and demonstrations. It has a fine range of trees and shrubs, and around 100 different species of birds have been recorded, including grebes, herons and owls.

People's Parks

Regent's Park, again, was originally monastic property, which Henry VIII

Fishing, swimming and boating are among the pleasures of the Serpentine, the lake in Hyde Park.

appropriated and used for hunting. Later it was let to dairy farmers, who supplied Londoners with much of their milk, butter and cheese until the leases ran out in 1811. John Nash was then employed to create the present park as a garden city. It was opened to the public in the 1830s.

By this time pressure was mounting for the provision of parks in the poorer areas of London, for the blameless recreation and improved physical and psychological health of the working class. In 1845 Victoria Park was opened to the public on some 200 acres (81ha) of land in Hackney. It was landscaped by Sir James Pennethorne, a pupil of John Nash, with fine trees and pleasant lakes.

Pennethorne also laid out Battersea Park, south of the Thames between Albert Bridge and Chelsea Bridge, on 200 acres (81ha) of common land where the great Duke of Wellington had once fought a duel. There were fairs there and gypsy encampments, which were all swept away when the salubrious new park opened in 1853. Almost a hundred years later, in 1951, new gardens were laid out there for the Festival of Britain. There is now a boating lake and a notable array of outdoor modern sculpture. Scenes from the life of Buddha are depicted on the Peace Pagoda, built by Buddhist monks in 1985.

Kennington Park, Southwark Park, Rotherhithe and Finsbury Park are

A peaceful Buddha in Battersea Park.

other examples of this type of improving municipal park, created for Londoners in the 1850s and 1860s. The laying-out of the embankments also provided an opportunity to construct gardens along the river, on land reclaimed from the Thames. Victoria Embankment Gardens, on either side of Hungerford Bridge, were opened in 1870. The 17th-century York Watergate, which is now in the gardens but originally opened onto steps down to the river, shows how much further inland the Thames reached in those days.

Brilliant yellow tulips brighten Regent's Park, bringing the country into town.

The Country in the Town

Further out from central London lie three more royal parks. These are Bushy Park, near Hampton Court, with its resplendent Chestnut Avenue and charming plantations; Greenwich Park, with the Royal Observatory; and Richmond Park, with its red and fallow deer, its ponds and woods, golf courses, polo and rugby pitches, riding and cycling paths. The deer provide venison for the Archbishop of Canterbury's table. The Isabella Plantation, fenced off against the deer, is a delightful woodland garden created mainly in the 1950s and 1960s, though first planted in 1831.

Other areas were originally commons, where tenants of the local lord had the right to pasture pigs and cattle, and collect firewood. Some 800 acres (324ha) of grassland and woods on Hampstead Heath, where wolves prowled in the Middle Ages, are now home to rabbits and foxes, owls and woodpeckers, herons and rare wild service trees. The heath was kept for public enjoyment only after formidable and protracted battles against landlords and 'improvers'. The same is true of Wimbledon Common, where every variety of British tree is said to grow, and which is also well known for its butterflies, fungi and grass snakes.

There is an enjoyable contrast between open areas of this kind, which are carefully kept wild, and artificially natural grounds created for stately mansions by great landscape architects such as 'Capability' Brown, Humphry Repton and others in the 18th century. Brown laid out the grounds of Syon House for the Duke of Northumberland with splendid lakes and trees, and part of Kew Gardens, including the rhododendron dell. Repton landscaped the grounds of Kenwood House, Hampstead, and was also involved in redesigning Golders Hill Park, on the heath's western edge. William Kent designed the gardens of Chiswick House, and also worked at what is now Gunnersbury Park.

Riders enjoy the famous Chestnut Avenue in Bushy Park (above), while in Wimbledon Park the windmill (left) has been a centre of attraction since it was built in 1817. It worked until 1860.

Cannizaro Park, just off Wimbledon Common, is another striking example of a landscape artfully contrived to look natural. It is named after the Duke of Cannizaro, a Sicilian nobleman who lived here in the early 19th century, and has been created by several generations of owners. The park has one of the best collections in the country of azaleas and rhododendrons, ablaze with colour in the spring. Among its other charms are a lake, winding woodland walks, huge clumps of bamboo and an aviary full of chattering, brightly coloured budgerigars.

London's parks are nothing if not varied. Avery Hill Park boasts a splendid Winter Garden of glasshouses, stocked with exotic trees and plants. Beside the Thames in Fulham, in the grounds of Fulham Palace, is Bishop's Park, which until 1973 was the official home of the Bishop of London. Clapham Common has football pitches, and hosts circuses, fairs and an annual horse show, while spring cherry blossom and ornamental lakes draw people to Brockwell Park, Tulse Hill.

Floral Fantasia

A surprising abundance of plant and animal life flourishes in London. More than 1,800 species of flowering plants and ferns have been recorded within 20 miles (32km) of St Paul's Cathedral in this century.

The ubiquitous London plane tree, which is resistant to traffic fumes, has been planted in the capital's streets and squares since the 1750s. Buddleia, rosebay willow herb and oxeye daisies sprout along railway embankments and on vacant lots.

Pigeons strut and coo in Trafalgar Square, and everywhere else as well. Seagulls are quite common, and vast flocks of starlings roost on buildings in central London, darkening the sky on expeditions to the country. The little London sparrows seem to have a chirpy cockney quality about them. Swans float regally on the Thames, peacocks parade in Holland Park and exotic waterfowl congregate on the lakes in St James's Park and Kew Gardens. Grey squirrels are in parks and gardens everywhere, while hedgehogs and foxes can be seen in the suburbs. Mice and rats are seen less often, but are nevertheless present everywhere, along with bats, butterflies and moths, rabbits and badgers.

Private gardens, patios and window boxes nurture everything from asters to zinnias. The great event of the gardening year in London is the Chelsea Flower Show, held since 1913 in May in the grounds of the Royal Hospital. Giant marquees shelter brilliant cascades of flowers and prodigious garden displays, while outside are tools, urns, garden furniture and gnomes galore.

The show is organised by the Royal Horticultural Society (which has its showpiece gardens outside London, at Wisley in Surrey). It was founded in 1804 with headquarters in Vincent Square, where there are still two exhibition halls and a notable horticultural library.

'Goffers' and Amazons

Cricket grounds like Lord's and the Oval are another ingredient of London's green scene. So are rugby and soccer grounds, bowling greens and, in the suburbs, golf courses.

The Royal Wimbledon Golf Club has its course on part of Wimbledon Common, where Julius Caesar's troops may have camped in the 1st century BC. The Royal Mid-Surrey, founded in 1892, has its course and clubhouse at Richmond, in the Old Deer Park. This

For a large city, London has a surprising range and variety of wildlife, from the friendly waterfowl in St James's Park (above) to the foxes sometimes glimpsed in private gardens (left).

borders Kew Gardens to the south and was once part of the park of Richmond Palace. The club professional in the 1920s was the legendary Henry Cotton, and its captain the future King Edward VIII.

Far more venerable is the Royal Blackheath Golf Club, the oldest in all England. A Society of Blackheath Golfers was founded as long ago as 1608 after James I's Scottish retinue had brought golf, or 'goff', to England with them. Goffers Road in Blackheath commemorates these pioneers. The club's present course, near Eltham Palace, was laid out by the great James Braid. Nearby is the ground of Blackheath Rugby Club, the oldest of its

kind in Britain, founded specifically for this purpose in 1858.

Blackheath itself — probably Bleak Heath originally — is a large area of open space to the south of Greenwich Park. It was here during the Peasants' Revolt in the 14th century that Wat Tyler drew up his army of rebellious peasants to hear the priest John Ball deliver his famous sermon: 'When Adam delved and Eve span, who was then the gentleman?' Jack Cade and his rebels gathered here in 1450. The two leaders are remembered in the names of Cade Road and Wat Tyler Road.

Roman Watling Street ran right through Blackheath, and centuries later highwaymen lurked along the high road, some of them to meet their end on the gibbet on Shooter's Hill. A team of female archers called the British Amazons practised on the heath in the 18th century, and it was also the scene of mass religious revival meetings at this time, addressed by Charles Wesley and George Whitefield. Today the woods and gorse thickets have been cleared away, and the heath has been tamed for the 20th century.

London's Statues

◆ ◆ ◆

Awealth of outdoor statues adds to the excitement of exploring London's streets. Many of them are the products of Britain's age of imperial ascendancy.

A statue is the central focal point of London for many visitors. The figure of *Eros* in Piccadilly Circus was unveiled in 1893 as a memorial to the Earl of Shaftesbury, the Victorian philanthropist who is also commemorated by Shaftesbury Avenue. Some people think that the statue is possibly a visual pun, with the god of love aiming to bury his shafts in the ground, but its brilliant sculptor, Alfred Gilbert, always denied that he had any such idea. Poised on one foot on a nautilus shell, with an elaborate helmet and the wings of a butterfly, *Eros* is made of aluminium. On the fountain below him are writhing dolphins and cupids.

Not very far away and well worth a look is another work by Gilbert, the memorial fountain to Queen Alexandra in Marlborough Gate, facing the east wall of St James's Palace. Another allegory of love, it was unveiled in 1932 by King George V, who reluctantly gave the eccentric sculptor a belated knighthood.

'Finest hour': Sir Winston Churchill gazes indomitably towards Big Ben.

Of Admirals and Actors

Another candidate for the title of London's hub is Nelson's Column in Trafalgar Square. The column itself is over 167ft (50m) high and the statue, by Edward Hodges Bailey, rises more than 17ft (5m) on top of that. It is said that 14 people sat down to a dizzying steak dinner on top of the column before the statue was hauled up into place. The admiral's empty sleeve is pinned to his coat, but there is no patch over his blind eye. His admirers were determined that Nelson should soar above the Duke of York, 124ft (38m) up on his column above Waterloo Place, but the highest statue of all in London is the figure of Justice on the Central Criminal Court, Old Bailey, which rises to 212ft (65m) above ground.

At the foot of Nelson's Column are four identical lions designed by Sir Edwin Landseer, and there are many other statues in and around the square. All the Englishmen, it has been pointed out, have their backs firmly turned on the National Gallery, including Charles I, looking down from his horse along Whitehall on an island in a sea of traffic. The equestrian figure of George IV, improbably riding bareback and stirrupless in a Roman toga, is by Sir Francis Chantrey and was originally intended to go on top of Marble Arch.

Behind the National Portrait Gallery stands the statue of the great actor, Sir Henry Irving, by Sir Thomas Brock, and on the traffic island in St Martin's Place is the memorial to the First World War heroine, Dame Edith Cavell, by Sir George Frampton. Brock and Frampton, with Alfred Gilbert, were leading figures of the New Sculpture movement in the late Victorian and Edwardian periods.

Fighting Men

Another favourite London statue is the equestrian figure of King Richard I in chain mail, brandishing his great sword on the back of his noble steed outside the Houses of Parliament in Old Palace Yard. Put in place in 1860, this heroic bronze is by Baron Carlo Marochetti, an Italian educated in France who came to

England in 1848. His good looks, charm and court connections in Paris gave him the entrée to high social circles and the favour of Queen Victoria and Prince Albert — to the jealousy of some native British sculptors. It was Marochetti who cast the Landseer lions for Trafalgar Square.

Near the Richard I statue, outside Westminster Hall, is the figure of Oliver Cromwell, with one of the best lions in London. By Sir Hamo Thornycroft, another leading New Sculpture figure, it dates from 1899.

Marochetti had meanwhile died in 1867, to be replaced as the pet hate of jaundiced British sculptors by Joseph Edgar Boehm, a Viennese of Hungarian descent who had settled in London in 1862. He became Sculptor in Ordinary to Queen Victoria, dominated the field of public monuments in London in the 1870s and 1880s, and was given a baronetcy in 1889.

It was Boehm who created the equestrian statue of the great Duke of Wellington at Hyde Park Corner. The 'Iron Duke' is the only person to be honoured with two equestrian statues in London. The other, by Chantrey, is outside the Royal Exchange in the heart of the City. The first monument erected to him was the 20ft (6.1m) figure of Achilles in Hyde Park, near Apsley House, by Sir Richard Wesmacott.

Physical Energy

There are several other notable statues in Hyde Park and Kensington Gardens. Arguably the finest is the ferociously vigorous *Physical Energy* by G F Watts.

Florence Nightingale, 'the Lady with the Lamp', in Waterloo Place. Beyond her is her friend and ally, Sidney Herbert.

Made in the 1880s (though not installed here until 1906), it symbolises the enterprise and progress of the age, with the rider at one with the natural order: his legs like roots, his head like the sun, his gaze searching the far horizon. It is in sharp contrast with the winsome *Peter Pan* of 1911, which is by Sir George Frampton. The Rima Monument of 1925, to the naturalist W H Hudson, is the work of Epstein, and *The Arch* by Henry Moore stands to the east of Long Water.

A stroll along Victoria Embankment will reward you with works by Brock, Sir William Goscombe John and Marochetti among others. Another good hunting ground for statues is Parliament Square. Here you can see statues of George Canning by Westmacott, Palmerston by Thomas Woolner, Smuts by Epstein, and a pugnacious Churchill by Ivor Roberts-Jones. Just off Pall Mall, Waterloo Place yields Burgoyne and Lawrence by Boehm, Captain Scott by Brock, Lord Clyde by Marochetti and Edward VII by Sir Bertram Mackennal. Not far away, the molehill which caused William III's horse to throw him, fatally, at Hampton Court is faithfully rendered in bronze beneath the hooves of the king's equestrian statue in St James's Square. The statue was erected more than a century afterwards, in 1807.

Heroes of our Time

In Leicester Square, Charlie Chaplin was unveiled in 1981 in his little man guise, with bowler hat and cane; he is by John Doubleday. A statue of Lord Dowding, the Battle of Britain commander, was unveiled in 1988 in front of St Clement Danes in the Strand, close to Sir Hamo Thornycroft's tremendous Gladstone monument. In Red Lion Square a bespectacled Fenner Brockway, the left-wing MP, waves an arm oratorically, primly observed from behind by the philosopher Lord Bertrand Russell.

George IV, his horse and a temporary passenger at rest in Trafalgar Square.

London

Area BY Area

London has evolved over the
centuries to no overall grand design
yet with many distinct areas, each
with its own history, associations and
flavour. When you visit one of the
places of interest on the following
pages, look at the map alongside and
explore the streets and other
attractions nearby.

Area BY Area

*Big Ben dominates Westminster, one of
London's most popular tourist areas*

⊖ WESTMINSTER
🚌 3, 11, 12, 24, 29, 53, 77A, 88, 159, C1
🚢 TOWER, GREENWICH AND THAMES BARRIER

Westminster Abbey

ATLAS REF 176 B3

◆ PARLIAMENT SQUARE, SW1 ◆

Westminster

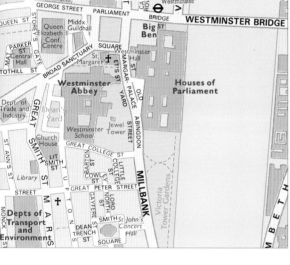

Hidden in Westminster Abbey, unknown to most visitors and seldom revealed, is one of Britain's most remarkable medieval art treasures. Craftsmen were brought from Italy in the 13th century to create the Great Pavement in the floor in front of the high altar. It is a marble diagram, whose geometric patterns make a symbolic picture of the universe as understood in the Middle Ages. The pavement is normally kept covered by a carpet for protection and is displayed only at intervals.

Westminster Abbey was the church of what was the British Empire. It is still the church of Great Britain. The crowded funerary monuments inside — some exquisite works of art, some banal in the extreme — are testimony to the hold it has always enjoyed over the national imagination. Here, not in far grander St Paul's, the British honour their dead. Here they crown their monarchs on an ancient wooden chair over a lump of sandstone. Here they buried their Unknown Warrior.

The first abbey church was built on the site some time before AD750. This was followed by a grander structure, erected by Edward the Confessor and consecrated in 1065. William the Conqueror was the first of a long line of monarchs of England to be crowned in the abbey. In 1245 the artistic King Henry III decided to rebuild the entire structure. This was the beginning of a tremendous building programme, which went on for 300 years. The last major addition was the superb Chapel of Henry VII, completed in 1519. For a brief period, from 1542 to 1556, the abbey was a cathedral — the seat of a bishop. Since then, however, it has been a 'royal peculiar' — an establishment resembling a cathedral, but with the sovereign, not a bishop, as its head.

Like all historic churches, the abbey has problems of tourist control and financial maintenance. It has solved them by charging a fairly substantial sum for entry into areas of special historic interest, while areas around the altar and the nave remain free of charge. During divine services all movement outside these areas is forbidden.

The **royal tombs** are, of course, the prime attraction of the abbey. Entrance to them is gained through a wicket in the north aisle, and access is allowed using a strictly controlled, one-way system based on topography, not chronology. Thus the tombs of Queen Elizabeth I and her cousin Mary Queen of Scots, separated by the width of Henry VII's Chapel, mark the beginning and the end of the itinerary. Near Mary's tomb an ancient wooden tablet bears the warrant of her son, James I of England and VI of Scotland, instructing the Dean and Chapter of Peterborough Cathedral to remove his mother's body from Peterborough to Westminster.

The **Chapel of Henry VII** has brilliant banners and painted 'achievements' adorning the 16th-century wooden stalls of the Knights of the Order of the Bath. Dominating the chapel, behind iron railings, is the tomb of Henry VII. One of the greatest funerary monuments in Europe, its effigy of the king was made by the Italian Renaissance sculptor Pietro Torrigiano, a contemporary of Michelangelo. The vaulted roof, completed in 1519, is an outstanding example of its kind.

A modern bridge leads from the Chapel of Henry VII into the very heart of the abbey — the **Chapel of St Edward the Confessor**. This was built over the apse of the original Saxon church. Here, behind the high altar, is the shrine of the saintly King Edward, with its escort of five kings and four queens. Among the tombs is that of Eleanor of Castile, with its exquisite effigy of the beautiful queen, created by order of her grieving husband, Edward I. His tomb lies only a few feet away — an immense, plain stone box, bearing the almost unreadable inscription, *Scottorum malleus* ('hammer of the Scots'). Nearby

Below: the south transept, with its medieval rose window and some of the great church's memorials of the illustrious dead. Poet's Corner is here, with the tombs of Chaucer and Spenser.

is the oak **Coronation Chair**, made for Edward by one Master Walter of Durham. People used to bribe the custodians to be allowed to sit in it. Below it is the ancient **Stone of Scone**, the coronation stone of the kings of Scotland. Edward I seized this from the Scots in 1297. In December 1950 a group of Scottish medical students succeeded in carrying it back to Scotland, but it was later returned. Other tombs in the chapel include that of Henry V, the hero of Agincourt, with its worn wooden effigy, and that of Edward III, looking like a magician with long hair and beard.

The **Grave of the Unknown Warrior** is just inside the entrance, at the west door. His body was buried here, in soil brought from the battlefields of France, on 11 November 1920. The so-called **Poets' Corner** is in the south transept. Here and nearby, the names of the great form a roll call of British history, art and science. Look for the tablet inscribed *O rare Ben Jonson*, marking the tomb of the great playwright. Does this mean exactly what it says, or rather *Orare* — 'pray for'? In the nave nearby are graves of great British scientists, including Sir Isaac Newton (1642–1727), the discoverer of the laws of gravity, and Ernest, Lord Rutherford (1871–1937), the father of atomic science.

It is well worth going on one of the guided tours, which will take you into areas that are accessible only under supervision. These include the superb, 14th-century **Jerusalem Chamber**. In a 700-year-old building that has been adapted and extended again and again over the centuries, there are also innumerable other corners and crannies which are worth exploring by the unaccompanied. Look for the enchanting **little cloister**, with its delightful fountain, near the **chapter house**. The chapter house, built about 1270, was once a meeting place for Parliament and was extensively restored in the 19th century. The Norman **undercroft** houses one of the most overlooked museums in Britain. Here are the death masks of a number of British monarchs, showing how they really looked — not as flattering official sculptors of the time portrayed them. Among them is that of Edward III, his face twisted by the stroke that killed him, and another of Katherine, the French wife of Henry V, who married the English king after his victory at Agincourt in 1415.

Open daily, 8.00am–6.00pm (closed except for nave and aisles on Sun). Free admission to all areas on Wed, 6.00pm–7.45pm; admission fees to some areas at other times.

Canaletto's painting of the Knights of the Order of the Bath in their finery, leaving Westminster Abbey in procession in 1749. The Chapel of Henry VII is the Order's chapel, and the banners of the knights hang above their stalls.

Westminster Abbey Area

St Margaret's, seen here with Big Ben in the background, has witnessed notable weddings in its time, including those of Milton, Pepys and Sir Winston Churchill.

St Margaret's

PARLIAMENT SQUARE, SW1
⊖ WESTMINSTER
ATLAS REF 176 B3
Standing in the shadow of the great Westminster Abbey, this enchanting little church nevertheless manages to lead its own life. It is a parish church of the city of Westminster. Since 1614 the House of Commons has adjourned here on certain occasions, when the Speaker sits in front of the lectern. Although founded in the 11th or 12th centuries, the church as it exists today is essentially the work of the early 16th century. The Duke of Somerset, Protector of England during the reign of the boy-king Edward VI (1547–1553), ordered the demolition of the church to provide stone for his grand new palace, Somerset House, but angry parishioners drove off the workmen.

Among the treasures of St Margaret's is the stained-glass east window, probably made to commemorate the marriage (which never took place) of Catherine of Aragon to Prince Arthur, elder brother of Henry VIII. William Caxton, the father of printing in England, is buried somewhere in the church or churchyard; in 1820 a tablet was erected to him on the right-hand side of the east door. Sir Walter Raleigh, beheaded in Whitehall in 1618, is buried in the chancel.
Open daily, 9.30am–5.30pm.

Houses of Parliament

PARLIAMENT SQUARE, SW1
⊖ WESTMINSTER
ATLAS REF 176 B3
The official name of the sovereign seat of British government is the New Palace of Westminster. This is because the building stands on the site of what was formerly the Royal Palace of Westminster. First occupied by Edward the Confessor, the Royal Palace of Westminster was, with the Tower of London, the principal residence of the monarch until Henry VIII acquired Whitehall Palace in 1529. The present remarkable building, a Gothic extravaganza, was begun in 1840. Queen Victoria opened the first Parliament here in 1852, and today the building is usually referred to as the Houses of Parliament. The architecture is the work of Sir Charles Barry, assisted by the ecclesiastical architect A W Pugin, who specialised in Gothic revivals.

Victoria Tower at the west of the building is 336ft (102m) high, and as such is the tallest square tower in the world. The monarch enters the great archway underneath for the State Opening of Parliament in November each year. A flag flying from the Victoria Tower by day, and a light shining from the clock tower by night, indicate when Parliament is sitting.

Opening arrangements are subject to constant change, so check first with a Tourist Information Centre (a list appears on p.153 of this book). During parliamentary sittings, tourists are allowed into the Houses of Parliament every day. Access to public galleries in the House of Commons and the House of Lords is gained from St Stephen's entrance.

Big Ben

PARLIAMENT SQUARE, SW1
⊖ WESTMINSTER
ATLAS REF 176 B3
The 320ft-(97m-) high clock tower of the Houses of Parliament contains probably the most famous, and certainly one of the most accurate, public clocks in the world. Although the tower is often called Big Ben, the name actually applies to the huge bell inside the clock itself. In the Second World War, Big Ben achieved an almost religious importance. Members of the Big Ben Society would gather in prayer as the great bell boomed out before the 9 o'clock news on the radio. The bell, weighing 13½ tons, is named after Sir Benjamin Hall, Commissioner of Works at the time the bell was hung in 1858. Each of the clock dials is 23ft (7m) in diameter: the figures are 2ft (0.6m) high and the hands 14ft (4.2m) and 9ft (2.7m) long respectively.

The Mother of Parliaments rises in Victorian grandeur to dominate the river. It replaced a building destroyed by fire in 1834.

Westminster Hall

PARLIAMENT SQUARE, SW1
⊖ WESTMINSTER
ATLAS REF 176 B3
This majestic chamber was part
of the Royal Palace of
Westminster, and it survived two
great fires of 1512 and 1834. It
was begun during the reign of
William Rufus in 1097, and was
further embellished under
Richard II in 1399, when the
superb hammerbeam roof was
created. The largest hall in
England when it was built, its
floor dimensions today remain
unchanged: 240ft (73m) long by
69ft (21m) wide. In 1649 King
Charles I was tried here. Today,
the hall is largely used for
ceremonial occasions.

Jewel Tower

ABINGDON STREET, SW1
⊖ WESTMINSTER
ATLAS REF 176 B3
Although historically part of the
Palace of Westminster, the Jewel
Tower is physically separate from
it, so the public can easily obtain
admission. This delightful little
moated tower was built in 1366
to act, in effect, as the king's strong
room for jewels, plate and the like.
Subsequently used as a record
office, it was restored, after
air-raid damage, between 1948
and 1956. The upper chamber
acts as a small museum for relics
associated with the palaces of
Westminster and Whitehall. Look
for the carved bosses on the
vaults on the ground floor.
   *Open daily, 10.00am–6.00pm
(10.00am–4.00pm in winter).
Closed on Mon in winter.*

Central Hall

TOTHILL STREET, SW1
⊖ ST JAMES'S PARK
ATLAS REF 176 B3
Built in 1912 as the headquarters
of the Methodist Church, the
Central Hall has a great dome which
is the third largest in London. The
hall can seat 2,700 people and is in
frequent use for general meetings.
The first meeting of the General
Assembly of the United Nations
took place here in 1946.

Parliament Square SW1

⊖ WESTMINSTER
ATLAS REF 176 B3
Although now a maelstrom of
traffic, Parliament Square was
originally laid out by Sir Charles
Barry, architect of the New Palace

of Westminster, to provide a garden
setting for Parliament. After
Piccadilly Circus and Trafalgar
Square, this is the most popular
tourist spot in the capital, with its
panoramic views of the seat of
government and the great Abbey.
   The numerous statues in the
square are of famous statesmen,
including Field-Marshal Smuts,
the staunch South African ally of
Britain in the Second World War.
Also among them is Sir Winston
Churchill, shown in old age but
still vigorous, facing the Houses
of Parliament. On the west side
of the square is a statue of
Abraham Lincoln, presented by
the American people in 1920.

Victoria Tower Gardens

MILLBANK, SW1
⊖ WESTMINSTER
ATLAS REF 176 B3
The building of the Thames
Embankment was one of the
great works of Victorian
engineering, and Victoria Tower
Gardens, though not particularly
attractive in themselves, provide
a fine view of the River Thames
and the buildings on the south
bank. They also possess a replica,
made in 1912, of Rodin's
Burghers of Calais, placed
dramatically in the shadow of the
vast Victoria Tower of the
Houses of Parliament.

*The flags fly bravely in
Parliament Square,
formerly a slum area
which was cleared in
the 1860s after the new
Houses of Parliament
had been built.*

⊖ WESTMINSTER

Whitehall

ATLAS REF 176 B4

◆ SW1 ◆

This broad, handsome road connecting Trafalgar Square and Parliament Square has all the major government departments on or near it. Whitehall takes its name from the Royal Palace of Whitehall, which Henry VIII took over from Cardinal Wolsey in 1529 and adapted for his own use. The palace was destroyed by fire in the 17th century, though Henry VIII's wine cellar still survives under the Ministry of Defence.

The best overall view of Whitehall can be obtained from the portico of the National Gallery in Trafalgar Square. From here you can see the Admiralty on the right (designed by Robert Adam in 1760), and at the far end of Whitehall the Houses of Parliament.

Great Scotland Yard, tucked away on the left-hand side of the street, was formerly the headquarters of the Metropolitan Police (who have now moved into new buildings in Victoria Street). In front of the Ministry of Defence is, appropriately, the statue of Field Marshal Montgomery, the Second World War commander, in characteristic posture. Near him is one of Sir Walter Raleigh, the great Elizabethan courtier, explorer and writer.

Military statues in Whitehall include, outside the old War Office, a mounted figure of the Duke of Cambridge in his plumed hat. He was Commander-in-Chief of the British Army for 40 years until 1895. Further down the street is Field Marshal Haig, also on horseback, in a 1937 statue by Alfred Hardiman which attracted almost as fierce criticism as the commander it represents. In front of the Ministry of Defence is Oscar Nemon's bronze of Field Marshall Montgomery, unveiled in 1980. The statue of Field Marshal Slim by Ivor Robert Jones was erected 10 years later.

10 Downing Street SW1

⊖ WESTMINSTER

ATLAS REF 176 B4

It is typical of the British that No. 10 Downing Street, the official residence of the Prime Minister, should appear to be a modest terraced house. Appearances are deceptive, however, for behind the reticent façade is a complex of rooms, some of great elegance, including the Cabinet Room on the ground floor. No. 10 Downing Street is connected to No. 11, the official residence of the Chancellor of the Exchequer.

Downing Street is named after its builder, Sir George Downing, who died in 1684. During major rebuilding at Nos 10 and 11, however, archaeological evidence came to light which showed that the area had been in more or less continuous occupation from Roman times onwards. Among the finds were the remains of a major Saxon hall, and the tennis court of Henry VIII's Palace of Whitehall. Until recently, public access to the street was freely permitted, and tourists liked to photograph each other in front of No. 10.

The street is closed to the public, but a view can be obtained from Whitehall.

Cabinet War Rooms

KING CHARLES STREET, SW1

⊖ WESTMINSTER

ATLAS REF 176 B3

Parallel to Downing Street, towards Parliament Square, is King Charles Street. At the far end from Whitehall, steps descend to a piece of wartime nostalgia, the rooms from which a small war cabinet directed the course of British involvement in the Second World War. The Cabinet Room itself is arranged as though for a meeting. Among the complex of rooms and passages is Churchill's bedroom, which also served as his office. He made some of his most important wartime broadcasts from the desks in the room (including one to the French in rather uncertain language, when, it is said, he had a French translator sitting on his lap). In the Map Room the Cabinet followed the global course of the war, while the Telephone Room kept Churchill in direct contact with the President of the USA.

Open daily, 10.00am-6.00pm.

The Cenotaph

WHITEHALL, SW1

⊖ WESTMINSTER

ATLAS REF 176 B4

'Cenotaph' literally means 'empty tomb'. The Cenotaph in Whitehall commemorates all servicemen of the British Empire and Commonwealth who were killed in both World Wars. Originally intended as a memorial to the First World War ('the war to end all wars'), the Cenotaph had a commemoration to the dead of the Second World War added to it in 1946. The design is by Sir Edwin Lutyens, and the monument was originally inaugurated on Armistice Day, 11 November 1920. Although somewhat fallen in public esteem today (men used to remove their hats when passing, but no longer do so), it is still the focus of the national remembrance service on the

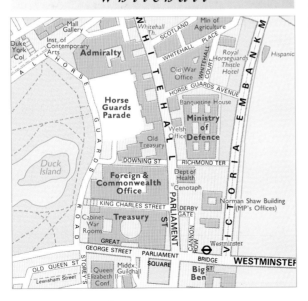

Whitehall

In remembrance of 'The Glorious Dead', the Cenotaph is adorned only by flags of the armed services and poppies.

second Sunday in November each year, when the monarch lays a wreath at its base.

Horse Guards

WHITEHALL, SW1
⊖ WESTMINSTER
ATLAS REF 176 B4

The Changing of the Guard here is one of the most popular tourist spectacles in London. On either side of the arch leading into the Horse Guards building is a trooper of the Household Cavalry, mounted on a horse trained to accept the endless, close proximity of inquisitive tourists. The troopers are posted from 10.00am to 4.00pm, but are relieved every hour. The Changing of the Guard takes place every day at 11.00am (10.00am on Sundays). Because of the popularity of the event and the relatively small viewing area, it is advisable to get there well before time.

The Horse Guards building, begun in 1742, stands on the site

The Household Cavalry in stately evolutions on Horse Guards Parade, the former tiltyard of Whitehall Palace and a scene of jousting.

of a guardhouse for Whitehall Palace. Passing through the arch today, you enter a large open space, Horse Guards Parade, where the **Trooping the Colour** takes place on the monarch's official birthday in June. Statues of outstanding commanders are placed around the parade, including a modern one to Earl Mountbatten of Burma, assassinated in 1979. The Guards Memorial is on the edge of Horse Guards Parade, near St James's Park.

Banqueting House

WHITEHALL, SW1
⊖ WESTMINSTER
ATLAS REF 176 B4

This is the finest example of pure Renaissance architecture in England. Built by Inigo Jones between 1619 and 1622 for King James I, it is one of the few surviving parts of the Royal Palace of Whitehall. Ironically, it was designed to display the splendour of the monarchy, shortly before the English decided to cut off their monarch's head. King Charles I commissioned the great Flemish artist, Peter Paul Rubens, to paint

nine immense allegories for the ceiling. The central panel shows the apotheosis of Charles's father, King James I of England (and VI of Scotland), while other panels show the benefits of monarchical government. The platform on which Charles I was beheaded was placed in Whitehall outside the Banqueting House and a bust of the king, erected in 1798, probably marks the site of the window through which he stepped for his execution.

Open Tue–Sat 10.00am–5.00pm, Sun 2.00pm–5.00pm. Admission fee.

Allegorical paintings by Rubens celebrate the benefits of good government on the ceiling of the Banqueting House.

⊖ PIMLICO
⊖ VAUXHALL
🚌 2B, 36, 77A, 88

Tate Gallery

ATLAS REF 176 B2

◆ ── MILLBANK, SW1 ── ◆

The Tate Gallery houses the national collections of a) British painting from the 16th century to the 19th, and b) foreign and British 20th-century painting and sculpture. Despite its ultra-conventional exterior, with Classical pillars and Renaissance replicas, this is the gallery most likely to enrage the conservative.

In the central halls, bemused visitors in the past have encountered neatly piled builders' bricks, broken slates arranged in a circle, and driftwood or flint stones arranged in patterns as 'works of art'. Deeper in the building you will encounter canvases with a single red line painted across them, or with white painted on white.

All the same, the Tate is a gallery where art is alive and vibrant. The place teems with young art students being led through the intricacies of Dadaism and Surrealism. In the restaurant and teashop you will encounter their elders, engaged in equally passionate discussion about some new exhibit. And there is much to discuss. Because the gallery includes contemporary art, the Trustees must look to the future when acquiring new works and decide whether an unconventional composition is a Picasso of the future.

Since 1989 the gallery has totally rearranged a substantial proportion of exhibits. Essentially, the intention is to provide a simple chronological path through the collection, tracing the development of British art from 1550 to the present day and the connections between British and foreign art in the 20th century. The Trustees have broken down the old-fashioned distinction between art before and after 1900.

The advantage of the new system is that it forces you to look again at old favourites in a new context, and it brings out works from the vast reserve. The disadvantage is that you never quite know where things are. If you are in quest of a particular school or artist, it is essential to pick up a copy of the free plan available in the foyer. The gallery also regularly publishes a free pamphlet, *Preview*, which describes forthcoming exhibitions and lectures.

In 1841 the Tate Gallery's collection was founded when Sir Francis Chantrey, a fashionable sculptor, left a substantial bequest to the Royal Academy to help build up a collection of British art. The present building, opened in 1897, was the gift of a wealthy sugar merchant, Sir Henry Tate. Over the past century, subsequent additions — all paid for by private benefactors — have substantially enlarged the floor area. The policy on acquisitions has also broadened. The display of British painting to give an overall survey from the 16th century to today is the Tate's prime objective, but many modern European and American works are also included in its collection.

The Tate publishes authoritative guides and catalogues, and from Monday to Friday there are free guided tours, all of which begin in the

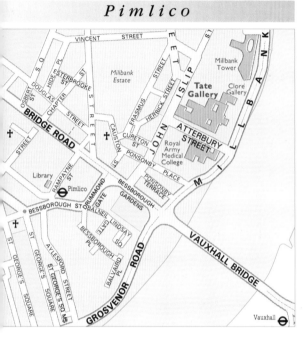

Pimlico

*Along the Embankment between Vauxhall Bridge and the Tate Gallery, near the Henry Moore statue **Locking Piece**, is a plaque on a buttress, marking the site of steps down to the river which until 1867 were used by convicts on their way to exile in Australia. They came from the prison which stood where the Tate is now. The biggest gaol in London, it was built in 1821 to put the ideas of Jeremy Bentham into practice. Inmates were kept in total silence and were put to work.*

The central hall of the Tate Gallery, designed in the 1890s by Sidney Smith. The gallery is involved in more or less non-stop controversy about what it should or should not be buying.

Rotunda. Visitors can also simply wander round with the gallery plan, for the presentation of the collection is admirably clear. There are more than 30 display areas, each with an overall theme or devoted to a single artist. In each area a large notice outlines the theme, drawing attention to any particularly important works. Individual works are also identified, with brief notes indicating anything important or unusual in their composition or history.

The best-known works include the mystical paintings of **William Blake**, the down-to-earth productions of **Hogarth**, **Constable's** enchanting visions of the English landscape and the perennially popular **Pre-Raphaelites**, as well as fine examples of **Gainsborough**, **Reynolds** and **Landseer**, and huge, apocalyptic works by **John Martin**. Among the modern paintings are works by **Augustus John**, **Francis Bacon**, **L S Lowry** and **David Hockney**. **Stanley Spencer's** two versions of the Resurrection, set in his village churchyard at Cookham-on-Thames in Berkshire, are also on display. **Picasso** and **Matisse** are both represented, as well as the **Cubists**, and **Surrealists** such as **Salvador Dali**.

In 1987 the generosity of a property developer, Sir Charles Clore, enabled the gallery to provide a proper setting for its **Turner collection**. Before this, much of the tremendous output of Britain's great artist was housed in different places. The Clore Foundation enabled an entire new wing, designed by James Stirling, to be built separate from the main block but connected to it. Here, for the first time, all of Turner's paintings belonging to the Tate are displayed. The Clore Gallery also has a study room devoted to the artist.

Of all the major institutions in central London, the Tate is the worst-served by public transport. There is only one bus which passes the main entrance, the 77A. It is best to reach the Tate Gallery from Pimlico underground station, which is only 20 minutes' walk away. The streets in between are interesting examples of Victorian middle-class housing, worthy of study in their own right. Laid out by the developer Thomas Cubitt in the 1840s, they established a tradition of good residential building in this area which has continued into the 20th century. One example of such developments is Dolphin Square, laid out in 1937.

Open Mon–Sat 10.00am–5.50pm, Sun 2.00pm–5.50pm.

*John Constable's famous and much-loved **Flatford Mill** (top) exemplifies the gallery's display of great British artists from the 16th century on, while Salvador Dali's **Lobster Telephone** (above) is an example of its modern art.*

⊖ ST JAMES'S PARK
🚌 11, 24 29, C1

Buckingham Palace

ATLAS REF 175 F3

◆ SW1 ◆

St James's Park

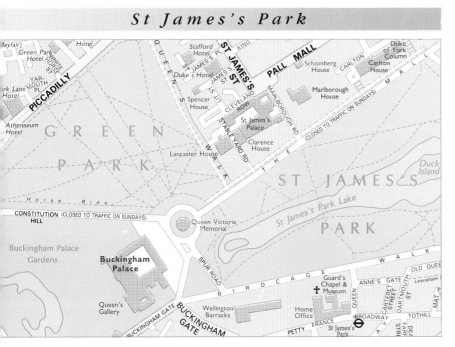

Queen Anne's Gate is worth a stroll not only for its 18th-century charm, but for its galaxy of distinguished past residents. Lord Palmerston was born at No. 20 in 1784 and the prime minister who lost the American colonies, Lord North, also lived in the street. Jeremy Bentham and John Stuart Mill both lived at No. 40 and the redoubtable Admiral Fisher, father of the dreadnought battleship, at No. 16. Note the rich variety of grotesque faces above the windows of the houses and the fire mark on No. 26.

Although Buckingham Palace, the principal residence of the monarch, is never open to the public, a surprising number of people know something about its interior and 40 acre (16ha) gardens. Every summer garden parties are held in the grounds, to which several hundred people from all walks of life are invited in recognition of their services to the community. In addition, young people who have successfully completed the Duke of Edinburgh's Award Scheme are invited, each with one parent, to the palace to the annual presentation of awards.

The core of the palace was built in 1702 as the town house of the Duke of Buckingham. George III bought it in 1761, but although it was altered and enlarged over the following years, it was not until the accession of Queen Victoria in 1837 that the palace became the principal royal residence in London. The imposing east wing which the public sees, built in a Classical style in 1913, is the work of Sir Aston Webb, who also designed the Queen Victoria Memorial at the top of the Mall. The family quarters are in the north wing, facing the grounds and as far away as possible from the hurly-burly of London. Under the present Queen the palace has become more of a family home than at any time in the past. The Prince of Wales was born here in 1948, followed by Prince Andrew in 1960 and Prince Edward in 1964. The **State Apartments** are in frequent use for investitures and state

banquets. They include the Throne Room, the State Ballroom and the Music Room.

The immense gravelled forecourt of the palace is patrolled by sentries of the Guards Division. Sentries also stand outside the railings, but the actual work of controlling crowds for the traditional **Changing of the Guard** is done by uniformed police.

The palace overlooks **St James's Park** and **Green Park**. There is an open space in front, to which vast crowds may gravitate at times of national importance. It was from the balcony of Buckingham Palace that the Royal Family, together with Winston Churchill, shared with an immense crowd the rejoicing at the end of the Second World War.

A favourite perching-place for younger members of the crowd is the immense **Queen Victoria Memorial**, in front of the palace. The sculptures, by Sir Thomas Brock, date from 1911. In them, he indulged the Edwardian love of allegory to the full. Courage and Constancy sit at the feet of Victory, while Truth, Motherhood and Justice jostle for places with the Arts and Sciences. Queen Victoria herself is seated facing The Mall.

Not open to the public. The Changing of the Guard takes place at 11.30am daily, or on alternate days from mid-Aug to Apr.

Buckingham Palace looks suitably regal from across St James's Park, with the Queen Victoria Memorial to the right. The scene is fundamentally a celebration of the might and grandeur of the British Empire.

Nearby . . .

The Royal Mews

BUCKINGHAM PALACE ROAD,
SW1
⊖ VICTORIA
ATLAS REF 175 F3
Built by John Nash in 1826, the
Royal Mews contains the Gold
State Coach, built in 1762, which
is used for coronations. It also
houses the Irish State Coach,
usually used for the State
Opening of Parliament, and the
Glass State Coach, used for family
occasions such as royal
weddings.
   *Open on Wed and Thu,
2.00pm–4.00pm. Closed during
Ascot week. Admission fee.*

The Queen's Gallery

BUCKINGHAM PALACE ROAD,
SW1
⊖ VICTORIA
ATLAS REF 175 F3
Originally the private chapel of
Buckingham Palace, the Queen's
Gallery was destroyed by
bombing in the Second World
War. It was rebuilt, and opened
to the public in 1961. Items on
display are drawn from the Royal
Family's private collection and
the Royal Library at Windsor, and
are changed from time to time.

Display items in the past have
included the shirt worn by King
Charles I on the day of his
execution, and the sketchbooks
and diaries of Queen Victoria.
   *Open Tue–Sat 10.30am–
5.00pm, Sun 2.00pm–5.00pm.*

The Mall SW1

⊖ CHARING CROSS
⊖ ST JAMES'S PARK
ATLAS REF 176 A4
The Mall connects the hustle and
bustle of everyday London with
the deliberate majesty of the
palace. It is separated from the
turmoil of Trafalgar Square by the
solidity of **Admiralty Arch**, and
terminates at the open space in
front of **Buckingham Palace**.
Great plane trees line it on each
side and, despite its width and
the speed of traffic, it is easy to
cross, for there are pedestrian
crossings linked to lights. On one
side are the refreshingly green
trees of **St James's Park**, on the
other the dignified, creamy-white
columns and façades of **Carlton
House Terrace**. All ceremonial
processions leaving Buckingham
Palace for Parliament,
Westminster Abbey or St Paul's
Cathedral pass along this
handsome boulevard.
   The Mall takes its curious
name from the French ball game
of *paille maille*, which King

Charles II introduced in England,
and which was played along the
length of The Mall when it was
first laid out in 1660. (Parallel to
The Mall is the street known as
Pall Mall, which owes its name to
the same pastime.) Sir Aston
Webb transformed The Mall in
1911, as part of the massive
Edwardian development of this
ceremonial area of London.
   Approaching The Mall from
Trafalgar Square, you see first on
the left a brutally functional
structure known simply as **The
Citadel**, built in 1940 and part of
the wartime Admiralty, to which
it is linked. On the right is
Carlton House Terrace. Just
before the steps leading to the
terrace is the **Institute of
Contemporary Arts (ICA)**,
tucked away beneath elegant
arches. Although it is a club, a
day-time ticket can be obtained,
which allows the casual visitor to
use its very civilised facilities.
These include a cinema and
theatre for avant-garde
entertainment, and a restaurant.
   Immediately next to the ICA
are the steps leading to the **Duke
of York's Column**, built by
Benjamin Wyatt in 1834. Almost
as impressive as Nelson's Column
in appearance, it commemorates
an ineffectual royal commander,
immortalised in the nursery
rhyme *The Grand Old Duke of
York/He had 10,000 men*. It was
paid for by a supposedly
'voluntary' donation of one day's
pay from every man in the British
Army. Further along are the
gardens of Marlborough House,
and St James's Palace.

*A troop of the
Household Cavalry
enters The Mall. This
stately boulevard was
part of the Edwardian
concept of a grand
ceremonial arena at
the heart of the
Empire's capital. It is
used for all royal
parades and
processions.*

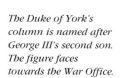

*The Duke of York's
column is named after
George III's second son.
The figure faces
towards the War Office.*

Buckingham Palace Area

One of London's most delightful views is the prospect along the lake in St James's Park to Horse Guards and Whitehall. The lake has long been famous for its wildfowl.

St James's Park   SW1

⊖ ST JAMES'S PARK
⊖ CHARING CROSS
ATLAS REF 176 A3/4

Within a few minutes' walk of one of the busiest urban areas in the world is a lake which plays host to a wider variety of wild fowl than most people will see in a lifetime. They are wild only in the sense that they look after themselves. In fact, they have become so accustomed to tourists, and so expectant of being fed, that the visitor almost has to shoo them away. On the bridge crossing the lake, regular visitors have trained sparrows actually to sit on their hands and feed. For the tourist with tired and fractious children, St James's Park is a godsend.

St James's Park was laid out for King Charles II by the French landscape gardener André Le Nôtre in 1662, but its history

goes back long before that. Originally, it was simply an open space just outside the city of Westminster, belonging to the hospital of St James the Less. When Henry VIII acquired the hospital (by purchase and not by his usual technique of sequestration) and converted it into St James's Palace, the open space nearby became a deer park. The architect John Nash, who redesigned much of the central area of London, laid out the park as it is today, together with the lake, in 1829.

Birdcage Walk   SW1

⊖ WESTMINSTER
⊖ ST JAMES'S PARK
ATLAS REF 176 A3

Birdcage Walk, together with The Mall on the north side, encloses St James's Park. It has a curious and attractive rural feeling, with the park on one side and the

houses and gardens of Queen Anne's Gate on the other. Birdcage Walk takes its name from aviaries which were established here during the reign of King James II; a number of decoy cages were also once placed here for the sport of King Charles II. **Cockpit Steps**, leading into Queen Anne's Terrace nearby, is another legacy of the sport of cockfighting.

Queen Anne's Gate   SW1

⊖ ST JAMES'S PARK
ATLAS REF 176 A3

London's attraction lies not only in its great set pieces, but in its quiet little corners, like this gem of a street. Considering the mayhem wrecked first by the Luftwaffe and then by post-war developers in this area, its survival is little less than a miracle. The street was built as a unit in 1704 and has scarcely

Several houses in Queen Anne's Gate have handsome wooden doorways. Lord Grey (commemorated by the blue plaque) was foreign secretary in 1914.

changed since. Outstanding are the exquisitely detailed carvings that decorate the wooden doorways of the houses. These were probably the work of woodcarvers accustomed to working on the elaborate poops and figureheads of ships of the Royal Navy, for a number of these craftsmen were discharged by the Admiralty at about the time the street was built. Some of the houses still retain iron link-snuffers beside their doors.

Although the houses are modest in appearance, they were home to many well-known people, including statesmen such as Lord Palmerston and Lord Grey, and the famous 18th-century actress Peg Woffington. The delightful, lively statue of Queen Anne near No. 13 was made during the Queen's lifetime, and was intended to be erected outside the church of St Mary-le-Strand. After her death in 1714 designs for the church were modified and the statue found a home here. The 18th-century house at the end of the street is the headquarters of the National Trust.

Wellington Barracks

BIRDCAGE WALK, SW1
⊖ ST JAMES'S PARK
ATLAS REF 176 A3
The headquarters of the Guards Division, Wellington Barracks were built in 1833. Here are stationed five regiments of Foot Guards (Grenadier, Scots, Irish, Welsh and Coldstream) who

together with the Household Cavalry make up the Household Brigade — units in direct attendance on the monarch. (The Household Cavalry is stationed in Hyde Park Barracks.)

The Guards Chapel (Royal Military Chapel)

BIRDCAGE WALK, SW1
⊖ ST JAMES'S PARK
ATLAS REF 176 A3
The Guards Chapel, which stands in front of Wellington Barracks, was first built in 1838. It was largely destroyed by bombs in the Second World War. The present building was rebuilt to a modern design in 1963.
Open Mon–Fri 10.00am– 3.30pm.

The Guards Museum

BIRDCAGE WALK, SW1
⊖ ST JAMES'S PARK
ATLAS REF 176 A3
Easy to overlook (for it is underground) this custom-built museum is well worth a visit. Covering three-and-a-half centuries, it contains exhibits about the Foot Guards' military and social history (many presented to the public for the first time). The museum as a whole provides a key to the complex military rituals centred around the monarch.
Open Mon–Thu 10.00am– 4.00pm. Closed on ceremonial days.

London Transport Headquarters

BROADWAY, SW1
⊖ ST JAMES'S PARK
ATLAS REF 176 A3
In the 1930s the London Passenger Transport Board led the world not only in its operation of public transport in the capital, both underground and above, but in what would now be called its image. Famous artists were commissioned to design transport posters and the map of the London underground system, designed during this period, has been copied in many other countries since. In 1929 the board commissioned the architect Charles Holden to design a building which would act as both administrative headquarters and an underground station. St James's Park station, with the London Passenger Transport Board's offices above, was the result.

Holden had the courage and vision to commission three controversial sculptors of the day, Jacob Epstein, Eric Gill and Henry Moore, to make sculptures for the façade. Epstein created the two grim figures *Night* and *Day* (symbolising the transport board's range of responsibilities), which can be seen just above the entrance in Broadway. The sculptures by Gill, Moore and other artists of the period are higher up on the wings and on the main building.

The Foot Guards on parade. With the Household Cavalry, the Guards make up the Household Division of ceremonial troops — though they are fighting soldiers as well.

Victoria

ATLAS REF 175 F2/176 A3

◆ SW1 ◆

Before the 1960s Victoria Street, running from Westminster Abbey to Victoria Station, was a splendid, ebullient example of turn-of-the-century architecture. Today it is a textbook example of how not to build in a city. The richly varied buildings were almost entirely swept away in the frantic 'development' that swept Britain in the 1960s and 1970s, and in their place came a canyon of glass and steel.

There are some survivals, and there has been one great gain. The front of Westminster Cathedral has been opened up with a well-planned square. The superb Albert pub, all plush and engraved glass, on the north side of the street, is an example of the style of building that once abounded here. Another survival is the Victoria Palace Theatre, built in 1911 and for many years the home of the zany comedy team *The Crazy Gang*. Opposite is an engaging little clock-tower, modelled on Big Ben when it was built in 1892 and now known as 'Little Ben'.

It is well worth leaving Victoria Street to explore the tangle of small roads running off it. These still have a life of their own. **Strutton Ground**, for instance, has a lively street market.

Westminster Cathedral

VICTORIA STREET, SW1
⊖ VICTORIA
ATLAS REF 176 A2

The seat of the Cardinal Archbishop of Westminster, this is the mother church of Roman Catholicism in Britain. Begun in 1896, the building was completed by 1903. A Byzantine style was chosen, instead of the then fashionable 'churchwarden's Gothic', in order not to compete with the genuine Gothic of Westminster Abbey at the end of Victoria Street.

As a deliberate matter of policy, the decoration of the interior has not been completed, so as not to put too great a financial burden upon the present generation. The marble cladding of the interior goes about halfway up, leaving the remainder of the 12 million bricks in the building uncovered. They will probably remain uncovered for the rest of this century.

Victoria Station was built on piles over the Grosvenor Canal, constructed in the 18th century, which ran south — through what were then uninhabited swamps — to the Thames between Chelsea Bridge and Grosvenor Bridge. The station is in two halves, originally the separate termini of the London, Brighton and South Coast Railway and the London, Chatham and Dover Railway. The wall between them was not broken through until the 1920s, after both companies had become part of the Southern Railway.

The immediate impression on entering the cathedral is of immensity and a solemn gloom, heightened by the dark bricks above the halfway level. There is an unrestricted view of nearly all the 342ft (104m) length of the building: the nave is 60ft (18m) across and as such is the widest in England, with arches 90ft (27m) high. In the distance the immense **sanctuary** is easily visible, for it is raised impressively nearly 5ft (1.5m) above the level of the nave.

The marbles and stone of the cathedral come from many countries. The yellow marble pillars supporting the canopy over the high altar of Cornish stone came from Verona. The dark green pillars which support the galleries came from Greece, while their beautiful white capitals, no two of which are alike, are from the quarries used by Michelangelo in Carrara. The two great columns at the west end of the nave are of deep red Norwegian granite, symbolic of the Blood of Christ. The 14 **Stations of the Cross**, carved on Hopton stone, are by the controversial British sculptor Eric Gill. Adorning the main piers, they are arguably the most outstanding works in the cathedral.

When the cathedral is completed, the marble will reach 30ft (9.1m) up the walls, and the roof will be covered in mosaic. Some indication of the cathedral's finished appearance can be obtained by looking at the now completed chapels. Of these, the **Lady Chapel** on the south side of the high altar is the most elaborately decorated. The body of John Southworth, who was hanged at Tyburn in 1654, was brought to the cathedral from France in 1930 and is now in a glass shrine in the **Chapel of St George**, situated on the cathedral's north side.

Eminent people buried in the cathedral include Cardinal Hinsley, who died in 1943 and whose tomb is in the **Chapel of St Joseph**, and Cardinal Heenan, who died in 1975 and is buried near the pulpit. The statue of St Peter is a copy of the statue in St Peter's, Rome.

If you have a head for heights, it is worth taking the lift up the **campanile**. On a clear day virtually all central London, from Victoria to St Paul's, is visible. The campanile is 273ft (83m) high and you can consequently look down on the towers of the far more historic Westminster Abbey.

Open 7.00am–8.00pm daily. Campanile open Eas–Oct, Wed–Sun 9.30am–5.00pm. Admission fee.

Victoria

The Bluecoat (Blewcoat) School

CAXTON STREET, SW1
⊖ ST JAMES'S PARK
⊖ VICTORIA
ATLAS REF 176 A3

William Greene, founder of what is now Watney's Brewery, established this school for the education of poor children in 1688. The Bluecoat School was named after the colour of the tunic worn by its pupils. The present building was erected in 1709 and is an architectural gem of its period. The exterior is of red-and-yellow brick, with elegant pilasters and a statue of a 'Blewcoat Boy' over the door. The interior consists of a single, pine-panelled room with a semi-basement. Tall, handsome pillars frame the door on the inside, and the original fireplace has been restored. The building was acquired by the National Trust in 1954. It is used today as a National Trust shop.

Open Mon–Wed and Fri 10.00am–5.30pm, Thu 10.00am–7.00pm.

Greycoat Hospital

GREYCOAT PLACE, SW1
⊖ ST JAMES'S PARK
⊖ VICTORIA
ATLAS REF 176 A2

Like the Bluecoat School, Greycoat Hospital was founded for the education of poor children, and again owes its name to the colour of the tunic worn by the pupils. Founded in 1698, it was enlarged and became a day school for girls in 1873. Badly bombed in the Second World War, it was rebuilt and enlarged in 1955. It is still a school, catering for 900 children.

The building is not open to the public, but the handsome front of the historic section, with its figures of 'Greycoat' children, is only a few feet from the pavement and plainly visible.

Victoria Station SW1

⊖ VICTORIA
ATLAS REF 175 F2

Before the age of air travel, Victoria Station was the gateway to Europe by way of Dover, with such famous trains as the *Golden Arrow* leaving daily for Paris. A tourist version of the *Simplon Orient Express* helps to maintain this link with the past. The station is on the Circle, District and Victoria underground lines, and there is a major bus station in the forecourt. Little of the Victorian atmosphere remains, for the station was rebuilt in 1909 and again in 1923. **The Grosvenor Hotel** immediately adjoining it, however, does retain some period interest.

Belgravia SW1

⊖ KNIGHTSBRIDGE
⊖ SLOANE SQUARE
⊖ VICTORIA
ATLAS REF 175 E2

Belgravia is essentially an upper-class suburb, laid out in the mid-19th century, with some of the finest domestic architecture in London arranged round its handsome squares and crescents. Although many of the mansions, particularly Belgrave Square, have been taken over by institutions, others are still in use as homes.

*Elgar's **Dream of Gerontius** had its first London performance in the newly completed Westminster Cathedral in 1903.*

The 'Blewcoat Boy', in 17th-century costume.

≷ ⊖ CHARING CROSS
⊖ LEICESTER SQUARE
⊖ EMBANKMENT
🚍 1, 3, 6, 9, 11, 12, 13, 15, 24, 29, 53, 77A, 88, 159
⚓ TOWER AND GREENWICH

National Gallery

ATLAS REF 172 B1

♦ TRAFALGAR SQUARE, WC2 ♦

Even if you do not want to see the pictures, it is worth climbing the steps to the handsome Classical portico of the National Gallery, for its Corinthian columns command one of the finest views in London, looking out over Trafalgar Square and down Whitehall. The views inside are finer still, however, and it would be a pity not to venture in to look at one of the world's best Old Master collections, with more than 2,000 paintings by artists from Giotto to Picasso.

Bequests, gifts and purchases over the last two centuries have enabled the collection to grow from modest beginnings. In 1824 King George IV, the painter Sir Thomas Lawrence and the connoisseur Sir George Beaumont helped to persuade the government of the day to buy a collection of 28 paintings for the nation. The collection had been assembled by John Julius Angerstein, a financier of Russian origin who had made a fortune in the City and died the previous year. His son offered the paintings to the government on Lawrence's advice.

The collection was put on display to the public in Angerstein's home at 100 Pall Mall (now the Reform Club). It included five Claudes — among them the ravishing *Seaport with the Embarkation of the Queen of Sheba*; Hogarth's sardonic *Marriage à la Mode* series; Raphael's portrait of *Pope Julius II*; two Rembrandts; Rubens's *Rape of the Sabine Women*; and the enormous *Raising of Lazarus* altarpiece by Sebastiano del Piombo, which is Number 1 in the National Gallery's catalogue.

Almost immediately, the collection was augmented by gifts. A clergyman named Holwell Carr gave Tintoretto's *St George and the Dragon* and Rembrandt's *Woman Bathing in a Stream*. Sir George Beaumont presented the gallery with more Claudes, a seraphic *Autumn Landscape* by Rubens and a Canaletto, *The Stonemason's Yard*. In the 1830s the gallery's committee acquired a magnificent Titian, *Bacchus and Ariadne*, and Caravaggio's famous *Supper at Emmaus*.

As the collection expanded, it outgrew its space — as it has gone on doing ever since. In 1832 the architect William Wilkins was commissioned to build a new home for the collection in Trafalgar Square, on the site where the royal stables of Whitehall Palace once stood. Completed in 1838, in Classical style with a dome and pepperpot turrets, it filled the whole north side of the square, but was only one room deep (Wilkins had very sensibly been forbidden to obscure the view of St Martin-in-the-Fields from the west). The gallery is far bigger now. It has been extended several times, most recently in 1991 when the Sainsbury Wing designed by Robert Venturi was completed.

In 1855 Sir Charles Eastlake, President of the Royal Academy, was appointed as the National Gallery's first director. He pursued a vigorous buying policy on trips to Italy until he died in harness 10 years later. Eastlake laid the foundations of the gallery's splendid holdings of Italian painters before Raphael, who up to that time were not highly regarded in Britain. His purchases included Uccello's *Battle of San Romano*, which once graced the bedchamber of Lorenzo dei Medici and, daringly, Bronzino's *Allegory with Venus and Cupid*.

Other favourites in the gallery today were acquired before the end of the 19th century: Holbein's *Ambassadors* double portrait; Botticelli's *Mars and Venus*; Baldovinetti's *Lady in Yellow*; Leonardo's wonderful *Virgin of the Rocks*; Raphael's *Ansidei Madonna*; and masterly Titians and Veroneses.

Already in 1842 the gallery had acquired Jan van Eyck's *Arnolfini Marriage* (with the artist seen reflected in the mirror). Under Eastlake's successor, Sir William Boxall, notable 17th-century Dutch and Flemish paintings were added with the acquisition of Sir Robert Peel's collection, including a celebrated Rubens, *Le Chapeau de Paille*. The gallery today has a substantial show of Dutch and Flemish painters,

Charing Cross

A fountain in Trafalgar Square shoots its spray into the sky, with the National Gallery behind.

from Rubens and Van Dyck to Vermeer, Cuyp, Hobbema, Hals and Rembrandt.

On the Spanish front the gallery is especially strong in Velázquez, with the *Rokeby Venus*, *Christ in the House of Martha and Mary* and others. They hang with striking El Grecos, Murillos and Zurbaráns, and the Goyas include the well-known portrait, *The Duke of Wellington*.

When the Tate Gallery was founded to cover British art of all periods and modern art (after 1900), many of the National Gallery's British exhibits were moved to Millbank. Some choice pieces were, however, kept firmly in Trafalgar Square. They included Constable's *Haywain* and *Cornfield*, paintings by Reynolds and Gainsborough, a splendid Stubbs and two of the best-loved of all Turners: *Rain, Steam and Speed* and *The Fighting Téméraire* — works representing the old age and the new.

Apart from Claude and Poussin, the National Gallery turned a dismissive eye on French art and remained aloof until well after 1900. In 1917 Sir Hugh Lane included Renoir's delicious *Umbrellas* and other major 19th-century French works in a bequest to the gallery, but it was so uninterested that Sir Hugh decided to leave them to the city of Dublin instead. The codicil to his will had not been completed when he died and so the pictures move back and forth between Dublin and London.

The lack of French paintings was overcome to some extent by the acquisition of works by Watteau, Boucher and Fragonard, as well as paintings by David and Géricault, and a tremendous Ingres portrait, *Madame Montessier*. There are also works by Van Gogh, such as *Sunflowers*, signed simply 'Vincent', and paintings by Monet, Manet, Degas and Renoir. There are several Cézannes and Seurat's *Bathers at Asnières*, with a Gustav Klimt of 1904 (the first work by Klimt acquired for any British collection), a Matisse portrait of 1908 and a Picasso cubist work of 1914. Some of the paintings would seem more at home in the Tate Gallery.

The gallery has its own specialist conservation department, responsible for the cleaning and preservation of pictures. In 1914 the beautiful *Rokeby Venus* was slashed with a meat cleaver by a suffragette and successfully repaired. In the 1980s a visitor fired a shotgun at Leonardo's magical cartoon of *The Virgin and Child with St Anne and St John the Baptist*. It too has been repaired, and is now on show again in a protective half-light. The gallery also runs special exhibitions and a free lecture programme. It has a shop and a restaurant.

Open Mon–Sat 10.00am–6.00pm, Sun 2.00pm–6.00pm.

Seurat's **Bathers at Asnières**, *which was purchased in 1924, is one of the best-loved paintings in the National Gallery's collection. It is a monumental work of the 1880s.*

National Gallery Area

Trafalgar Square WC2

⊖ CHARING CROSS
ATLAS REF 172 B1

Every Christmas an immense fir tree, presented by the Norwegians in thanks for British help during the Second World War, is erected in Trafalgar Square. Carollers sing under the illuminated tree, and the ceremony sums up the role of this great open space. It is, in effect, the village green of London. Here people congregate spontaneously on New Year's Eve, for political demonstrations, or to feed the innumerable pigeons which are an essential part of the scene.

The square was laid out on the site of the former royal mews by Sir Charles Barry, architect of the Houses of Parliament, in the 1840s, well over a quarter of a century after Nelson's victory at Trafalgar in 1805. **Nelson's Column**, over 167ft (50m) high, was erected in 1843 and designed by William Railton. The immense 17ft (5m) high statue of Nelson is the work of E H Bailey. Four bronze reliefs on the base of the monument, cast from French cannon captured at Trafalgar, illustrate Nelson's battles at Cape St Vincent, the Nile, Copenhagen and Trafalgar. The four great lions are by Sir Edwin Landseer.

The oldest statue in the square is the equestrian one of Charles I. Cast in 1633, it was ordered to be destroyed for the value of the metal it contained during the English Civil War, but survived and was erected on its present site in 1675. Just behind the statue a bronze plaque marks the official centre of London. Other statues in the square are those of two Victorian generals, Sir Charles Napier and Sir Henry Havelock. The fountains are modern, built in 1948 to the design of Sir Edwin Lutyens. The so-called 'Imperial Standards of Length' set in the north side of the square are of antiquarian interest.

Separating the square from the tranquillity of St James's Park is **Admiralty Arch**, erected in 1910. On the east side is **South Africa House**, with its lively sculptures of animals.

Looking up Whitehall to Nelson's Column, with double-decker buses crowding London's 'village green'.

National Portrait Gallery

ST MARTIN'S PLACE, WC2
⊖ CHARING CROSS
ATLAS REF 172 B1

Physically adjacent to the National Gallery, the National Portrait Gallery is another legacy of the 19th-century impulse to collect and display. Unlike the National Gallery, however, the prime consideration of the National Portrait Gallery is not artist but subject. It is, in effect, the nation's family album, containing more than 7,000 portraits in various forms of Britain's outstanding men and women, past and present. The collection began in 1856, but the building itself was not erected until 1896, The collection is arranged approximately in order of date. Unless you are in quest of a particular period or person, the best thing to do is to go to the second floor (there is a lift) where the sequence begins, and work your way downwards.

Open Mon–Fri 10.00am–5.00pm, Sat 10.00am–6.00pm, Sun 2.00pm–6.00pm.

St Martin-in-the-Fields

ST MARTIN'S PLACE, WC2
⊖ CHARING CROSS
ATLAS REF 172 B1

Dominating St Martin's Place, this is the parish church of the Royal Family, for Buckingham Palace falls within its parish. The present church, the work of James Gibbs, was built between 1721 and 1726, and its beautiful Classical front shows the influence that Sir Christopher Wren had on the architect. Inside, there is a royal box and an Admiralty box, for St Martin's is also the parish church of the Admiralty, on the other side of Trafalgar Square.
Duncannon Street occupies the site of a churchyard where the 17th-century actress and royal mistress, Nell Gwyn, was buried.

Charing Cross WC2

⊖ EMBANKMENT
⊖ CHARING CROSS
ATLAS REF 172 B1

This is the area where Whitehall, the Strand and Trafalgar Square meet, the very heart of London. It takes its name from a cross which the grieving Edward I erected to his wife Eleanor in 1291. Although she died in Nottinghamshire, her body was brought to Westminster Abbey to be buried, and at every place where the coffin rested, an Eleanor Cross was raised. The last of these was erected on the site now occupied by the statue of Charles I in Trafalgar Square. Charing is a corruption of *chère reine* (dear queen). The cross in front of the railway station is a reasonably accurate replica, erected in 1863 to mark the building of the station.

The Savoy Hotel and Theatre

STRAND, WC2
⊖ CHARING CROSS
ATLAS REF 172 C1

East of Trafalgar Square, on the south side of the Strand, is the Savoy, a network of streets, courts, rows and places of the same name. They stand on the site of a palace built here in 1245 by the Earl of Savoy.

The Savoy Hotel was opened in 1889 by Richard d'Oyly Carte, who first staged the operettas of Gilbert and Sullivan in the adjoining theatre between 1881 and 1889. The Savoy was the first public building in the world to be lit by electricity, and today it is still one of London's most elegant and luxurious hotels, with many period features and two famous restaurants.

Leicester Square WC2

⊖ PICCADILLY CIRCUS
⊖ LEICESTER SQUARE
ATLAS REF 172 B1

Architecturally a mess, but socially lively, Leicester Square is the centre of London's theatreland and includes some of the largest cinemas in the country. Named after an Earl of Leicester who had a house nearby in the 17th century, the square was laid out as early as 1665, but in its present form it dates from 1897, when its open space was turned into gardens. Previously, Leicester Square was known as Leicester Fields and was a favourite place for duels. Today, a copy of the statue of Shakespeare in Westminster Abbey stands in the middle of the garden, and there is a lively statue of Charlie Chaplin nearby. Half-price seats to same-day shows in West End theatres are sold from a booth on the west side of the square. Although the queue is sometimes very long, this is one way of getting an evening's entertainment in London for a good price.

Dominated by giant cinemas, Leicester Square has been largely closed to traffic. The Empire Cinema was built in the 1920s on the site of the old Empire Music Hall.

◒ COVENT GARDEN
◒ LEICESTER SQUARE

Covent Garden

ATLAS REF 172 B1

♦ WC2 ♦

Traditionally, the English have always disliked town planning, preferring to work on a piecemeal basis until everything seizes up. It is fortunate therefore that when Francis Russell, the 4th Earl of Bedford, obtained permission to develop the area around Covent (or 'Convent') Garden in 1631, he com-

missioned Inigo Jones as architect. Jones had spent time in Italy and had returned to England full of the ideals of the Italian Renaissance. He planned a Classical Italian piazza and church for the area, surrounded by arcaded houses. Although he was initially hampered by his patron's parsimony, he eventually achieved his aim.

In Covent Garden conjurers, jugglers and buskers have taken the place of the market porters and flower girls of Victorian and Edwardian days.
In the portico of St Paul's Church, facing Covent Garden Piazza, is a plaque which marks the site where in 1662 Samuel Pepys witnessed the first recorded Punch and Judy show in London. A pub in the old market building is called the Punch and Judy.

St Paul's

COVENT GARDEN, WC2
◒ COVENT GARDEN
◒ LEICESTER SQUARE
ATLAS REF 172 B1
Inigo Jones planned this church

Covent Garden

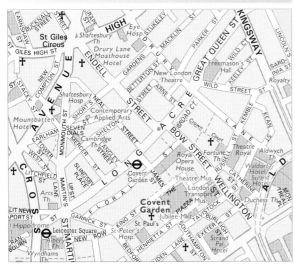

as the focal point of Covent Garden Piazza (today it is all that survives of his work). His patron, the 4th Earl of Bedford, was anxious about costs and insisted that he wanted 'nothing more than a barn'. Jones made the magnificent reply, 'Well then, you shall have the handsomest barn in England.' His work lived up to this boast, for the church is a curious mixture of plainness and magnificence.

St Paul's, Covent Garden, was the first place of worship built in London since the Reformation and was inevitably involved in controversy. Inigo Jones wanted the entrance in the east, facing the Piazza, and designed the splendid portico of the church for this purpose. However, the ecclesiastical authorities of the day insisted that the altar should be in the east, and so visitors enter the church from the west, from behind as it were. St Paul's is frequently called the 'actor's church' because of its many

associations with the theatre, and there are a number of memorials to members of the profession in the very plain interior. The Irish dramatist George Bernard Shaw used the portico for the opening scene of *Pygmalion*, and today it serves as a kind of impromptu stage for outdoor theatre.

Covent Garden Market

COVENT GARDEN, WC2
◒ COVENT GARDEN
◒ LEICESTER SQUARE
ATLAS REF 172 B1
In 1831 a number of substantial but elegant buildings, designed by Charles Fowler, appeared in the centre of Inigo Jones's Piazza. These were the buildings of the vegetable market which, until 1974, formed the core of one of London's liveliest areas. The market porters, with their baskets towering above their heads, were as much part of the London scene as the Beefeaters of the Tower of London. Very late-night

The former garden of the monks of Westminster Abbey is now a haven of more urban recreation.

revellers, or very early morning travellers, could take advantage of Covent Garden's market privilege whereby pubs were opened at 5.00am for 'bona-fide market traders'. All this went when the post-war passion for tidying up inner-city areas banished the market to Vauxhall. The huge, empty, financially valuable area was scheduled for development — that is, for transformation into office blocks — but a vigorous local campaign fought off the threat. In 1980 the market buildings and those surrounding the Piazza were restored and adapted, and now house shops, wine bars, restaurants and museums. There is also a wide variety of outdoor entertainment, from buskers to street theatres. For the tourist wandering around London, the market provides a pleasant interlude of free and light-hearted entertainment.

Open during normal trading hours. Markets include antiques (Mon), general goods (Tue–Fri) and crafts (Sat and Sun).

Royal Opera House

BOW STREET,
COVENT GARDEN, WC2
⊖ COVENT GARDEN
⊖ LEICESTER SQUARE
ATLAS REF 172 B1
It says something about the British that they should place their only opera house in the middle of a vegetable market. Before Covent Garden fruit and vegetable market was moved,

elegantly clad opera-goers were obliged to make their way through cabbage stalks, rotting oranges and other debris to their evening's entertainment.

The first building on this site was erected by the theatrical manager John Rich, who opened with a production of Congreve's *Way of the World* in 1731. This theatre and its successor both burnt down, and the present theatre was built by E M Barry in 1858. The portico has a determinedly Classical appearance, and Barry also managed to incorporate sculptures by the Neoclassicist John Flaxman, the first professor of sculpture of the Royal Academy, into his design. These had been saved from the previous building. Originally known simply as the Covent Garden Theatre, the Royal Opera House was given its new name in 1939 and has since been the principal home of opera and ballet in Britain. Though is is heavily subsidised, prices for perfomances are high and seats are booked well in advance.

Photographers' Gallery

GREAT NEWPORT STREET, WC2
⊖ COVENT GARDEN
⊖ LEICESTER SQUARE
ATLAS REF 172 B1
The Photographer's Gallery houses changing displays of the work of professional photographers.
Open Tue–Sat 11.00am–7.00pm.

London Transport Museum

COVENT GARDEN, WC2
⊖ COVENT GARDEN
⊖ LEICESTER SQUARE
ATLAS REF 172 B1
Occupying the building that was Covent Garden Flower Market, the London Transport Museum gives an excellent picture of the triumphs and problems of London's transport system over the past century-and-a-half. On display are old faithfuls of public transport, including a reconstruction of the very first omnibus, operated by George Shillibeer in 1829, and a 'knifeboard' horse bus, whose passengers sat back-to-back on the roof. There is also a collection of early steam locomotives, an example of the first underground railway of 1863 and a number of working displays.
Open daily, 10.00am–6.00pm. Admission fee.

Theatre Museum

TAVISTOCK STREET, WC2
⊖ COVENT GARDEN
⊖ LEICESTER SQUARE
ATLAS REF 172 B1
The Theatre Museum occupies the basement of the old Covent Garden Flower Market. Opened in 1987, a substantial part of its display consists of theatre bills, costumes, paintings and mememtos of famous players.
Open Tue–Sun 11.00am–7.00pm. Admission fee.

Seven Dials WC2

⊖ LEICESTER SQUARE
⊖ COVENT GARDEN
ATLAS REF 172 B2
In Charles Dickens's time this was one of the roughest, toughest areas of London, notorious for its poverty and crime. It is the focal point of seven streets and takes its name from a column with seven dials on it, which stood here in the 18th century. A new column was erected in 1987.

Theatre Royal

DRURY LANE, WC2
⊖ COVENT GARDEN
ATLAS REF 172 C1
This is one of the oldest theatre sites in London. The first theatre here was destroyed in the Great Fire of 1666 and was replaced by one designed by Sir Christopher Wren. A third theatre, built in 1794 and managed by the great dramatist, Richard Sheridan, also burnt down.

The present building, with its portico and Ionic colonnade, is the largest theatre in London. Inside it is sumptuously furnished, and there are numerous monuments to former exponents of the dramatic arts. Today, many of the productions are musicals and hit shows.

No longer going anywhere, red double-decker trams stand in their ranks in the London Transport Museum.

⊖ PICCADILLY CIRCUS
⊖ TOTTENHAM
  COURT ROAD
⊖ OXFORD CIRCUS

Piccadilly Circus

ATLAS REF 172 A1

◆ W1 ◆

For over 40 years, ever since the Second World War, a debate has been going on about what to do about Piccadilly Circus. The most famous spot in London, once known as the 'hub of the Empire', Piccadilly Circus is also the most disappointing when what could be is compared with what is. The views from this point are superb. Southwards are the soaring towers of Westminster; westwards, dignified Green Park; northwards, the splendid curve of Nash's Regent Street; and eastwards, the bright lights of theatreland. But the central area, Piccadilly Circus itself, lacks form and feeling. The best time to see it is undoubtedly at night, when the crude advertisements of the day become a mass of swirling neon lights, generating an air of excitement in the thronging crowds and bringing the area to life.

The introduction of gaslight to London in 1814 was the beginning of Piccadilly Circus's career as a centre of entertainment, and it was laid out in its present form towards the end of the 19th century. The underground station, with its distinctive architecture, was rebuilt in 1925. The station became shamefully run down, but a major restoration programme ending in 1989 restored its trim appearance. Outside is Sir Alfred Gilbert's *Eros*, erected in 1893 as a monument to the 7th Earl of Shaftesbury, a philanthropist and social reformer. Gilbert chose to cast the figure in aluminium, the first time this metal had ever been used for a statue. Contrary to popular opinion, *Eros* is not firing his arrow into Shaftesbury Avenue, but into Regent Street. The statue has become an emblem for the West End of London.

Piccadilly Circus

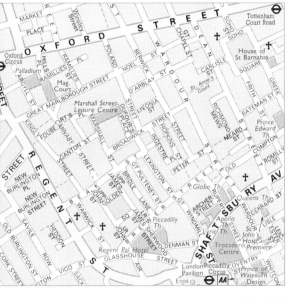

Karl Marx, author of **Das Kapital**, *lived for several years in the 1850s at No. 28 Dean Street (above the Quo Vadis restaurant). He and his wife, five children and maid squashed into two small rooms, in tatty but cheerful disorder. They were desperately poor and Marx wrote at one point that for 10 days the family had lived on nothing but bread and potatoes. He used to walk from here to the British Museum every day to pursue his research in the Reading Room.*

Eros aims his bow against a background of gigantic advertising signs in Piccadilly Circus (right), while at night (inset) the Christmas shopping lights blaze in Regent Street.

Regent Street W1

⊖ PICCADILLY CIRCUS
⊖ OXFORD CIRCUS
ATLAS REF 172 A1

Laid out by John Nash between 1813 and 1816, Regent Street is one of London's most successful attempts at planning on a large scale. Named after the Prince Regent (later King George IV), it was designed to connect the Regent's town house, Carlton House, with his properties in what is now Regent's Park. The buildings which Nash designed have nearly all been rebuilt, few to their benefit, but the street itself sweeps in a splendid curve through the very heart of London's West End. The famous **Café Royal**, situated near Piccadilly Circus, was rebuilt in 1928 but retains something of the plush appearance which attracted Bohemians such as the Victorian playwright and satirist Oscar Wilde and the 20th-century Welsh portrait painter Augustus John.

Liberty

REGENT STREET, W1
⊖ OXFORD CIRCUS
⊖ PICCADILLY CIRCUS
ATLAS REF 171 F1

A shoppers' paradise, with an immense range of high-class goods under one roof, Liberty is also an astonishing architectural landmark. Built in 1924, it displays an exuberant but unified front to Regent Street. The front on Great Marlborough Street, running at a right-angle off Regent Street, has been designed to give the appearance of a Tudor house. The medieval theme is continued in the clock over Kingly Street, where every hour St George appears and attacks the dragon.

Carnaby Street W1

⊖ OXFORD CIRCUS
ATLAS REF 171 F1

The sartorial revolution among young people in the 1960s began here, and a quirk of fashion turned a dreary backstreet into a household name. A number of small shops catered for tastes in colourful or outrageous clothes and as the public flocked in, street traders decided to band together to provide a unified image for the street with coloured pavings, ornamental arches and the like. There is little to be seen here of the sixties' revolution today.

Soho W1

⊖ TOTTENHAM COURT ROAD
⊖ PICCADILLY CIRCUS
⊖ LEICESTER SQUARE
ATLAS REF 172 A2

Soho, the centre of London's entertainment industry, owes its cosmopolitan atmosphere to the fact that is was the area where French Protestant refugees settled in the late-17th century. Bounded by Oxford Street, Shaftesbury Avenue, Regent Street and Charing Cross Road, it is a maze of small streets which have survived both air raids and developers and retained their identity. As well as countless restaurants, pubs and clubs, both respectable and dubious, Soho still possesses good 18th-century domestic architecture. Some of the best examples can be seen in **Broadwick Street** and **Meard Street**. **Berwick Street** has a raucous street market, while **Wardour Street** is the centre of the British film industry. **Soho Square** is a dignified area with a pleasant garden. Laid out for Charles II in 1681, it has his statue in the centre.

Shaftesbury Avenue W1

⊖ PICCADILLY CIRCUS
⊖ LEICESTER SQUARE
ATLAS REF 172 A1/B2

Part of the great 19th-century programme of improvement in central London, Shaftesbury Avenue was carved through some of the worst slums in 1886. It was named after Lord Shaftesbury, the great Victorian social reformer. Many theatres are situated on or near it, including the Lyric (1888), the Apollo (1901) and the Globe (1906).

Trocadero

PICCADILLY, W1
⊖ PICCADILLY CIRCUS
ATLAS REF 172 A1

At the southern point of Shaftesbury Avenue, where it joins Piccadilly Circus, is the Trocadero, a modern complex of shops, restaurants and exhibitions in a rebuilt Edwardian shell. Among the attractions is the **Guinness World of Records**, which shows in dramatic, three-dimensional form the various superlatives – the world's longest, biggest, smallest, loudest and so on.

Open daily, 10.00am–12.00 midnight (Guinness World of Records 10.00am–10.00pm). Admission fee to certain parts.

Rock Circus

LONDON PAVILION
PICCADILLY CIRCUS, W1
⊖ PICCADILLY CIRCUS
ATLAS REF 172 A1

Part of the Tussaud's Group, the Rock Circus is housed in a modern shopping complex, the London Pavilion. It features waxworks of pop stars, computer-linked to records. A 20-minute show consists of animated figures playing and singing as if in a live concert.

Open Sun, Mon, Wed and Thu 11.00am–9.00pm, Tue 12.00 noon–9.00pm, Fri and Sat 11.00am–10.00pm. Admission fee.

Chinatown

SOHO, W1
⊖ PICCADILLY CIRCUS
⊖ LEICESTER SQUARE
ATLAS REF 172 A/B1

Chinatown began spontaneously in a group of small streets south of Shaftesbury Avenue, when a number of Chinese families moved in. Subsequently it developed into a sophisticated area of entertainment, including restaurants and shops, while still retaining ethnic charm. **Gerrard Street** and **Macclesfield Street** have been pedestrianised and are at the heart of Chinatown. **The Chinese New Year** is celebrated here with street decorations and processions in January or February each year.

The Palace Theatre in Cambridge Circus advertises a long-running musical. The surrounding area of Piccadilly and Soho is the principal theatre, night-club and red-light district in London.

GREEN PARK
9, 14, 19, 22, 25, 38

St James's Palace

ATLAS REF 176 A4

◆ PALL MALL, SW1 ◆

Overshadowed by the more obvious glamour of nearby Buckingham Palace, where crowds straining for a glimpse of royalty are entertained by the balletic Changing of the Guard, St James's Palace tends to be ignored by many on the tourist circuit. Unlike most royal palaces St James's has a public highway, Marlborough Road, running beside it. From the road you can look straight into **Friary Court**, where heralds traditionally proclaim the accession of a new monarch. Sentries from the Guards' Division patrol it, and as the palace is also the headquarters of the Honourable Corps of Gentlemen at Arms and of the Yeomen of the Guard, it is the centre of much colourful activity. The Yeomen of the Guard, the monarch's personal bodyguard, wear Tudor-style uniforms.

Originally the palace was a leper hospital, outside the medieval boundaries of London. Henry VIII bought it and rebuilt it as a manor house, and his massive brick tower still dominates the building. Set in green countryside, the palace became very popular with successive monarchs. The Commonwealth turned it into a prison in the mid-17th century, but Charles II restored it and used it both for State purposes, and as convenient lodgings for his many mistresses. When the Royal Palace of Whitehall burned down in 1698, St James' became the principal royal residence in the kingdom. Legally it remains so, which is why foreign ambassadors are accredited 'to the Court of St James'.

West of the palace, facing Stable Yard, is **Clarence House**, built by the architect John Nash in 1829 for the Duke of Clarence (later King William IV). In this century it became the home of the young Princess Elizabeth (later Queen Elizabeth II) and Princess Anne was born here. It has more recently been the home of Queen Elizabeth the Queen Mother.

St James's Palace is not open to the public, but the Chapel Royal holds Sunday services at 8.30am and 11.15am, to which all are welcome. Clarence House is not open to the public.

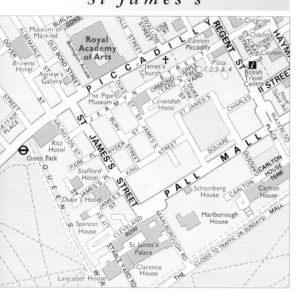

St James's

A statue of Athene and a copy of the Parthenon frieze dignify the Athenaeum Club.

In the courtyard of Burlington House, the premises of the Royal Academy, is a statue of Sir Joshua Reynolds by Alfred Drury, erected in 1931. It is garlanded with flowers every year to mark the opening of the Summer Exhibition. The great man, who is shown with his brushes and palette, and looking suitably creative, was the first President of the Academy when is was founded in 1768.

Nearby . . .

Marlborough House

PALL MALL, SW1
GREEN PARK
ATLAS REF 176 A4

On the corner of Marlborough Road and Pall Mall is Marlborough House, built by Christopher Wren in 1709 for the great Duke of Marlborough. After the death of Sarah, Duchess of Marlborough in 1744, the house became the home of various members of the Royal Family, the last being Queen Mary, widow of King George V. After her death in 1953 the house was turned into a Commonwealth conference centre.

In Marlborough Road, almost adjoining Marlborough House

and immediately opposite St James's Palace, is **Queen's Chapel**. Designed by Inigo Jones in 1623, it was the chapel used by Charles I's Queen, Henrietta Maria.

Further along Marlborough Road is Sir Alfred Gilbert's delightful **memorial** to Queen Alexandra, consort of Edward VII, erected in 1932.

Marlborough House is not open to the public. Members of the public may, however, attend Sunday services in Queen's Chapel from Easter to the end of July.

St James's Street SW1

GREEN PARK
ATLAS REF 176 A4

There is a superb view from the upper, Piccadilly end of this handsome street, taking in the

massive tower of St James's Palace and the park beyond. The street survived the attentions of the Luftwaffe and post-war developers and is essentially of the late-18th and early-19th centuries.

Some of the most famous London clubs are to be found here, including **Brooks's**, built in 1778, and the **Carlton Club**, built in 1826. The smaller roads opening off St James's Street are worth exploring, in particular **St James's Place**, with its 18th-century town houses leading off the west side. **Spencer House** in St James's Place, the sumptuous town house of the Princess of Wales's ancestors, has been magnificently restored at a cost of £18 million and is open to the public.

Full of smart little shops, Burlington Arcade opened in 1819. In earlier days the porters were always old soldiers of the Tenth Hussars.

Pall Mall   SW1

⊖ GREEN PARK
⊖ PICCADILLY CIRCUS
ATLAS REF 176 A4

This is the heart of London's clubland. The massive buildings, intended to reflect the wealth and influence of their members, give the street its dignified but ponderous appearance. On the corner of Pall Mall and Waterloo Place is the doyen of the clubs, the **Athenaeum** (built in 1830), with its golden statue of Athene and a Classical frieze. Next comes the **Travellers' Club** (built in 1832 – originally members had to prove they had travelled overseas, at least 500 miles from London) and then the **Reform Club**. The oldest building in the street (No. 82) is 17th-century **Schomberg House**, which was the home of the great portrait painter Thomas Gainsborough in the 18th century.

Royal Academy of Arts

PICCADILLY, W1
⊖ PICCADILLY CIRCUS
⊖ GREEN PARK
ATLAS REF 172 A1

This imposing building is a double attraction: it is one of the last of the great mansions which once lined Piccadilly and it is also the headquarters of the 'art establishment' in Britain. Built in 1713 as the town house of the 3rd Earl of Burlington (from which it takes its official name of Burlington House), it became the home of the Royal Academy of Arts after considerable alterations in 1869. In addition, the building houses a number of other learned societies, including the Society of Antiquaries and Linnaean Society. The rooms of these various societies contain historic treasures, but are not open to the general public. The well-known Royal Academy Summer

Exhibition is held annually and regularly attracts popular interest.

Open daily, 10.00am–6.00pm. Admission fee to exhibitions.

Burlington Arcade

PICCADILLY, W1
⊖ PICCADILLY CIRCUS
ATLAS REF 172 F1

Run as a somewhat self-conscious survival of the art of gracious living, Burlington Arcade comes complete with liveried attendants known as beadles who, it is said, have orders to eject anyone who whistles or runs. It is well worth a visit for its architecture and merchandise. First built in 1819 and containing 72 shops, it can be regarded as a forerunner of modern shopping malls It is interesting to cross the road and compare it with Piccadilly Arcade, built a century later for a less-exclusive public.

St James's Palace Area

Museum of Mankind

BURLINGTON GARDENS, W1
⊖ PICCADILLY CIRCUS
⊖ GREEN PARK
ATLAS REF 171 F1
Officially the Ethnographic
Department of the British
Museum, the contents of the
Museum of Mankind were once
tucked away on an upper floor
there, and rather resembled an
up-market junk shop with the
exhibits all crammed into a small
space. In 1972 the department
was moved into its present
elaborate building (erected in
1869) to allow better display.

The incredible wealth of
material from Africa, the
Americas and the Pacific is still
there, tucked away behind the
scenes. What the general public
sees are selections from the
reserve stock, including an Aztec
crystal skull and New Guinea
masks, displayed like the jewels
in nearby Bond Street. The
museum has become deservedly
famous for lively exhibitions
which illustrate man's
relationship to his fellows and his
surroundings.

Because many of the artefacts

*The Museum of
Mankind's collections
contain material from
the indigenous peoples
of Africa, America and
the Pacific.*

were acquired from Third World
countries under dubious
circumstances in the 19th
century, the museum has become
the target of demands for
restitution. Two of its collections
in particular, the Ashante Regalia
and the Benin Bronzes, have
been the centre of controversy.
The Ashante Regalia is claimed
by Ghana because the treasures
were looted from Kumasi (now
part of Ghana) by a 19th-century
expedition under Sir Garnet
Wolseley, and the Nigerians
claim the Benin Bronzes for
similar reasons. Items from both
collections are on permanent
display.
*Open Mon–Sat 10.00am–
5.00pm, Sun 2.30pm–6.00pm.*

St James's

PICCADILLY, W1
⊖ PICCADILLY CIRCUS
ATLAS REF 172 A1
This was the last of 55 London
churches designed by Sir
Christopher Wren in the 17th
century. It was the only one built
on a completely new site (with
all the others he had to adapt his
design to an existing foundation)

and of all his churches, it was one
he liked best. In it he pursued his
idea that a Protestant church
should be an 'auditory', in which
it was possible both to hear as
well as to see the preacher.

St James's is a church which,
quite literally, has grown up with
its area. When Wren began
building it in 1676, Piccadilly
was not yet in existence. Henry
Jermyn, Earl of St Albans, had
leased the whole of the area
around St James's Palace for
development and he
commissioned Wren to build a
church to serve the new estate.

The building was consecrated
in 1684, the entrance then being
from what is now Jermyn Street.
It was heavily damaged in an air
raid in 1940 and after major
restoration by Sir Albert
Richardson it was rededicated in
1954. The beautiful ceiling was
restored by using plaster casts
taken from fragments salvaged
after the air raid; elsewhere,
drawings of the original church
were used as a guide. Despite the
heavy damage, survivals include
some of the most important
works of the sculptor and
woodcarver Grinling Gibbons,
among them the beautiful marble
font, the altarpiece and the organ
case. The churchyard was laid
out as a garden to commemorate
the courage of Londoners in the
'Blitz', at the expense of Viscount
Southwood, a newspaper
proprietor.

Jermyn Street SW1

⊖ PICCADILLY CIRCUS
ATLAS REF 172 A1
Running parallel to the south side
of Piccadilly, this street is named
after Henry Jermyn, who
developed the area in the 17th
century. It is still a 'village street'
of small, if extremely expensive
and fashionable shops, selling
everything from shoes to
cheeses.

Fortnum & Mason

PICCADILLY, W1
⊖ PICCADILLY CIRCUS
⊖ GREEN PARK
ATLAS REF 172 A1
Fortnum & Mason must be one of
the great institutions of London.
Staff on the ground floor still
wear morning clothes, but in
other ways the shop is

Mr Fortnum and Mr Mason in 18th-century costume on the handsome clock, designed by Berkeley Sutcliffe, which was installed above the shop in 1964.

innovative. For example, its buyers were the first to place an order, in 1886, with a young man called H J Heinz. Founded in 1707 by Hugh Mason, a small grocer, and William Fortnum, a footman at the court of Queen Anne, the shop's association with royalty has continued over the centuries, adding no little to its fortunes. There is probably no luxury food that is not in stock, and it is literally an education to wander through the displays. The proprietors have always had a lively sense of publicity; when windows were broken by suffragettes in 1914, they sent food to the culprits in gaol. In 1964 a clock with revolving figures of Mr Fortnum and Mr

Mason was erected above the shop's entrance. It never fails to attract the attention of passers-by.

Faraday Museum

ALBEMARLE STREET, W1
⊖ GREEN PARK
ATLAS REF 171 F1
Situated in the basement of the Royal Institution (No. 21) where Michael Faraday practised as professor of chemistry, the Faraday Museum contains historic apparatus belonging to Faraday and others, and boasts a reconstruction of the laboratory where his most important discoveries were made.
    Open Tue–Thu 1.00pm–4.00pm.

Floris, founded in Jermyn Street in 1730 by a Spanish barber, sells perfume.

St James's Square SW1

⊖ PICCADILLY CIRCUS
ATLAS REF 176 A4
Although it was first laid out in the 1660s, this beautiful square is virtually a textbook example of 18th-century architecture. Outstanding among the mansions is **Chatham House** (No. 10 on the north side), built in 1726 by Henry Flitcroft and now the home of the Royal Institute of International Affairs. No. 20 on the west side is the work of the 18th-century architect Robert Adam. In the north-west corner at No. 14 is the **London Library**, founded by Thomas Carlyle in 1841. Although the garden in the centre of the square is officially private, it has generously been opened to the public by residents. The equestrian statue is of King William III.

Carlton House Terrace SW1

⊖ CHARING CROSS
ATLAS REF 176 A4
The best view of this terrace is from The Mall, where rows of gleaming Classical pillars rear up like a cream-coloured cliff. The terrace was laid out by John Nash between 1827 and 1832 to provide mansions for statesmen and the aristocracy (Gladstone lived at No. 11). Most are now occupied by institutions, such as the Royal Society at No. 6.

⊖ BOND STREET

Mayfair

ATLAS REF 171 E/F1

◆ W1 ◆

Mayfair

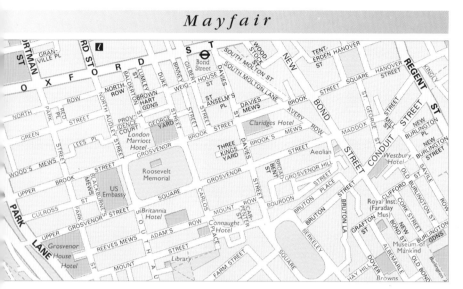

Mayfair is worth exploring for the mews that run behind its main streets. Three Kings Yard and Adam's Row, for example, are close to Grosvenor Square. In the 18th century, when the area became fashionable, wealthy residents kept their coaches and stabled their horses in the mews. The upper rooms were occupied by the coachmen and grooms. Much of the area was rebuilt between 1870 and 1900 by the Duke of Westminster. The little alleys have been altered into smart maisonettes, garages and offices, but they retain the charm of a more spacious age.

The fashionable area of Mayfair is a paradox because, like Pimlico, Bloomsbury and several other London districts to which people refer, it does not officially exist. Mayfair is not even a postal district. The area is generally accepted as being the large rectangle bounded by Oxford Street on the north, Regent Street on the east, Piccadilly on the south and Park Lane on the west. Elegant residences, some of them small places, have given way to hotels, offices and expensive shops, but the area has still managed to retain its exclusive air.

Mayfair had modest beginnings. The area first began to develop when an annual may fair, previously held in the Haymarket, was moved to a site near Hyde Park Corner in 1688. This is now Shepherd Market, a charming enclave with pavement tables, named after the 18th-century architect Edward Shepherd, who leased land here to stall-holders and booth-keepers during the first fortnight in May.

During the 18th century, with the growth of the West End, Mayfair developed rapidly. The district was the creation of great landlords whose names are still remembered – the Grosvenors (of Grosvenor Square), the Berkeleys (of Berkeley Square), Sir Thomas Bond (of Bond Street), and the Curzons (of Curzon Street). Fortunately they were men of taste, and their preference for Classical designs resulted in a dignified pattern of streets and squares.

Of the great houses that were once Mayfair's pride, few have survived. Lord Burlington's Piccadilly mansion is now the home of the Royal Academy; the Duke of Cambridge's house has become the Naval and Military Club; and Devonshire House is a new building with an old name.

Bond Street W1

⊖ BOND STREET
⊖ GREEN PARK
ATLAS REF 171 F1

Mayfair's most expensive and fashionable street of shops runs between Piccadilly and Oxford Street. For people exploring Mayfair, this is a convenient artery from which to branch off. Three hundred years old in 1986, the street has two parts — **Old Bond Street**, to the south (planned by Sir Thomas Bond), where Thomas Agnew and Sons can be found among the fine art dealers — and **New Bond Street**, further to the north, where Asprey, the gold- and silversmiths, sell anything from a jewel box to a gold-plated toothbrush. The international auctioneers Sotheby's can be found at No. 35.

Famous past residents of Bond Street include the Scottish author and biographer, James Boswell, Emma, Lady Hamilton (the mistress of Horatio, Lord Nelson), and the great Victorian actor, Sir Henry Irving.

Berkeley Square W1

⊖ GREEN PARK
ATLAS REF 171F1

Berkeley Square has a romantic aura. The central gardens have fine plane trees and on the west side are some original houses from the 1730s, when the square was laid out and named after Lord Berkeley of Stratton, a Royalist commander in the Civil War. Among them, No. 44 (now the Clermont Club) is notable. The hand of developers has not been kind to the east and south sides of the square, where Devonshire House once stood. This building was demolished in 1924; only the grounds were left.

Grosvenor Square W1

⊖ BOND STREET
ATLAS REF 171 E1

London's largest square after Lincoln's Inn Fields, Grosvenor Square was the main feature of a 100 acre (40.5ha) estate developed by Sir Richard Grosvenor in the 18th century. The first of the fine, fashionable

Rebecca at the Well, among the Berkeley Square plane trees.

buildings went up in 1725. The last of the original buildings disappeared in 1968, but the

square has been tastefully rebuilt to retain a residential appearance. This is a corner of an English field that is for ever American. John Adams, the first United States Ambassador to London, lived in a house on the north-east corner, while the great American financier John Pierpont Morgan lived at No. 12. No. 20 was used as US army headquarters in the Second World War, when Grosvenor Square became known as Eisenhower Platz. Today the whole of the west side is occupied by the **US Embassy**, built in 1961 by Eero Saarinen, which (despite its golden eagle, threatening to swoop) does not unduly upset the square's general design. The main, dominating statue is that of Franklin D Roosevelt by Sir William Reid Dick. The statue of the great American wartime President, wearing a cloak and leaning on a stick, was unveiled by his widow in 1948.

Park Lane W1

☯ MARBLE ARCH
☯ HYDE PARK CORNER
ATLAS REF 171 E1/175 E4
What are now the fronts of some of the older houses in Park Lane were the backs in the 18th century. Today, Park Lane is a

three-lane carriageway running from Marble Arch south to Hyde Park Corner, along the eastern boundary of Hyde Park. Several major hotels now stand on the sites of important 18th-century residences, from which they have taken their names. Examples are **Grosvenor House Hotel**, built on what was the site of the Grosvenor family home; the **Dorchester**, which has replaced Dorchester House; and the Londonderry Hotel, which is on the site of Londonderry House.

East of Park Lane, behind the Dorchester, is **Grosvenor Chapel** in South Audley Street. Built by the Grosvenor Estate in the 18th century, it was used by US forces in the Second World War. The 18th-century politician and reformer, John Wilkes, is buried here.

St George's

HANOVER SQUARE, W1
☯ OXFORD CIRCUS
ATLAS REF 171 F1
Completed in 1725, St George's Hanover Square acquired a reputation as a fashionable church for society weddings during the 18th and 19th centuries. The marriages of many famous people have taken place here — including that of Emma,

Lady Hamilton, in the 18th century.

St George's was one of the first churches in London to be adorned with a Classical portico and bronze hunting dogs. The 18th-century Scottish author, James Boswell, wrote that he was distracted during a Sunday sermon here by the lovely Duchess of Grafton.

Savile Row W1

☯ PICCADILLY CIRCUS
ATLAS REF 171 F1
Synonymous since the middle of the 19th century with exclusive gentleman's tailoring, Savile Row is still home to some of the finest outfitters in the world. Among the renowned names are Gieves & Hawkes at No. 1 and Hardy Amies at No. 14.

No. 14 was also the last home of the Georgian playwright Richard Brinsley Sheridan (1751–1816).

Running from Burlington Gardens to Conduit Street, Savile Row is named after Lady Dorothy Savile, whose husband, the 3rd Earl of Burlington, developed the area behind his mansion in Piccadilly from 1717 onwards as a 'little town'. Several fine houses at the southern end of Savile Row have survived.

Tightly packed traffic in Park Lane, with the Dorchester Hotel in the background, one of London's ritziest areas. Park Lane was originally an inconspicuous road running beside Hyde Park.

⊖ HYDE PARK
CORNER

Hyde Park Corner

ATLAS REF 175 E4

◆ W1 ◆

The large, intolerably busy traffic round-about on which five roads converge and which 150,000 vehicles pass a day, makes Hyde Park Corner more of a hazard than an attraction for sightseers. This is a pity, as there are a number of interesting historical features to make a visit worthwhile.

In the 18th century a turnpike collecting tolls stood near here, on a road to the west. This was where town and country met. Apsley House, just east of the turnpike, consequently became known as 'No. 1, London'. It is still a building of importance. Separated from it by the entrance into Hyde Park are a delicate Regency gateway and a graceful Classical screen, designed in the early 19th century by Decimus Burton, a pupil of John Nash.

Burton's more dominating structure, on the island at Hyde Park Corner, is Wellington Arch. The arch forms a landmark at the top of Constitution Hill, the gently sloping road that leads from Hyde Park Corner to Buckingham Palace. Park Lane, Piccadilly, Grosvenor Place, Grosvenor Crescent and Knightsbridge all converge with Constitution Hill at Hyde Park Corner.

Hyde Park Corner

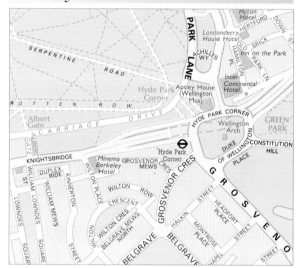

Apsley House (The Wellington Museum)

PICCADILLY, W1
⊖ HYDE PARK CORNER
⊖ KNIGHTSBRIDGE
ATLAS REF 175 E4

The survival of Apsley House epitomises the hero whose London home it was — the Duke of Wellington. The victor of Waterloo was not a soldier to surrender ground. Apsley House, built by Robert Adam in 1771–8 for Baron Apsley, became the Duke of Wellington's home in 1817. He lived here throughout the time that he was Prime Minister (1828–30) and until his death in 1852. Presented to the nation in 1947, the house is very much as it was in his lifetime, rather than being a formal museum.

Relics and paintings of the 'Iron Duke's' campaigns are the main items of interest to visitors, and the most impressive room is the **Waterloo Gallery**, where the Duke held a banquet every year to commemorate his greatest victory. It now displays magnificent paintings. On the table in the **Dining Room** is the silver Portuguese Service, presented to the Duke in 1816 by the Prince Regent of Portugal and one of the great treasures of the house. Two huge canvases in this room graphically depict hand-to-hand fighting at Waterloo.

Open Tue–Sun 11.00am–5.00pm. Admission fee.

At the Hyde Park Corner end of Piccadilly, on the south side of the street, there is still a stout wooden beam supported on two uprights. This is a relic of days gone by, a porter's rest. A man carrying a heavy load on his back could rest it on the beam, still tied to his back, for a breather before going on his way.

'No. 1, London', the Duke of Wellington's town house, stands calmly beside the traffic hurtling round Hyde Park Corner.

Wellington Arch

HYDE PARK CORNER, W1
⊖ HYDE PARK CORNER
ATLAS REF 175 E3

Dominating Hyde Park Corner is Wellington Arch, designed by Decimus Burton in 1858 as a triumphal entrance to Hyde Park. It was moved to the centre of the traffic island towards the end of the 19th century, in order to give Constitution Hill an architectural climax. Until 1883 the arch was surmounted by a colossal, 40-ton statue of the Duke of Wellington, so large that eight people are said to have once dined inside the horse. When the arch was put on its present axis, the statue was banished to Aldershot. The top of the arch remained bare until *The Quadriga* was placed on it in 1912. This work, showing the Angel of Peace descending into a Chariot of War drawn by four prancing horses, is by Captain Adrian Jones.

Among the lesser-known features of the arch is a police station — this is inside, and is the second smallest in London, after the one in Trafalgar Square.

A more modest **statue of Wellington** (astride Copenhagen, the horse that carried him at Waterloo) can be seen on a plinth in front of Apsley House. This is the work of the 19th-century British sculptor Sir Joseph Edgar Boehm; the statue was cast from captured French guns. The soldiers at each corner represent a British Grenadier, a Black Watch Highlander, a Welsh Fusilier and an Enniskillen Dragoon.

The military flavour of the area is enhanced by the 1927 **Machine Gun Corps Memorial** (with a statue of David flanked by Vickers machine guns), which was brought here in 1952. It is close to the **Royal Artillery Memorial** — a work consisting of an enormous block of Portland stone surmounted by a life-size stone Howitzer.

Green Park

PICCADILLY, W1
⊖ GREEN PARK
ATLAS REF 175 F4

Triangular Green Park consists of about 53 acres (21ha), with Piccadilly and Constitution Hill converging on two of its sides. The park derives its name from the fact that its main feature is grass and trees. It is largely devoid of flowers; according to tradition, this is because it was

used as a burial ground for lepers in the Middle Ages.

Rotten Row

HYDE PARK, SW1
⊖ HYDE PARK CORNER
ATLAS REF 175 E4/174 C4

King William III rode here regularly during the late-17th century, and this part of Hyde Park became known as the *route du roi* — hence Rotten Row. During the 18th and 19th centuries, Rotten Row was a most fashionable place to walk. It runs through Hyde Park in a straight line, from Hyde Park Corner almost as far as the Albert Memorial in Kensington Gardens. It is still used by horseriders today, although much of the surrounding stabling has disappeared.

Knightsbridge SW7

⊖ KNIGHTSBRIDGE
ATLAS REF 175 D3

On the north side of Belgravia, Knightsbridge includes the **Grenadier** public house in Wilton Row among its places of interest. The pub was once a billet for Wellington and his officers, and there is still a mounting block outside today. Old Barrack Yard nearby was the site of cavalry barracks until the 1840s.

At Albert Gate, leading into Hyde Park, is the **French Embassy**, one of two large buildings designed by Thomas Cubitt in the early 19th century.

The two buildings were nicknamed 'the two Gibraltars' when they were built, because, it was said, they would never be taken. In fact one of the buildings was leased soon after completion to George Hudson, the 'Railway King'.

Albert Gate stands on a bridge over the River Westbourne, where, it is said, two knights fought a duel in medieval times — hence Knightsbridge.

Part of the impressive Royal Artillery Memorial. The howitzer is angled to bombard the Somme battlefields in France.

Riders in Rotten Row. When it was first laid out, lamps were hung from trees all the way along, to deter highwaymen.

⊖ KNIGHTSBRIDGE
🚌 9, 10, 14, 19, 22, 30, 52, 74, 137, 503, C1

Harrods

ATLAS REF 175 D3

◆ BROMPTON ROAD, SW1 ◆

In 1834 the Royal Palace of Westminster burned down, the hansom cab first appeared on the streets of London, and a modest grocery and tea merchant's business opened in Cable Street, Stepney. London had plenty of other grocers and tea merchants, and the proprietor of this one does not seem to have been particularly ambitious, but he was competent at his business and he opened another branch, 15 years later, in Eastcheap in the City of London.

Knightsbridge

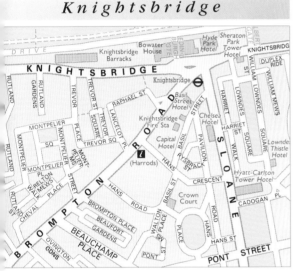

Harrods stands on the Brompton Road, now very smart, but in the 18th century a country footpath across the fields to the village of Brompton. The area to the north, around Montpelier Square, was first developed in the 1820s with quite modest houses. By the end of the century it had become a fashionable place. A heraldic eagle perches on the porch of No. 1 Montpelier Square. Harriette Wilson, the notorious 19th-century courtesan, lived at No. 1 Trevor Square for a time. Just to the east was Knightsbridge Green, which 150 years ago was still the green of the village of Knightsbridge. It sported a maypole as late as 1800.

The City in those days still had a large resident population and numerous shops. Only gradually, during the second half of the 19th century, did the residents and the shopkeepers move out, to be replaced by the financial institutions and offices which dominate the City today. The owner of the Cable Street and East-cheap grocer's shops was one of the first to move westwards to an outlying district which, in the 18th century, had been haunted by highwaymen and regarded as barely civilised. The area was known as Knightsbridge and the man who acquired a shop there in 1853 was Charles Henry Harrod.

Harrod took over a house and grocer's shop belonging to Philip Henry Burden at an address known as 8 Middle Queen's Building (now part of Brompton Road). The arrangement may have come about as a result of Burden's financial difficulties — it is possible that he owed Harrod money — but the two men seem to have been friends and to have come to an amicable agreement. Harrod's son, Charles Harrod, recognised the exciting potential of the new shop. The West End was turning into a fashionable place, and it was not long before he took over the business from his father and began to expand it into a major concern.

The 1860s saw the beginning of a revolution in retailing. The era of the department store had arrived, and shopkeepers began to extend their premises to offer customers the opportunity to do all their shopping under one roof. William Whiteley boasted of opening the largest store in the world in Westbourne Grove in 1863. Meanwhile, Charles Harrod attracted more customers to Middle Queen's Building and, by 1868, the shop boasted a new façade, 16 assistants, and new departments dealing in patent medicines, perfumes and stationery. Turnover, which had

been about £20 a week in 1853, had now risen to £1,000 a week.

Expansion continued during the 1870s and 1880s, and the Harrod family moved out of the premises to allow more room for merchandise. Harrods grew bigger by the year, and by 1880 100 staff were employed. Department-store shopping had by now become a favourite activity, and customers would travel up to London by train for the day, returning home in the evening laden with purchases and generally satisfied that the excursion had been a treat rather than a chore. By now Harrods aimed to supply its customers with virtually anything.

The best-known shop in the world occupies an entire block. It has a fine Edwardian terracotta façade and is five storeys high.

In the midst of success Harrods suffered a disaster when a fire broke out in December 1883, totally destroying the building and stock. There are two conflicting accounts of what happened next. One says that Charles Harrod immediately rented premises across the road and assured customers with outstanding Christmas orders that they would only suffer a slight delay. The other speaks of a despondent Harrod and an acquaintance called Edgar Cohen, who stepped in to save the situation. It *is* clear that the Christmas orders were attended to, and that the Christmas trade that year was the best yet. The fire also provided the opportunity to create a new and magnificent, purpose-built department store.

The new five-storey building opened in 1884. Within a short time Charles Harrod had retired, Edgar Cohen had taken over and Harrods had become a limited company under the general managership of Richard Burbidge, who decided that the still-growing shop should occupy a 4½ acre (1.8ha) site between Hans Crescent and Hans Road. By 1912 he had achieved his aim, and the familiar Doulton terracotta façade was in place.

Although Harrods has often been described as a 'top people's store', its Latin motto, *Omnia, omnibus, ubique,* proclaims that it will supply all things to everyone, everywhere. All aspects of human life are catered for by the shop, which offers its customers everything from printed christening invitations to funeral arrangements. Customers may bank at Harrods and keep their valuables in the safe deposit. It was once said that the pet department could supply everything from a mouse to an elephant, and when quarantine and export restrictions are favourable, exotic creatures can still be obtained.

Today Harrods is one of the most famous shops in the world. It has become legendary as a department store because of its high level of service and top-class merchandise, with no less than 20 acres (8ha) of goods, arranged on five floors and staffed by some 4,000 assistants (rising to 5,000 at Christmas and during the two annual sales). There are 300 departments, 18 of which belong to the famous and elegantly tiled **food and meat halls** on the ground floor. Here, among many other things, 500 different cheeses and 130 types of bread are for sale. Customers have a choice of 50 lifts and 11 restaurants and bars. At night, the façade of the building is illuminated by 11,500 light bulbs, supplied by the store's own generators.

The shop which was taking £1,000 a week in 1868 now has a *daily* turnover of about £1.1 million. The average number of customers is estimated at 35,000 per day, rising to an astonishing 300,000 on the first day of the famous January sale. In 1898 Harrods installed the first escalator in London, and since then business has never stood still.

W J Neatby designed Harrods' fabulous Art Nouveau tiled food halls, with their mouth-watering mosaics.

⊖ SLOANE SQUARE

Chelsea

ATLAS REF 174 C1

◆ SW3 ◆

When Thomas Carlyle moved into his new home in Cheyne Row, Chelsea, in 1834, he described the riverside village as 'a singularly hetereogeneous kind of spot, very dirty and confused in some places, quite beautiful in others, abounding in antiquities and the traces of great men.' Over 150 years later his description still holds good, even though London has long since engulfed the village. Parts of Chelsea are depressing, particularly those hampered by traffic. But where Chelsea is beautiful, it is very beautiful. It was born of the river — the name Chelsea means 'a landing place for chalk' —

and the river still gives it its character. And it still 'abounds in the traces of great men'.

Chelsea is London's true Bohemia, far more so than commercial Soho, or Hampstead with its self-conscious charm. In the snug Victorian pubs of Chelsea you may rub shoulders with leading figures in the worlds of art and communications. Residents have a strong sense of local patriotism. The borough was merged with Kensington in 1963 to become the Royal Borough of Kensington and Chelsea. Fortunately a lively local group, the Chelsea Society, helps to maintain the area's sense of identity.

James Bond, secret agent 007, lived in Royal Avenue, Chelsea, according to the chronicler of his exploits, Ian Fleming. This pleasant street runs south off the King's Road to Burton's Court, an open area of playing fields. There is a fine view of the front of the Royal Hospital from here, and the pillars of the handsome gateway are topped by trophies of arms. This was originally the main gateway to the Royal Hospital.

Royal Hospital

ROYAL HOSPITAL ROAD, SW3
⊖ SLOANE SQUARE
ATLAS REF 175 E1

One Chelsea institution whose name is familiar to everyone is the Royal Hospital, with its Chelsea Pensioners: old soldiers wearing spectacular uniforms and spending the evening of their days in one of Christopher Wren's masterpieces. The hospital is an architectural gem, built on a human scale. Aware that he was designing a home for the old and infirm, Wren ensured that the treads of the steps

should not be more than 3in (75mm) high.

The hospital was founded in 1682 by Charles II, using the Hôtel des Invalides (which Louis XIV had established in Paris in 1670 for infirm veterans of his army) as a model. Some 500 men, called 'in-pensioners', live in the hospital, but a great number of 'out-pensioners' also receive financial help from the foundation. The 'in-pensioners' are provided with food, accommodation and clothing daily. They are divided into six companies, each under an officer. The colourful scarlet frock-coat worn by the pensioners is a uniform that dates back to the time of the Duke of Marlborough (1650–1722).

The oldest parts of the hospital, and those into which visitors are allowed, are the **Figure Court** and the **north range** of buildings. The Figure

Court takes its name from the statue of Charles II by Grinling Gibbons which stands at its centre. The statue is decorated with oak boughs on Founder's Day (29 May), to commemorate Charles's escape on this day after the Battle of Worcester, when he hid from the Roundheads in an oak tree. A handsome pillared portico leads into the **Octagon Porch** from which the Great Hall (where the pensioners dine) and the Chapel lead off. The imposing **Great Hall** contains an immense mural of Charles II on horseback. Among the other portraits is one of a pensioner, William Hiseland, who married for the third time at the age of 100 and died aged 112. The body of the Duke of Wellington lay in state in the hall in 1852, before his funeral at St

Sir Christopher Wren's Royal Hospital buildings combine dignity and comfort.

Chelsea

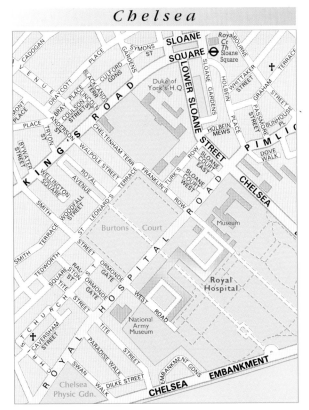

Paul's. The **Chapel**, completed in 1687, is much as Wren designed it. Visitors are welcome to join in the services. When the hospital was first built, its grounds went all the way down to the Thames, but they now cease at Chelsea Embankment.

Grounds open daily, 10.00am–dusk. Museum, Chapel and Great Hall, Mon–Sat 10.00am–12.00noon and 2.00pm–4.00pm (Sun 2.00pm–4.00pm, summer only).

National Army Museum

ROYAL HOSPITAL ROAD, SW3
⊖ SLOANE SQUARE
ATLAS REF 175 D1
Close to the Royal Hospital, this modern museum illustrates the history of the British Army from the 16th century to modern times. Included are contemporary weapons and equipment as well as historical ones. There is an excellent library of works on British military history.
Open Mon–Sat 10.00am–5.30pm, Sun 2.00pm–5.30pm.

Chelsea Physic Garden

SWAN WALK, SW3
⊖ SLOANE SQUARE
ATLAS REF 175 D1
Founded in 1673 by the Society

of Apothecaries for research into medicinal plants, Chelsea Physic Garden was given to the society by Sir Hans Sloane in 1722 (his statue, by Michael Rysbrack, stands in the garden). In 1732 cotton seed from the garden was sent to America, from which sprang the entire cotton industry of the southern states.
Open mid–Apr to mid–Oct, Wed and Sun 2.00pm–5.00pm, and daily during the Chelsea Flower Show. Admission fee.

Chelsea Old Church

CHEYNE WALK, SW3
⊖ SLOANE SQUARE
ATLAS REF 174 C1
The casual visitor might not give this rebuilt church a second glance, for its dignified exterior is dull and gives no indication of its rich history. Heavily bombed in 1941, Chelsea Old Church's most important feature, the **More Chapel**, has fortunately survived. It was built by Chelsea's most famous resident, Sir Thomas More, in 1528. The capitals of the pillars are believed to be the work of More's friend, Hans Holbein the younger, and are one of the earliest examples of Renaissance architecture in England. The church possesses some of the finest Tudor monuments in England, which have been skilfully restored after bombing.

Sloane Square SW3

⊖ SLOANE SQUARE
ATLAS REF 175 E2
The name of this square has entered the English language as a synonym for the pretentiously fashionable, perhaps because 'Sloanes' come here to shop.
The **Royal Court** theatre on the east side of the square was built in 1888, and has gained a reputation for avant garde productions. Opposite the underground station is the large store of **Peter Jones**, whose present building dates from 1935.

Carlyle's House

CHEYNE ROW, SW3
⊖ SLOANE SQUARE
ATLAS REF 174 C1
Interesting as the home of one of Britain's greatest writers, Thomas Carlyle, this small museum is also a good example of the modest, but well-designed, Georgian houses in the locality. Carlyle lived here with his wife from 1834 until his death in 1881. Maintained by the National Trust today, the house looks much as it would have done in Carlyle's lifetime.
Open Apr–Oct, Wed–Sun and BH Mon, 11.30am–5.00pm. Admission fee for non-National Trust members.

Window-shopping in the King's Road. Tourists visit this street to see fashions, as much on the shoppers as in the shops.

*Head of Thomas Carlyle, at the Chelsea house where the sage lived and wrote **The French Revolution, Heroes and Hero-Worship** and **Past and Present**.*

South Kensington

ATLAS REF 174 c2

◆ SW7 ◆

A lack of logic characterises many London names. This area, lying between Kensington proper and Belgravia, bounded on the north by Kensington Gore and on the south by the Cromwell Road, should really be called East Kensington. It contains some of the world's most famous museums, but it is not an area that invites casual strolling, for it is laid out in the grand manner, with no places for relaxation. Unless you wish to study Victorian monumental architecture in detail, the best plan is to go straight to the museum or other building of your choice.

South Kensington is a testimony to Victorian confidence and belief in education. Above all, it is a monument to Queen Victoria's earnest young husband, Prince Albert, for it was born of the Great Exhibition of 1851 and this was largely inspired by him. It is said

South Kensington

[map showing Imperial College, Science Museum, Victoria & Albert Museum, Natural History Museum, Royal College of Art, Cromwell Road, Thurloe Place, Brompton Road, South Kensington station, etc.]

Brick, terracotta and mosaic: the V & A.

that one person in six in Great Britain visited the exhibition, and the profits were used to buy 88 acres (36ha) just south of Hyde Park, where buildings designed to further the Prince Consort's ideals were erected. They included three great museums and a number of colleges of art and science, among them Imperial College. The appropriately named Exhibition Road was built to run through the heart of the area.

Opposite the Cromwell Road front of the Victoria and Albert Museum, outside the Ismaili Centre, is a small garden. In it is a memorial to the thousands of men, women and children who at the end of the Second World War were forcibly repatriated to the Soviet Union and Eastern European countries, there to meet imprisonment, torture and death. Dedicated in 1986, the memorial replaces an earlier one which was vandalised.

Victoria & Albert Museum

CROMWELL ROAD, SW7
⊖ SOUTH KENSINGTON
ATLAS REF 174 c3

This vast, handsome, ebullient building is the perfect symbol of Victorian Britain, in both its architecture and its contents. Known affectionately as the V & A, it plays a vital and frequently controversial role in modern applied art today, more than 100 years after its foundation.

The V & A grew over the better part of a century. The nucleus of its colossal collection was formed by a selection of objects displayed at the Great Exhibition, whose original purpose, 'the application of fine art to objects of utility', still pervades the institution. The collection was first established at Marlborough House but, under Prince Albert's influence, it was moved to this site in 1857. As the collection grew, so the building expanded. The purely 19th-century façade is the one facing Exhibition Road; the main façade, on Cromwell Road, was designed by Sir Aston Webb

between 1899 and 1909. The foundation stone was laid by Queen Victoria herself in 1899, and the museum was completed in 1909, eight years after her death. The vast lantern which forms a conspicuous feature above the entrance is designed to resemble an imperial crown, as if to mark the high point of the British Empire.

The museum is vast (covering 12 acres or 5ha) and its contents are immensely varied, ranging from 19th-century English watercolours to 9th-century reliquaries. The V & A has always regarded itself as an educational institution and although there has been controversy about its policies in the past, the public benefits from the changing exhibitions that are held here. The bedrock of the museum, however, is formed by the permanent exhibitions. **The Nehru Gallery of Indian Art**, for instance, had a setting inspired by the courts of the Mogul Emperors, in which exquisite miniatures, the personal wine cup of the Emperor Shah Jehan (carved from white jade), weapons and textiles are displayed.

The museum is particularly rich in domestic furniture, including the vast and famous **Bed of Ware**, mentioned in Shakespeare's *Twelfth Night*. Visitors can enter complete rooms saved from demolished houses. Students often come to the museum to study the remarkable, life-size plaster casts of Classical statuary, or to visit the **National Art Library**, the **Print Room**, or the **Picture Library**.

In addition to this great central collection, the V & A also administers a number of branch museums, including the Museum of Childhood in Bethnal Green. The Geological Museum is an integral part of the V & A (see p. 80–1).

Open Mon–Sat 10.00am–6.00pm, Sun 2.30pm–6.00pm. No admission fee, but an optional donation is requested.

Natural History Museum

CROMWELL ROAD, SW7
⊖ SOUTH KENSINGTON
ATLAS REF 174 c3
There are 65 million specimens and 1 million books and manuscripts in this museum, making up the world's most complete collection of natural history material. The museum's collection continues to grow at the enormous rate of 300,000 specimens a year. Such figures might well be daunting, but the Natural History Museum has benefitted, perhaps more than any other, from new techniques in museum display, which set out to explain, instead of letting the visitor wander blindly from one case to another. Since the 1970s the museum has concentrated on showing a series of self-contained exhibitions, rather than attempting to show off all of its millions of specimens in old-fashioned cabinets. The **Central Hall**, with its huge dinosaurs, and the **Whale Hall** are survivors from older, unmodernised exhibitions.

The building itself is as remarkable as anything inside it. Designed by Alfred Waterhouse, and built between 1873 and 1881, it could almost be mistaken for a cathedral. The effect is deliberate, for the intention was to provide a building 'for housing the works of the creator'. Everything is here, from the duck-billed platypus to samples of mineral deposits; from fossils, to a model of the human embryo. The museum has named one entire gallery 'creepy-crawlies', where its incredible

collection of arthropods, including a nightmarish model of a scorpion, is on display.

Modern computer technology is employed to enable visitors, particularly children, to find things out for themselves by operating visual display units. The great attractions, though, are still the traditional ones, such as the enormous skeleton of the dinsosaur *Diplodocus*, or the life-size model of a blue whale suspended from the Whale Hall ceiling. Among the riches on display is the detail of the building itself, with its enchanting little sculptures of animal and plant life adorning the walls and pillars. The museum's guidebook gives an overall picture of the collection and is an admirable souvenir.

Open Mon–Sat 10.00am–6.00pm, Sun 11.00am–6.00pm. Admission fee.

Two dinosaurs: the skeleton and the Natural History Museum's superb hall.

The Natural History Museum's Romanesque-style entrance is covered in terracotta slabs with animals, birds and fishes moulded in relief.

South Kensington

Science Museum

EXHIBITION ROAD, SW7
⊖ SOUTH KENSINGTON
ATLAS REF 174 C3
The Science Museum began life in 1857, at the height of the Industrial Revolution. The museum is both a child of that event and a record of it.

Originally part of the Victoria & Albert Museum, the Science Museum grew so rapidly that in 1909 it assumed an identity of its own. While other museum buildings in the area display the exuberance of Victorian architecture, the Science Museum reflects the austere, not to say bleak, values of our own time. The first part of the building was completed in 1928 and the second major block, overlooking Exhibition Road, in 1963.

In the East Hall the visitor encounters the extraordinary **Foucault Pendulum**. Devised in 1851 to demonstrate the rotation of the earth (it does so by virtue of its immensely long suspension), it still fascinates adults and children alike, and provides a kind of leitmotif for the museum — entertainment (and education) through the demonstration of scientific laws.

The museum's collections fall under three main headings: industry, science and society. Under the general description of

Futuristic displays on show in the Science Museum often look like modernistic works of art. The museum covers the development of technology from early steam engines to the Space Age.

energy converters the museum displays a series of engines, from 'Puffing Billy' of 1813, the world's oldest surviving locomotive, to the eight-engined *Black Arrow* rocket, designed to put Britain's second satellite into orbit in 1971.

Imaginatively, the museum uses works of art to demonstrate industrial history, such as *Coalbrookdale by Night*, painted in 1801 and showing the glow of industrial furnaces in what was still rural landscape. In the museum's science section, you can follow the development of computers from the first mechanical devices to today's split-second operations. There is also an example of the German coding machine, *Enigma*, used in the Second World War. Also on display are mathematical formulae worked out in three-dimensional forms, frequently producing results indistinguishable from some modern works of art.

In the areas devoted to society, visitors can follow the contribution made by science everyday life, and to medicine in particular. Transport is dealt with by exhibits showing the evolution of transport technology, from sailing ships to modern aircraft. The general theme of the exhibition is the implications of a more mobile society. An interesting exhibit

here is the 1958 Ford Edsel 'gas guzzler', which gave only 15 miles to the gallon and was a commercial failure as a result.

The museum also organises lectures, changing exhibitions and 'hands-on' displays, dealing with subjects such as the Food Pyramid and the Energy Bike.

Open Mon–Sat 10.00am–6.00pm, Sun 11.00am–6.00pm. Admission fee.

Geological Museum

EXHIBITION ROAD, SW7
⊖ SOUTH KENSINGTON
ATLAS REF 174 C3
The Geological Museum is sited between the Natural History Museum and the Science Museum. Officially, it is a part of the V & A (see pages 78–9). It is also the headquarters of the **British Geological Survey**, founded in 1835 to provide a comprehensive geological map of Britain. The museum was established shortly afterwards, in 1837. It originally occupied a house in Whitehall, to which specimens collected by the survey were taken for inspection. In 1851 the collection was moved to Jermyn Street and in 1935 — the centenary of the British Geological Survey — it occupied its present building.

Perhaps even more than the Natural History Museum, the

Geological Museum has benefitted from modern techniques of display. You might expect displays of mineral deposits and geological structures only to be of interest to specialists, but parts of the Geological Museum are stunning, almost like a jeweller's with their glittering displays of gemstones. Some of the exhibits are purely decorative, such as the threatening mask of an Aztec god and the richly decorated Murchison snuffbox. Others show the evolution of fossil ammonites, which provide geologists with an invaluable time key. An animated film portrays the different geological environments in which minerals and rocks are found. The exhibition of British fossils answers several questions, such as where are fossils found? How are they named? What exactly are they? The display called 'The Story of the Earth' traces the evolution of the planet.

An interesting facet of the museum is that it houses one of the greatest collections of building stones in Europe and restorers of ancient buildings often refer to the museum to find stones to match the colour and texture of originals.

Open Mon–Sat 10.00am–6.00pm, Sun 11.00am–6.00pm. Admission fee.

Brompton Oratory

BROMPTON ROAD, SW7
⊖ SOUTH KENSINGTON
ATLAS REF 174 C3
An oratory is 'a congregation of secular priests living together in a community without vows' and was the invention of the 16th-century Italian saint, Filippo de' Neri. The sumptuous structure in Brompton Road, inspired by the mother church of the Order of St Philip Neri in Rome, was designed by Herbert Gribble in 1878. It was formally opened by Cardinal Manning in 1884, in the presence of 16 bishops, 250 priests and the representatives of 17 religious orders. The most conspicuous features of the heavily decorated interior are the side chapels, each with distinctive ornaments, such as carvings, mosaics and paintings. In front of the **Chapel of St Philip** is a wax effigy of the saint, containing a relic from his body. Brompton Oratory is famous for its music, and for its magnificent organ in particular.

Open daily, 7.00am–8.00pm.

Baden-Powell House

CROMWELL ROAD, SW7
⊖ GLOUCESTER ROAD
ATLAS REF 174 B2
Baden-Powell House is the headquarters of the Scout Association (formerly the Boy Scouts). It is also a memorial to 'B P', Baron Baden-Powell, who founded the Boy Scouts Association in 1908. The house contains many mementoes associated with Baden-Powell, and there is a statue of him outside by Don Potter.

Open daily, 7.00am–8.00pm.

Ismaili Centre

CROMWELL GARDENS, SW7
⊖ SOUTH KENSINGTON
ATLAS REF 174 C2
Opposite the V & A, the Ismaili Centre was built in 1985 for the Aga Khan Foundation and has an art gallery and reading rooms, as well as a prayer hall. In the small public garden outside, there is a memorial to those who were sent back to the USSR against their will at the end of the Second World War.

Open Mon–Fri 9.30am–5.30pm.

The Baroque façade of Brompton Oratory gleams in Portland stone. The Oratorians were first brought to England by Cardinal Newman in 1848, and the building is one of London's leading Roman Catholic churches.

⊖ HIGH STREET
   KENSINGTON
⊖ SOUTH
   KENSINGTON
🚌 9, 10, 52, C1

Royal Albert Hall

ATLAS REF 174 c3

◆ **KENSINGTON GORE, SW7** ◆

Hligh up in the great dome of the Royal Albert Hall floats a collection of what appears to be severely abstract modern art. The objects, in fact, are designed to improve the acoustics of the great building. Ever since it

A statue of Prince Albert on a 42ft (13m) high column stands with the Royal Albert Hall beyond.

Kensington

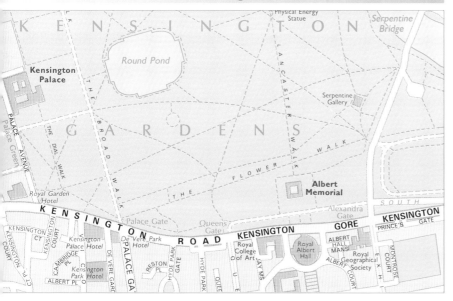

West of the Royal Albert Hall, Queen's Gate is worth strolling down for its handsome Victorian houses. Further down is St Augustine's Church.

Some of the best sculpture of its period surrounds the Albert Memorial.

was opened, more than a century ago, people have joked that audiences get two orchestras for the price of one: one on stage, the other in the echo of the ceiling.

The Royal Albert Hall is one of London's best-loved buildings. Here, annual Promenade Concerts (founded by Sir Henry Wood in 1895 and given in the Royal Albert Hall since 1941) disprove the charge that the British are not musical. Every year on the Saturday before

Remembrance Sunday, old soldiers gather here to remember their fallen comrades. Businesses hire the hall for social functions, and fans swarm in to attend boxing matches. Some of the season's most prestigious balls also take place here.

The official title of the building is the Royal Albert Hall of the Arts and Sciences, and, like the Kensington museums, it was built following the success of the Great Exhibition of 1851. Prince Albert was the enthusiastic patron of the Great Exhibition and it is entirely appropriate that this majestic, if rather startling building was built on a site acquired by the proceeds and dedicated to his memory. Queen Victoria laid the foundation stone on 20 May 1867 and opened the completed building, designed by Captain Francis Fowke and Lieutenant-Colonel Henry Scott, on 29 March 1871. The hall is, in effect, an enormous covered amphitheatre, more than 150ft (46m) high, capable of accommodating up to 8,000 people. Outside there is a mosaic frieze by the students of the South Kensington School of Art, illustrating the triumph of the arts and the sciences.

The interior is not only spectacular but also practical. Boxes are arranged one above the other in three tiers and high above them all are the 'gods', where impecunious music-lovers can hear the same music as wealthy patrons.

Visitors are allowed inside the Royal Albert Hall when it is not in use.

Nearby . . .

Albert Memorial

KENSINGTON GORE, SW7
⊖ HIGH STREET KENSINGTON
⊖ KNIGHTSBRIDGE
ATLAS REF 174 c3

Whatever the opinion of the sophisticated, this is an enjoyable confection, glittering with mosaics, gilding and multi-coloured stones, and smothered with statuary. There is no doubt as to whom the monument is dedicated, for Prince Albert is depicted sitting under the spectacular canopy. The figure is an excellent portrait of the handsome, serious-minded man and, as it has been protected by the canopy for more than a hundred years, it is still in good condition. The book Albert holds is not the Bible, but the catalogue of the Great Exhibition. The memorial is the work of a famous architect, Sir George Gilbert Scott, and was erected between 1863 and 1876. It is 175ft (53m) high and approached by a dignified flight of steps, 121ft (37m) wide. The four continents are shown at the corners, and the figures around the pedestal (175 in all), represent prominent artists and scientists of the day.

The Serpentine

HYDE PARK, W2
⊖ KNIGHTSBRIDGE
ATLAS REF 174 c4/175 d4

A good approach to this attractive lake in Hyde Park is from Alexandra Gate on Kensington Gore. Look for the magnificent iron Coalbrookdale gates on the left, just inside the park, one of the last survivals of the Great Exhibition of 1851. Londoners owe the Serpentine to Caroline of Ansbach, consort of King George II. Looking out at Hyde Park from Kensington Palace one day in 1730, she realised that a number of small ponds in the marshy ground could be turned into one attractive waterway, and the Serpentine was the result. Although not very large (about 40 acres or 16ha), the Serpentine changes character dramatically along its length. East is The Dell, an enchanting little water garden, while on the north side there is a boating lake. There is a swimming area (Lido) on the south side, and an Italian Garden on the west. Long Water connects with the Serpentine at Serpentine Bridge.

Serpentine Gallery

KENSINGTON GARDENS, W2
⊖ KNIGHTSBRIDGE
ATLAS REF 174 c4

The Serpentine Gallery was erected as a teahouse in 1907, but in 1972 it was launched by the Arts Council as a platform for contemporary art and sculpture, with frequently changing exhibitions.

Open daily, 10.00am–5.00pm (10.00am until dusk in winter).

Peter Pan Statue

KENSINGTON GARDENS, W2
⊖ LANCASTER GATE
ATLAS REF 174 c4

The statue is on the west side of Long Water, not far from the Italian Garden. It is an engaging piece of Edwardian whimsy, showing the hero of the story with assorted characters.

Royal College of Art

KENSINGTON GORE, SW7
⊖ KNIGHTSBRIDGE
⊖ HIGH STREET KENSINGTON
ATLAS REF 174 b3

Immediately next door to the Royal Albert Hall, but utterly different from it in spirit, is the Royal College of Art. Originally called the School of Design when it was founded in 1837, the college today is housed in a stark modern building designed by H T Cadbury-Brown and Sir Hugh Casson between 1960 and 1964.

Royal Geographical Society

LOWTHER LODGE
EXHIBITION ROAD, SW7
⊖ SOUTH KENSINGTON
ATLAS REF 174 c3

Some of the most famous and exciting expeditions, including the conquest of Everest, were planned in this building, which the society (founded in 1830) moved into in 1913. The work of Victorian architect Norman Shaw, who also designed Albert Hall Mansions nearby, Lowther Lodge was erected as a private house in 1870.

The society's musuem is not open to the public. The Map Room, with its collection of over half a million maps and atlases, is open Mon–Fri 10.00am– 1.00pm and 2.00pm–5.00pm.

Knightsbridge Barracks

KNIGHTSBRIDGE, SW7
⊖ KNIGHTSBRIDGE
ATLAS REF 175 d3

The headquarters of the Household Cavalry, Knightsbridge Barracks houses two regiments, the Life Guards (distinguished by a scarlet tunic with blue collars and cuffs) and the Blues and Royals (distinguished by blue tunics with scarlet collars and cuffs). The building, dating from 1970, is by Sir Basil Spence, the architect of Coventry Cathedral.

A summer afternoon in Hyde Park, with the Serpentine in the background. It took 200 workmen to dig out the lake and its formal opening was on 1 May 1731.

Royal Albert Hall Area

The main axis of Kensington, where Church Street comes down the hill to join the High Street. The Victorian Church of St Mary Abbots takes its name from the abbots of Abingdon, who built the first church here in the 12th century.

Kensington High Street W8

⊖ HIGH STREET KENSINGTON
ATLAS REF 174 A3
If you want to sample the full flavour of Kensington, go into the parish church of **St Mary Abbots** in the High Street. In 1866 the architect Sir George Gilbert Scott (who also designed the Albert Memorial in Kensington Gardens) was commissioned to build a 'truly magnificent' church here, to replace the dilapidated 17th-century building. Today, visitors approach the church via a massive stone cloister, and the interior is the epitome of Victorian opulence. Here there is plenty of evidence of Empire, with memorials to British men and women who lived and died in half the known globe.

Until the mid-19th century, Kensington was a country village. From 1820 to 1833 William Cobbett, the pugnacious politician and pamphleteer, had a farm on the site of what is now High Street Kensington underground station. **Kensington Church Street**, which begins on the corner of the High Street beside St Mary Abbots, still has a slightly countrified air.

Kensington Palace

KENSINGTON GARDENS, W8
⊖ HIGH STREET KENSINGTON
ATLAS REF 174 A4
A country house that became a royal residence, Kensington Palace is partly a museum today. It still contains accommodation for members of the Royal Family, as well as 'grace and favour' apartments, which are the personal gift of the monarch to a subject. They are usually allocated to pensioners who have served the Crown.

When William of Orange became King William III of England in 1688, he bought a country house near the village of Kensington to escape the hurly-burly of London. He paid £20,000 for it and afterwards spent £60,000 transforming it into a palace with the help of the great architect, Sir Christopher Wren. The south front overlooking the ornamental gardens appears today much as when Wren left it. Close to London, but set in countryside, Kensington Palace subsequently became a favourite royal residence. William III and his wife, Queen Mary, both died here; so did George II and Queen Anne. The future Queen Victoria was born here in 1819.

The **State Apartments** were restored and reopened to the public in 1975. On the ground floor is the **Red Saloon**, where the young Queen Victoria held her first Privy Council in 1837.

Kensington Palace, seen across its formal garden. It was built by Sir Christopher Wren.

The **Court Dress Collection** is here, and in adjoining rooms. Look out for the collection of dresses worn by Queen Victoria, which range from the sprigged muslins of girlhood to the widow's weeds of old age. The beautiful **Queen's Staircase**, leading to the **Queen's Gallery**, is the work of Sir Christopher Wren. The gallery and the rooms on the first floor contain a large collection of portraits and the rooms themselves are excellent examples of 17th-century domestic architecture. They include decorative work by the early 18th-century architect and painter, William Kent, and carvings by Grinling Gibbons, a pupil of Wren. On the first floor is the room in which the young Princess Victoria was told she

For children of all ages: Peter Pan in Kensington Gardens.

was Queen. It contains a number of personal mementoes, and the cradle used by her children.

In the grounds outside is the **Orangery**, a striking building of 1704, attributed to Sir Christopher Wren but probably designed by Nicholas Hawksmoor.

Open Mon–Sat 9.00am–4.50pm, Sun 1.00pm–4.50pm. Admission fee.

Kensington Gardens W8

⊖ HIGH STREET KENSINGTON
ATLAS REF 174 B4
Kensington Gardens should not be confused with **Kensington Palace Gardens** (otherwise

known as 'Millionaire's Row'), which run from Kensington High Street to Notting Hill Gate and are mostly occupied by foreign embassies. Kensington Gardens adjoin the western edge of Hyde Park. Although they were once the private gardens of the palace, they are now open to the public. They are beautifully laid out, and the **Flower Walk** is particularly attractive. Model boats can sail on the **Round Pond**. Elsewhere British nannies can be seen, members of a vanishing species, dressed in sensible clothes and wheeling their well-bred charges in solid perambulators.

Linley Sambourne House

18 STAFFORD TERRACE, W8
⊖ HIGH STREET KENSINGTON
ATLAS REF 174 A3
Built in 1868, the house is maintained by the Victorian Society as a typical example of an upper middle-class residence of the period. It is named after its former owner, Mr Linley Sambourne, a successful artist who died in 1910.

Open Mar–Oct, Wed 10.00am–4.00pm, Sun 2.00pm–5.00pm. Admission fee.

Leighton House

HOLLAND PARK ROAD, W14
⊖ HIGH STREET KENSINGTON
ATLAS REF 185
Once the home of Lord Leighton, the immensely popular Victorian painter who died in 1896, the house is now a centre for Victorian studies. Built in 1866, it was designed by Leighton as a fantasy Moorish palace. The highlight of the interior is the **Arab Hall**, with its walls clad with ornate Islamic tiles. Examples of Leighton's work,

along with paintings by his contemporaries, are on display.

Open Mon–Sat 11.00am–5.00pm (Mon–Fri 11.00am–6.00pm during special exhibitions). Admission fee.

Commonwealth Institute

KENSINGTON HIGH STREET, W8
⊖ HIGH STREET KENSINGTON
ATLAS REF 185
Founded as the Imperial Institute in 1887, the Commonwealth Institute is an information centre for Commonwealth affairs, staging exhibitions and promoting economic studies. There is an excellent library and reading room.

Open Mon–Sat 10.00am–5.00pm, Sun 2.00pm–5.00pm.

Holland Park W8

⊖ HIGH STREET KENSINGTON
⊖ HOLLAND PARK
ATLAS REF 185
One of London's best-kept secrets, this delightful green area with its attractive gardens complete with peacocks is a remarkable survival from a leisured past. At its heart is **Holland House**, a Jacobean mansion built in 1605, which became the centre for a political and literary set under the formidable Lady Holland in the 19th century. The great novelist, Charles Dickens, was among those who attended her fashionable soirées. The house was badly bombed in the Second World War, but part of the original building has been incorporated into a youth hostel, dedicated to the late King George VI. There are a number of survivals in the grounds, including the Orangery, the Ice House and the Ballroom.

Model sailboat buffs come from miles around to try out their prized vessels on the Round Pond in Kensington Gardens. The pond owes its existence to the landscaping enthusiasm of Queen Caroline, consort of George II in the 18th century. In those days the land here formed the private grounds of Kensington Palace. When the gardens were later opened to the public, it was at weekends only to begin with and only respectable, decently dressed persons were admitted. Soldiers, sailors and servants were not allowed in.

Madame Tussaud's

ATLAS REF 171 E3

◆ MARYLEBONE ROAD, NW1 ◆

Among the scores of famous, beautiful, sinister or talented figures at Madame Tussaud's is a bust which invariably attracts attention. It is of a little old lady wearing glasses and a poke bonnet — Madame Tussaud, who modelled herself eight years before her death in 1850.

She was born Marie Grosholtz in Strasbourg in 1761. Her widowed mother became housekeeper to a talented artist, Dr Philippe Curtius, who exhibited wax figures in the fashionable Palais Royal. Curtius took a fancy to his housekeeper's little daughter and taught her his art. She learned quickly. At the age of 17 she modelled Voltaire, and later became art tutor to the French royal family. During the French Revolution she was called upon to take death masks of notable victims of the guillotine, including King Louis XVI and Queen Marie Antoinette. These are on display in the museum's Chamber of Horrors, along with the original guillotine blade.

Madame Tussaud's collection grew steadily. In 1802 conditions in France became so bad that she decided to take her exhibition on a tour of major English cities. In 1835 she set up a permanent exhibition of historical and contemporary figures in Baker Street. Following her death in 1850 her sons inherited the business. Her grandsons commissioned the present building for the exhibits, which opened in Marylebone Road in 1884.

The oldest figure on display is Sleeping Beauty, modelled by Madame Tussaud's mentor Philippe Curtius in 1765. It is actually a portrait of Madame du Barry, the celebrated mistress of Louis XV, who went to the guillotine in 1793.

As ever, the chief attraction at Madame Tussaud's is the **Chamber of Horrors**, which includes gruesome exhibits, such as a recreation of a Victorian back street with the corpse of one of Jack the Ripper's victims in it. There is a garotte on display, as well as a working model of the guillotine, and an electric chair. Tussaud's strives for grisly authenticity. In 1878 the exhibition acquired a genuine gallows from Hertford Gaol, and the Chamber of Horrors includes them in its display, along with models of famous 20th-century murderers, such as John Christie and Dr Crippen. A model of George Smith, the 'brides in the bath' murderer, leans over a victim in the actual tub in which he drowned them.

Model-making techniques have changed little over the past 200 years, and the exhibition includes a model of sculptor Mark Richards, shown working on a figure. He is the first person employed by Madame Tussaud's to appear in wax — apart from the lady herself. Making a figure can take up to three months. Each subject is created by translating hundreds of measurements and photographs into three-dimensional form. Eyes must be specially made, and real human hair is painstakingly inserted into the wax head a strand at a time, to create a natural effect.

Historic and contemporary figures, such as the Queen, are on permanent display. Others are changed with fashions, especially those of well-known subjects in the field of entertainment. It has been said that an entertainer's popularity can be gauged by how long his or her figure remains on display at Madame Tussaud's. A subjects is often photographed standing beside his or her finished model, and this is a rigorous test of the sculptor's art. Again and again, it is virtually impossible to tell which figure is real from the photograph. As far as possible, subjects are modelled from life, and they usually supply clothes for the figure. One exception was the artist Pablo Picasso. Having seen the likeness of Rembrandt in Madame Tussaud's in Amsterdam he decided that since Rembrandt gave no sitting — and the likeness was good — there was absolutely no need for him to do so.

Open Mon–Fri 10.00am–5.30pm, Sat and Sun 9.30am–5.30pm. Admission fee.

A plaque on No. 1 Dorset Square, at the corner with Melcombe Street, marks the building from which Free French and British agents left London during the Second World War for devious and highly dangerous forays into occupied France. Plaques across the road recall that before the houses were built in the early 19th century the square was the site of Thomas Lord's first London cricket ground, where the MCC was founded in 1787.

Baker Street and Marylebone

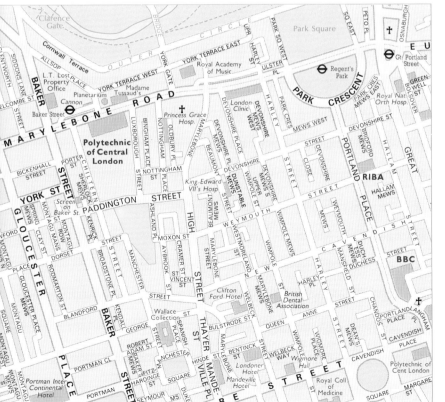

Bluff King Hal and some of his womenfolk are among the perennially popular, large-as-life figures thronging the halls of Madame Tussaud's.

Nearby . . .
The Planetarium

MARYLEBONE ROAD, NW1
⊖ BAKER STREET
ATLAS REF 171 E3

It was an air raid in the Second World War that made this spectacular exhibition possible. In September 1940, the first 1,000lb (454kg) bomb dropped on London fell on Madame Tussaud's cinema in Marylebone Road, totally destroying it. During the 1930s Madame Tussaud's directors had planned to create just a small planetarium, but the destruction of the cinema and a decline in cinema audiences eventually encouraged them to build one of the world's largest planetariums on the site. It was opened on 19 March 1958 by the Duke of Edinburgh in the presence of the Astronomer Royal, an impressive recognition of the Planetarium's authenticity. Today, the Planetarium is an entertainment and a place of educational importance.

The great copper dome has become one of London's landmarks. It is actually a number of domes of different materials, one inside the other. The innermost dome is a giant projection screen with 2½ million perforations for acoustic and ventilation purposes. Optical projections need very clean air to be effective, and it is important, too, that the 5,000 beams of light which pass at any one time from the projector to the dome cannot be seen.

In the early days of the Planetarium, programmes were given 'live' by a team of narrators. Live shows are still given to schools, but the general programme is recorded and automated, so that more complex effects can be produced.

'A cloudless night sky every day' is a good description of the Planetarium's inner dome. For once, stars can be seen in all their clarity, and the first glimpse of the artificially produced night sky never fails to bring a gasp of wonderment from the audience. The sky is produced by a Zeiss star projector (named after Carl Zeiss, who installed it in 1958).

In 1980 an **Astronomer's Gallery** was introduced, which traces the development of astronomy from ancient times to man's landing on the moon on 21 July 1969. An interesting fact conveyed by the display is that because the moon has no atmosphere or wind, the astronauts' footprints will last as long as the moon itself.

Shows: Mon–Fri 12.20pm– 5.00pm, Sat and Sun 10.20am– 5.00pm. Admission fee.

221B Baker Street W1

⊖ BAKER STREET
ATLAS REF 171 D3

The fictional detective, Sherlock Holmes, was said to live at this address in Sir Arthur Conan Doyle's famous novels. Today, tourists are attracted to No 221B (which is part of the Abbey National's headquarters), to admire the plaque erected here. (In fact, the Abbey National employs a member of staff full-time to answer letters that are sent to Sherlock Holmes at this address!)

A short distance away, at 239 Baker Street, there is a small museum dedicated to Sherlock Holmes, which describes itself as '221B Baker Street'.

221B Baker Street museum open daily, 10.00am–5.00pm. Admission fee.

The wonders of space are vividly conveyed at the London Planetarium, and the brilliance of the night sky can be far more fully experienced than in the real world outside.

Madame Tussaud's Area

Marylebone High Street
W1

⊖ REGENT'S PARK
⊖ BAKER STREET
ATLAS REF 171 E2

The area around Marylebone High Street was laid out from 1708 onwards, when the Duke of Newcastle bought the manor house of the village of St-Mary-le-Bourne and began to develop the area into an estate. Henrietta Place was named after the Duke's daughter, while her husband, Edward Harley, Earl of Oxford and Mortimer, gave his name to Harley and Mortimer Streets. Bentinck Street and Portland Place were named after Harley's son-in-law, William Bentinck, Duke of Portland.

Despite two centuries of development, the original grid plan in the squares and streets around Marylebone High Street is still discernible. The latter is an attractively narrow, winding little road with a high proportion of residential accommodation, plus small shops and restaurants. **Harley Street**, to the east, has retained its Georgian terraces. A residential air lingers, even though this street has been a centre for top doctors and private clinics since the 1850s.

Wimpole Street W1

⊖ REGENT'S PARK
⊖ BAKER STREET
ATLAS REF 171 E2

Wimpole Street is famed for its romantic associations, for it was here that the Barrett family lived in the mid-19th century. The poet Robert Browning courted the ailing Elizabeth Barrett here in the face of disapproval from her father. The whole story is told in the film, *The Barretts of Wimpole Street.*

Marylebone Station

BOSTON PLACE, NW1
⊖ MARYLEBONE
ATLAS REF 171 D3

Marylebone's handsome railway station made its appearance in 1899. It was built for the convenience of wealthy Victorian commuters from the Chilterns and was much admired by the late poet, Sir John Betjemen. It was the last mainline station built in London and was originally constructed for the Great Central Railway.

Wallace Collection

HERTFORD HOUSE,
MANCHESTER SQUARE, W1
⊖ BOND STREET
ATLAS REF 171 E2

Manchester Square is characteristic of Georgian Marylebone, a quiet oasis with a green garden in the middle (the garden is not open to the public). On the north side of the square is a large and handsome building, Hertford House, built between 1776 and 1788 and now housing one of London's lesser-known, but most important museums, the Wallace Collection. The collection was established by the Marquesses of Hertford, who were great art collectors from the late-18th century onwards. After the death of the 4th Marquess in 1870, the house and collection went to his illegitimate son, Sir Richard Wallace. He enlarged the already impressive collection and turned Hertford House into a showcase for it. His widow, Lady Wallace, bequeathed the house and its contents to the nation in 1897.

Much of the charm of the Wallace Collection is that it is housed in what was a private mansion, and it reflects two centuries of good taste. Even the superb toilet facilities are those of the 19th century, with their lavish deployment of brass and marble. The balustrades of the **Grand Staircase** were made for Louis XV, and one of the rooms contains the marriage commode of Marie Antoinette. The collection is arguably one of the finest of French art outside France, and it is almost overwhelming in richness, including paintings, armour, furniture and ornaments. It has an outstanding display of European and Oriental arms and armour and a number of engaging paintings by Europeans of the Middle East. Perhaps its most famous possession is *The Laughing Cavalier* by the 17th-century Dutch portrait painter, Frans Hals. Other great paintings include works by French 18th-century masters such as François Boucher, Jean Watteau and Jean Fragonard. There are also works by Rembrandt and Rubens, Titian and Canaletto, Velázquez and Reynolds.

Among the furniture are superbly ornate Rococo pieces, a notable example being a rolltop desk by J J Reisener, the 18th-century French cabinet-maker and master of marquetry and ebony work. This example of his craftsmanship was made for the King of Poland in the 1760s. A collection of elaborate French 18th-century boxes are worthy of attention, as are the Italian Renaissance terracotta sculptures and the unique collection of wax portraits. Sèvres porcelain, Italian majolica and Limoges enamels are among the treasures to be admired here.

Open Mon–Sat 10.00am–5.00pm, Sun 2.00pm–5.00pm.

Marylebone grew up around the Church of St Mary le Bourne (the bourne was the Tyburn stream) in medieval times. Marylebone High Street (below) was laid out in the 18th century and boasts some fine terraces.

*Frans Hals's **Laughing Cavalier** is just one of many treasures in the Wallace Collection. Its outstanding works of art were purchased by the Marquesses of Hertford in the 18th and 19th centuries, and were bequeathed to the nation in 1897.*

Exhibits in the British Dental Association Museum prove how grisly going to the dentist was in the past — as this cartoon demonstrates.

British Dental Association Museum

64 WIMPOLE STREET, W1
⊖ BAKER STREET
⊖ OXFORD CIRCUS
ATLAS REF 171 E2

Some of the exhibits in the British Dental Association Museum might seem more appropriate in Madame Tussaud's Chamber of Horrors. They show, however, the astonishing ingenuity employed in the past in the search for the conquest of pain. Among the objects on display is a clockwork drill, made about 1860, complete with a key to wind it up. Exquisite steel dental instruments, decorated with gold leaf and mother-of-pearl, were made for the Prince of Wales (later King Edward VII) in the 19th century. There is also a reconstruction of a dental surgery of 1899. Ever since the British Dental Association Library was established in the 1920s, dental practices and individuals have donated items of historical interest to its collection and the museum was founded in 1934.

Today the museum possesses over 10,000 items of historical interest and its visitors' book shows that a lively interest is taken in it by visiting members of the general public, as well as by the dental profession.

Open Mon–Fri 9.00am–5.00pm.

⊖ REGENT'S PARK
🚌 30, 135, C2

Regent's Park

ATLAS REF 171 D/E4

◆ NW1 ◆

Designed by John Nash for the Prince Regent (afterwards King George IV), Regent's Park became a model for public parks around the world. It was originally planned as a kind of garden city, an attractively rural setting for private villas and terraced housing. The terraces were named in honour of the Prince Regent's brothers. A lake was constructed in the west, fed by the Tyburn stream, and the park was completed by 1825. Ten years later it was opened to the public for the first time.

These neatly painted narrowboats on the canal are used today as houseboats.

The Terraces

Nash's original plans were considerably more extensive and spectacular than the work actually carried out before the money ran dry. All the same, Regent's Park was a pioneering piece of town planning and the elegant terraces, designed by Nash and his protegé Decimus Burton, remain among the most admired in London. The most individual of them is Sussex Place, with its line of pointed cupolas. The most extravagant is Cumberland Terrace, which is handsomely ornamented with statues.

Outer and Inner Circles

The park is roughly circular in shape. Nash originally meant to build terraces all round the perimeter, but they actually occupy three of the four sides, leaving Regent's Canal to border the park on the north. Inside the perimeter is the Outer Circle, a carriage drive almost 3 miles (4.8km) in length. Inside this again is the Inner Circle road.

From Regent's Park tube station, visitors can cross the Outer Circle and stroll all the way north across the park on the **Broad Walk**. This pleasant promenade, with fine views of Cumberland and Chester Terraces, leads to the buildings of the zoo. It continues the line of Portland Place, Nash's grand ceremonial approach to the park.

From Baker Street tube station, York Gate opens on to the southern end of the boating lake. Beyond is **Regent's College**. This was formerly occupied by Bedford College, founded in 1849 and the world's first university college for women, which moved out of London to Egham in Surrey in the 1980s.

The Inner Circle road encompasses **Queen Mary's Gardens**, named after George V's consort. Beyond the elaborate 1930s gates are flower beds, a lily pond, a waterfall and one of the best rose gardens in Britain, with something like 20,000 specimens.

One of Regent's Park's finest vistas is from the Outer Circle looking down York Gate to the Classical portico of St Marylebone parish church. The church was completed in 1817 and John Nash took advantage of this to alter his plan for York Terrace, which was originally to have been a single building. He now built the terrace in two halves with a gap between them, to create today's splendid prospect. To make the view from the park even grander, Nash moved all the York Terrace front doors to the back.

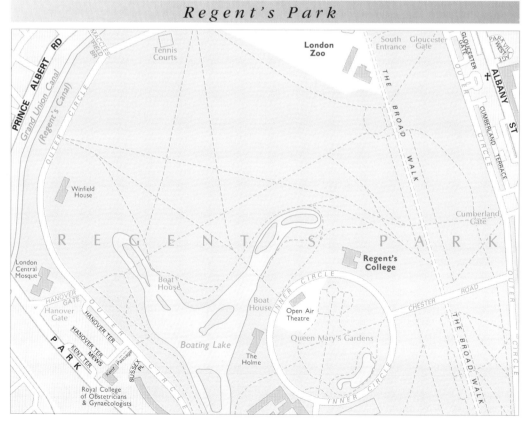

Regent's Park

The open-air theatre is also inside the Inner Circle. Outside, close to the boating lake, is **The Holme**, a villa designed by the 18-year-old Decimus Burton for his father, James Burton, who was Nash's builder. A little to the north, **St John's Lodge** was designed by Nash and enlarged by Sir Charles Barry in the 1840s. It has a secluded and tranquil garden.

The **boating lake** has an island with a heronry, scarcely disturbed by people enjoying themselves in hired rowing boats. A bird sanctuary to the north shelters much of the park's wealth of birdlife, which includes more than 80 species of wild birds.

The Central London Mosque

Over at the western side of the park, by Hanover Gate, is the Central London Mosque, designed by Sir Frederick Gibberd in the 1970s. Its gleaming copper dome and tall minaret make an exotic contrast with the Classical grandeur of Nash's Hanover Terrace close by. To the north is **Winfield House**, built in 1936 for the Woolworth heiress Barbara Hutton and now the American ambassador's residence.

The Canal

The Regent's Canal was completed in 1820 to link the Grand Union Canal at Paddington with the Thames. It was laid out by Nash, who was one of the investors in it. There is enjoyable walking along the towpath and barge trips are available.

The Open-Air Theatre

Attending a performance at the open-air theatre can be a delightful experience on a summer evening. Playgoers are advised to take sweaters and rugs with them, but surprisingly few performances are rained off. The theatre opened in 1932 and Vivien Leigh, Deborah Kerr and Jack Hawkins have all appeared here. The auditorium seats more than 1,000 and Shakespeare is a speciality; *A Midsummer Night's Dream* is often performed.

London Zoo

By the early 1990s falling attendances, shrinking revenue and a change in the public's attitude to zoos had made the future of London Zoo painfully uncertain. The number of visitors had halved since the 1950s. The zoo was losing £2 million a year and it seemed clear that whatever its long-term future might prove to be, it could not continue on the same lines as in the past. A possible solution was to keep some of the animals in Regent's Park, with the zoo becoming principally a heritage and conservation centre.

In more than 150 years in Regent's Park the zoo entertained and instructed millions of visitors — especially children — and built up a solid reputation for scientific work and successful breeding programmes. The Zoological Society of London was founded in 1826 and its area in the park was laid out by Decimus Burton in the following year. With monkeys, bears, zebras,

beavers and kangaroos on display, it quickly established itself as a popular attraction.

During the 19th century the zoo opened in succession the world's first reptile house, first aquarium and first insect house, while adding more and more animals. Already in 1843 a popular draw was a chimpanzee named Lady Jane, who sat at a table and drank tea from a cup. A hundred years later a gorilla named Guy was a star attraction, but probably the zoo's most famous animal of all was Chi Chi, the giant Chinese panda which arrived in 1958.

Besides a thoroughly engaging collection of animals, the zoo build up another fascinating and important collection — of buildings. The **clock tower** at the centre of the layout, and the **giraffe house**, were both designed by Decimus Burton. The **Mappin Terraces**, a miniature mountain intended mainly for bears, date from 1914 and mark an important stage in the move away from cages to more natural settings for animals. In 1934 the penguins were given a concrete pool, designed by the architect Berthold Lubetkin.

Post-war buildings of note include the **Snowdon Aviary** and the **Elephant House**, with its eccentric roofline, designed by Sir Hugh Casson. The **Charles Clore Pavilion** for small mammals was opened in 1967, with a special section given over to nocturnal animals. In the end the buildings may prove to be the zoo's most enduring legacy to London.

Penguins pose for an interested gallery at the zoo. Their pool is a 1930s modernist creation in concrete.

Cumberland Terrace with its handsome portico is the grandest in the park.

⊖ OXFORD CIRCUS
⊖ BOND STREET
⊖ MARBLE ARCH

Oxford Street

ATLAS REF 171 E1/F2

◆ W1 ◆

Always a main route between London and the west, Oxford Street was a Roman road. It owes its name to the Earls of Oxford, who once owned land on the north side. Early in the 18th century it was still a country road, notorious for the cut-throats who lurked along it. Urban development started at its eastern end in 1739, and by 1800 it was built up along its entire length. It began to turn into a major shopping street in the 19th century.

From the 12th century to the 18th, Tyburn (at the western end of the street) was a famous place of execution, where crowds would gather to watch the ghoulish spectacle of a criminal being hanged. The gallows, or Tyburn Tree, stood on what is today a traffic island at the junction with Edgware Road. A plaque marks the site today where so many formerly suffered.

To the south of Oxford Street lies Mayfair, to the north Marylebone. East of Oxford Circus, where John Nash's Regent Street cuts across Oxford Street, is a 'garment district' of small clothing firms. The four identical quadrants surrounding Oxford Circus were designed by Sir Henry Tanner and built between 1913 and 1928.

The number of underground stations along this mile-long (1.6km) length of road underlines its importance as a traffic artery. Oxford Street has resisted all attempts to cosmeticise it and many of its buildings, mostly retail outlets, are nondescript. The pavements provide a version of street theatre, with hawkers displaying their wares from suitcases.

Oxford Street

Marble Arch

OXFORD STREET, W1
⊖ MARBLE ARCH
ATLAS REF 171 D1

This vital junction, where the main north-south artery of Edgware Road and Park Lane meets the east-west artery of Oxford Street and Bayswater Road, is one of London's planning disasters. Created in the 1960s, when the sole objective of road engineers was to move the greatest body of traffic at the highest possible speed with the fewest possible delays, at no matter what cost to urban fabric, Marble Arch is equalled in sheer inhumanity only by Hyde Park Corner to the south.

Marble Arch stands at the centre of an island, beside an attractive water feature created in an attempt to humanise the locality. Modelled on the Arch of Constantine in Rome, Marble Arch was designed by the architect John Nash in 1828 as the triumphal beginning of a processional way from Buckingham Palace. The archway proved too narrow for the State Coach, however, and the whole construction was moved to its present site in 1851, when Buckingham Palace was enlarged by Queen Victoria.

Today the arch stands in splendid isolation amid the traffic. If you can make your way through the underpass and onto the island, you will find that the arch is decorated with reliefs by Richard Westmacott and Edward Baily.

Only members of the royal family and the King's Troop of the Royal Horse Artillery are permitted to pass through the portals of Marble Arch, at the end of Oxford Street.

Right: the Selfridges building, with its façade of towering Ionic columns, occupies an entire block along Oxford Street.

Speakers' Corner

HYDE PARK, W2
⊖ MARBLE ARCH
ATLAS REF 171 D1

This is the extreme north-east corner of Hyde Park, which at one time abutted Marble Arch. The three sites in London where public speaking is permitted today — Speakers' Corner, Lincoln's Inn Fields and Tower Hill — were all once sites of public executions. A tradition of public speaking has arisen at these places probably due to the 'last words' customarily permitted to the executed.

The best time to visit Speakers' Corner is on Sunday afternoons, when you will hear every kind of speaker possible, from near-lunatics to budding young politicians and famous public figures. The crowds gather around one speaker or another, and an ability to continue a line of argument in the face of frequently noisy heckling is a severe test of skill. The police are in evidence, but they usually take no action unless obscenity or violence are threatened.

Selfridges

OXFORD STREET, W1
⊖ MARBLE ARCH
ATLAS REF 171 E2

Towering among the nondescript buildings of Oxford Street like a liner among tugs is Selfridges department store. Built in 1908 by an American businessman, Harry Gordon Selfridge, its exterior is an outstanding piece of Edwardian commercial architecture. The dominant feature is an immense clock supported by *The Queen of Time* by the sculptor Gilbert Bayes. The shop has spectacular window displays, particularly at Christmas.

British Broadcasting Corporation (BBC)

LANGHAM PLACE, W1
⊖ OXFORD CIRCUS
ATLAS REF 171 F2

As the headquarters of an organisation which is not only world-famous, but has undoubtedly shaped the pattern of public broadcasting throughout the world since its foundation in 1922, the BBC building is curiously subdued. Indeed, were it placed in any other locality, you could pass it by. However, its situation on a corner means that the great, grey, bland cliff of its façade is visible from a distance. Built in 1931, the most distinguished aspect of its exterior is *Prospero and Ariel*, sculpted by the controversial British artist, Eric Gill. The Entrance Hall contains another statue by Gill — *Orpheus* — with a pompous Latin inscription expressing the ideals of Lord Reith, the first Director-General of the BBC.

All Souls

LANGHAM PLACE, W1
⊖ OXFORD CIRCUS
ATLAS REF 171 F2

The building of the BBC robbed this curious little church of its primary function. The great British architect, John Nash, intended All Souls to be the focal point of Regent Street as it swept northwards to Regent's Park. Built between 1822 and 1825, the church aroused much adverse comment due to its curious design; a completely round nave surrounded by pillars on the outside, crowned by a sharp-pointed steeple. A famous caricature of the period depicted Nash impaled on the steeple, accompanied by the caption 'Nashional Taste!!!'

In 1975 the church was altered to become an evangelical centre. During the rebuilding, the floor was substantially lowered, revealing the inverted brick arches of Nash's foundations. These have been left exposed for visitors to look at, and to create a dramatic effect.

All Saints

MARGARET STREET, W1
⊖ OXFORD CIRCUS
⊖ GOODGE STREET
ATLAS REF 171 F2

All Saints Church is a product of the Victorian ecclesiastical architect at his most confident and most ebullient. Built in 1859, the church was the work of William Butterfield, who designed nearly 100 places of worship.

He was one of the most ruthless 'restorers' of his time, but here he had the chance to express his ideas, unencumbered by the need to recognise the work of a predecessor. The interior is a riot of colour, with frescoes, marbles, mosaics and stained glass all 'drumming the praise of the Lord into you', in the words of the great architectural historian, Nikolaus Pevsner.

The circular portico of All Soul's Church was designed to be a visual pivot at the point where Regent Street curves round to enter Langham Place.

The Virgin and Child in the High Victorian Church of All Saints, Margaret Street.

Portland Place W1

⊖ REGENT'S PARK
ATLAS REF 171 F3

Originally laid out in the 1770s by Robert Adam and his brother James as an enclave for the wealthy, this was once one of the handsomest Georgian streets in London. However, most of the houses have been rebuilt over the years and the original grandeur has now been spoiled. On the east side, Nos 46–48 by James Adam remain.

⊖ RUSSELL SQUARE
⊖ TOTTENHAM
COURT ROAD
🚌 8, 10, 14, 14A, 22B,
24, 29, 38, 55, 503

The British Museum

ATLAS REF 172 B2

◆ GREAT RUSSELL STREET, WC1 ◆

The British Museum was founded in 1753 with the modest aim of representing the whole range of world culture. It succeeded to such an extent that some branches are now housed in separate buildings: the dispatch of the natural history section to the museum at South Kensington was an early move in the 1880s.

Today there are some 4 million exhibits displayed in the British Museum's galleries, which spread over a 14-acre (5.6ha) site, and about 4 million people come to see these exhibits every year. A few go away battered and bewildered, having attempted to race round everything. It cannot be done. The museum offers guided tours, which pick out the highlights of some of the collections and serve as a good general introduction, and these can be recommended. There are also gallery talks given by experts in particular fields. Visitors who prefer to explore on their own may do so. There are free gallery plans available, and further advice on navigation through the vast network of galleries and corridors may be obtained from the Information Desk.

This was the first secular, national and public museum in the world, and it was originally financed by money raised from a public lottery. The funds purchased 75,575 objects for the nation which had been assembled by Sir Hans Sloane (1660–1753), a physician and voracious private collector. Sloane had once owned a house in Bloomsbury Place, and it was in this area that the Trustees of the new museum looked for suitable premises. They rejected Buckingham House (the building which was to become Buckingham Palace) as impractical, and eventually settled on Montagu House, a somewhat dilapidated 17th-century building, which was eventually demolished to make way for the museum as we know it today.

Even in the early days there was too much for visitors to see, and too little time in which they could see it. Visitors were admitted by ticket, five at a time, and were escorted by a guide. The tickets were free on application, but the demand for them was enormous and touts, recognising a lucrative market, soon began to obtain their own supplies to sell to the highest bidder. One man, rushed through in 30 minutes, protested that the collection, which in those days was mostly concerned with items of natural history, merited at least 30 days' study.

Bloomsbury

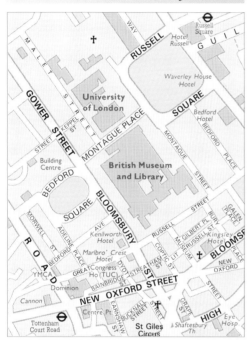

The word 'Bloomsbury' probably comes from the name of the medieval manor of Blemund'sbury, which was bought by the Earl of Southampton in 1545. Today the area is dominated by the buildings of London University.

Behind the British Museum's stately portico, constructed in the 1840s, is a treasure trove of objects ranging from Egyptian mummies to Elgin Marbles.

Although it initially lacked funds, the museum was soon recognised as a worthy cause, and gifts poured in. Some, listed in the museum's Book of Presents, could hardly be described as just what the Trustees had always wanted (a starved cat and rat, for example, and a chicken with two heads); others, such as George II's gift of the Royal Library of the Kings and Queens of England, founded in 1471, were of enormous value. The Royal Library brought with it the obligation of copyright deposit. This means that a copy of every book and newspaper published must be submitted to it, as it is the national collection.

It soon became clear that Montagu House was too small to house all the antiquities and manuscripts in the museum's possession. In 1804 work began on new galleries for the Townley Collection of Greek and Roman Antiquities, but still more space was needed to do justice to the amazing items which were acquired during the early years of the 19th century — the most famous and notorious being the Elgin Marbles, sculptures removed from the Parthenon and Erechtheum in Athens by Lord Elgin in 1802, purchased by Parliament in 1816 and viewed by the Greek Government and others today as property which should be returned to Greece.

By the 1820s the British Museum had acquired a reputation for the excellence of its Greek and Roman antiquities, and it was decided that these should be housed in a suitably imposing building in Classical style. Robert Smirke, the architect chosen to design the new building, planned a monumental sequence of galleries arranged around an open courtyard, but this failure to make use of space was criticised. The courtyard was soon enclosed and turned into the circular domed **Reading Room**, famous today as the place where the German political philosopher Karl Marx wrote *Das Kapital*. Smirke's Classical building has provoked strong feelings — some praise its magnificent, imposing character and impressive façade, with its giant Ionic columns; others criticise it as cold and absurd. Originally designed so that objects could be illuminated by daylight falling through skylights, the building still serves its purpose well.

The British Museum today is far more than an extensive collection of objects. It is a centre for research and scholarship and undertakes conservation work; it publishes books, runs study tours and answers queries from people seeking expert information about rare objects in their possession.

The various departments include Coins and Medals; Prints and Drawings; and Egyptian, Greek and Roman, Prehistoric and Japanese Antiquities, each responsible for many thousands of exhibits. It would be impossible to name any single outstanding item among so many. The Egyptian Galleries are particularly popular, and the Rosetta stone always attracts attention. It is a slab of black basalt just over 3ft (1m) high, dating from the reign of Ptolemy V (196BC) and inscribed in Egyptian and Greek. Its discovery in 1799 led to the decipherment of Ancient Egyptian hieroglyphics.

People who find Egyptian mummies revolting might prefer to wonder at the amazingly opulent finds of the Sutton Hoo ship burial. These include Saxon torques and silverware, probably for an East Anglian king, which were uncovered by archaeologists working on a 7th-century site in Suffolk in 1939. Other visitors to the British Museum may wish to study the art of Piranesi, Dürer and Botticelli, or to admire the magnificent colouring of Islamic pottery and tiles in the John Aldis Gallery. The museum has owned the superbly illuminated Lindisfarne Gospels since its foundation in 1753, and these works offer a thrilling glimpse of rich artistry in a 7th-century monastic community in north-east England.

Today, the British Museum continues to expand and ranks as one of London's most popular tourist attractions. It is a museum to return to again and again, and of which it is impossible to tire.

Open Mon–Sat 10.00am–5.00pm, Sun 2.30pm–6.00pm.

The Nereid Monument from Xanthos in Asia Minor is among the British Museum's collection of Greek and Roman antiquities, one of the strongest in the world.

British Museum Area

The Senate House of London University towers 210ft (64m) above Bloomsbury. Built in the 1930s, the masterpiece of architect Charles Holden, it was designed to accommodate changing needs. Even the floors can be raised and lowered.

Bloomsbury and Bedford Squares WC1

✪ EUSTON SQUARE
✪ RUSSELL SQUARE
ATLAS REF 172 B2

The concept of the town square, with attractive gardens, tall leafy trees, and carefully tended flower beds was an important part of the planning of Bloomsbury in the late-18th and early 19th centuries. The surviving squares account for much of the area's special atmosphere today. Tavistock Square still has an attractive public garden, and blue plaques on several houses recall meetings of members of the Bloomsbury Group, a select circle of avant-garde English writers and artists (among them the famous novelist Virginia Woolf and her sister Vanessa Bell) who lived in the area between 1904 and 1939.

Bedford Square is still magnificent — this is the place to see a sumptuous array of splendid doorways and elegant sash windows, dating from the last quarter of the 18th century. Many old-established book publishers have their offices here. **Bloomsbury Square** was redeveloped at the beginning of the 19th century. The gardens were the work of Humphry Repton, the late-18th century landscape gardener.

University College

GOWER STREET, WC1
✪ EUSTON SQUARE
ATLAS REF 172 A3

London University began in Bloomsbury in 1828, with the opening of University College, housed in fine Greek-revival buildings by William Wilkins. University departments can be found in many of Bloomsbury's gracious Georgian houses, but the university's ambitious building programme has also been responsible for the destruction of much that was once elegant. The massive, white **Senate House**, located behind the British Museum in Malet Street, is visible from many points in the area.

The Percival David Foundation of Chinese Art

53 GORDON SQUARE, WC1
✪ EUSTON SQUARE
✪ RUSSELL SQUARE
ATLAS REF 172 A3

The Percival David Foundation is one of London University's several art collections. Opened in 1952, the foundation consists of nearly 2,000 pieces of Chinese ceramics of outstanding quality.
Open Mon–Fri 10.30am–5.30pm.

The Jewish Museum

WOBURN HOUSE,
UPPER WOBURN PLACE, WC1
✪ EUSTON
✪ EUSTON SQUARE
ATLAS REF 172 B3

The Jewish Museum is housed on the first floor of Woburn House. The room is crammed with portraits and precious objects associated with the Jewish way of life.

One of the most astonishing pieces is the carved wooden synagogue ark which dominates one end of the room. It dates from the 16th century and is thought to have come from a synagogue in Venice. By some curious process it came to Britain and was discovered during the 1930s serving as a wardrobe in a servant's bedroom in Chillingham Castle, Northumberland.

The museum has a wealth of fine silverware, including some splendid ornate Chanukah lamps, used in the celebration of the annual Feast of Lights. Among the many other precious items on display are a number of amulets, including a very rare golden one with an inscription in Greek, which is thought to date from the 8th century.
Open Tue–Thu (and Fri in summer) 10.00am–4.00pm, Sun (and Fri in winter) 10.00am–12.45pm. Closed Mon, Sat and Jewish holidays.

The Thomas Coram Foundation for Children

40 BRUNSWICK SQUARE, WC1
✪ RUSSELL SQUARE
ATLAS REF 172 B3

Originally known as the Foundling Hospital until its name was changed to the Thomas Coram Foundation in 1954, this was a charity established in 1739 by Captain Thomas Coram. Coram had been appalled at the sight of young children living destitute in London on his return to England after some years spent in the American colonies. His foundation aimed to provide 'the maintenance and education' of such unfortunates.

Today visitors to the foundation may visit the museum and art gallery. William Hogarth, one of the first governors, hoped that the presentation of various works of art to the foundation would attract the public and help raise funds.

The original buildings were demolished in 1926, but visitors may admire some 120 paintings in a room built on the site in 1937. They include works by Hogarth, Sir Joshua Reynolds and Thomas Gainsborough, as well as an organ keyboard and scores used by Handel.

Coram's Fields, part of the old Foundling Hospital grounds, are now a large park with a zoo, where adults must be accompanied by a child!

Museum and art gallery open Mon–Fri 10.00am–4.00pm. Admission fee.

Pollock's Toy Museum

1 SCALA STREET, W1
⊖ GOODGE STREET
ATLAS REF 172 A3
Benjamin Pollock (1856–1937) was famous for his toy theatres and his name lives on in this museum and shop devoted to all manner of toys. Arranged in six rooms, rather like a doll's house, the museum offers a glimpse into the childhood of past generations. Exhibits include a 4,000-year-old Egyptian mouse

— apparently a genuine toy — and many more animals, puppets and mechanical devices. There are dolls, puppets, and many of Pollock's own theatres on display.

Open Mon–Sat 10.00am–5.00pm. Admission fee.

Dickens's House

48 DOUGHTY STREET, WC1
⊖ RUSSELL SQUARE
⊖ CHANCERY LANE
ATLAS REF 172 c3
Charles Dickens lived here with his wife and children between 1837 and 1839. He worked on *Pickwick Papers, Oliver Twist, Nicholas Nickleby* and *Barnaby Rudge* here. The death in this house of his sister-in-law, Mary Hogarth, inspired the description of Little Nell's death in *The Old Curiosity Shop*. Today the house is the headquarters of the Dickens Fellowship and attracts visitors from all over the world.

Open Mon–Sat 10.00am–5.00pm. Closed on public holidays. Admission fee.

Centre Point

ST GILES' CIRCUS, W1
⊖ TOTTENHAM COURT ROAD
ATLAS REF 172 B2
A 400ft (122m) office block

above a plaza with an ornamental pool and shops, Centre Point was notorious as a building that was deliberately kept empty by its developers while property values soared in London. Completed in 1967, it is regarded by some as the most hideous building in the capital, while others have suggested that it should be listed as an architectural landmark.

The British Telecom Tower

CLEVELAND STREET, W1
⊖ GOODGE STREET
⊖ WARREN STREET
⊖ GREAT PORTLAND STREET
ATLAS REF 172 A3
When it opened in 1964 the Post Office Tower (as it was then called) was the tallest building in London at 619ft (189m). It was erected to enable television and radio broadcasting to work effectively above the surrounding buildings, but it soon became a landmark in its own right, attracting thousands of visitors eager to look down on the capital from the vantage point of its famous revolving restaurant. The tower is no longer open to the public, although it continues to function. A needle of concrete and glass, it is topped by transmitters and radio masts.

Pollock's Toy Museum in Scala Street is itself a kind of doll's house of children's playthings over the centuries.

⊖ HOLBORN
⊖ CHANCERY LANE

Holborn

ATLAS REF 172 c2

◆ WC1, EC1 ◆

Holborn, the district which runs from Shaftesbury Avenue to Newgate, takes its name from the 'old bourne' that was once part of the River Fleet. Created a borough in 1900, Holborn technically ceased to exist in 1965 when it was gobbled up by the Borough of Camden. However, Holborn is the name applied today to the area around High Holborn, Holborn and Holborn Viaduct. The locality continues to have literary, scholarly and legal associations. To the north-west is Bloomsbury, while the Inns of Court are situated to the north and south.

Holborn is an interesting and varied area for visitors to stroll about at will. It has several peaceful squares and an informal, unpretentious atmosphere.

Holborn

Running north from Holborn, the street called Hatton Garden is named after Sir Christopher Hatton, friend and courtier of Elizabeth I. He did indeed have a garden here: a beautiful rose garden which he leased from the bishops of Ely. Today the street is famous for its diamond dealers, one of the world's major concentrations of the trade. The great diamond house of De Beers has its London office on Holborn Viaduct close by.

Spring daffodils freshen the dusty legal air of Lincoln's Inn, the oldest of London's Inns of Court.

Lincoln's Inn WC2

⊖ HOLBORN
⊖ CHANCERY LANE
ATLAS REF 172 c2
One of London's four Inns of Court, where lawyers have chambers and students train for the legal profession, Lincoln's Inn was founded in the 13th century.

It has occupied its present site since the 15th, and is an interesting place historically. The best approach is through the **Tudor gatehouse** bearing the arms of King Henry VIII, in Chancery Lane. The **chapel** stands on an open undercroft with Gothic vaulting, and **New Square** nearby has a quiet, cathedral-close charm. There are more than 70,000 law books in the Victorian library in Lincoln's Inn; founded in 1497, this collection of legal books is the oldest and most comprehensive in the country.

Lincoln's Inn open Mon–Fri 9.00am–6.00pm. Great Hall and Old Hall open Mon–Fri 9.00am–12.00noon and 2.30pm–6.00pm. Permission to visit the chapels and halls may be obtained from the Porter's Lodge, 11a New Square, WC2.

Sir John Soane's Museum

13 LINCOLN'S INN FIELDS, WC2
⊖ HOLBORN
ATLAS REF 172 c2
A gateway from Lincoln's Inn leads into Lincoln's Inn Fields. This is one of London's largest squares, and is believed to have been laid out by the 17th-century Palladian architect, Inigo Jones. On the north side, in three houses converted into one, is the unusual, comparatively little-known museum created by Sir John Soane in the early 19th century. When this rather eccentric architect of the Bank of England died in 1837, he left instructions that his house with its collection of antiquities should become a museum, on condition that it remained in its state of romantic disorder.

On different floors and around unexpected corners is a wealth of treasures, including the beautiful alabaster Egyptian sarcophagus of Seti I, a pharaoh who died in 1,290BC. There are also two 18th-century works by Hogarth, *The Election* and *The Rake's Progress*, and thousands of architectural drawings.

Open Tue–Sat 10.00am– 5.00pm. Permission is needed to study drawings in the library.

The Old Curiosity Shop

13-14 PORTSMOUTH STREET, WC2
⊖ HOLBORN
ATLAS REF 172 c2
Housed in a building of about 1567, the Old Curiosity Shop is at the south-west corner of Lincoln's Inn Fields. Selling souvenirs, it takes its name from Charles Dickens's famous Victorian novel, and claims to be London's oldest shop.

Gray's Inn WC1

⊖ CHANCERY LANE
ATLAS REF 172 c3
Gray's Inn, with gardens stretching from High Holborn to Theobald's Road, has a **Great Hall** where barristers and students dine several times a year. The hall (built in 1560 and well restored since it was damaged in 1941) saw the first performance of Shakespeare's *Comedy of Errors* in 1594. The layout of the gardens is ascribed to the Elizabethan statesman Sir Francis Bacon (1561–1626), one of the inn's most distinguished former members, whose statue is on the lawn. Other famous members of the inn in Tudor times were the poet and soldier Sir Philip Sidney and Queen Elizabeth I's Secretary of State, Sir Francis Walsingham.

Exterior open daily 9.00am– 2.00pm, gardens Mon–Fri 12.00 noon–2.30pm. For permission to see the Great Hall, apply at the Porter's Lodge, 10 South Square, WC1.

Holborn Viaduct EC1

⊖ CHANCERY LANE
ATLAS REF 173 D2
Holborn Viaduct is an iron bridge, 1,400ft (427m) long and 80ft (24m) wide, built to span the valley of the River Fleet and Farringdon Street in 1896. Very much in the decorative Victorian tradition, it has bronze statues of historic City notables and four Italian Gothic gazebos at the corners. **Holborn Circus** nearby, with its five-road crossing, was built as part of the viaduct scheme and has an equestrian statue of Prince Albert, Queen Victoria's consort.

St Andrew's Church

HOLBORN CIRCUS, EC4
⊖ CHANCERY LANE
ATLAS REF 173 D2
The ancient Church of St Andrew, first mentioned in AD951, was badly damaged by fire in 1941 but has been well restored. It enjoys associations with many great men of the past, including the 18th-century philanthropist, Sir Thomas Coram, the Regency literary critic, William Hazlitt, and Benjamin Disraeli, the Victorian statesman.

St Etheldreda's Church

ELY PLACE, EC1
⊖ CHANCERY LANE
ATLAS REF 173 D2
Just off Holborn Circus, this is the oldest Roman Catholic church in Britain and Holborn's oldest building.

It began as a small chapel in 1251 and subsequently became the property of the Bishop of Ely. St Etheldreda's is named after its 7th-century Abbess, part of whose hand is preserved here. In an alley nearby, between Hatton Garden and Sly Place, the Mitre Tavern displays the trunk of a cherry tree around which Queen Elizabeth I and a courtier, Sir Christopher Hatton, are said to have danced.

London Silver Vaults

CHANCERY LANE, WC2
⊖ CHANCERY LANE
ATLAS REF 172 C2
These unexpected underground bazaars gliter with antique silver, displayed by retailers. The Silver Vaults were opened in 1952 in basements which had previously housed the famous Chancery Lane Safe Deposit.
   Open Mon–Fri 9.00am–5.30pm, Sat 9.00am–12.30pm. Closed on Bank Holidays.

Red Lion Square WC1

⊖ HOLBORN
ATLAS REF 172 C2
Off Theobald's Road, Red Lion Square was the creation of a get-rich-quick builder, Nicholas Barbon, a doctor by profession but notorious as London's first speculative developer. He laid out the square in 1684 on what had been a 17-acre (6.8ha) paddock. This literally involved him in a pitched battle with lawyers from Gray's Inn, who complained that their view had been spoilt.

The square has associations with the 19th-century Pre-Raphaelite artists, for Dante Gabriel Rossetti, William Morris and Edward Burne-Jones all had rooms at No. 17 in the 1850s. Morris opened up a showroom for his fabric designs at No. 8, where he also set up a kiln in the basement for firing tiles and stained glass.

St Sepulchre-without-Newgate

NEWGATE STREET, EC1
⊖ CHANCERY LANE
ATLAS REF 173 D2
This is the largest of the City of London's parish churches, with a chapel dedicated to musicians and many musical associations. On the Feast of St Cecilia, the patron saint of music, (22 November), the choirs of St Paul's, Westminster Abbey, Canterbury Cathedral and the Chapel Royal gather here to honour the saint with a special service.

From outside this church condemned men from Newgate Prison were carted off to execution at Tyburn in the 17th and 18th centuries. Part of a door to an underground passage, through which the sexton would go to pray with the prisoners, can still be seen.

The Old Curiosity Shop was the home of Little Nell, the heroine of Dickens's novel. The shop is one of the few remaining Elizabethan buildings in London.

⊖ TEMPLE
⊖ ALDWYCH

Strand and Aldwych

ATLAS REF 172 c1

◆ WC2 ◆

Until the late-17th century the City of London and the City of Westminster were two quite distinct entities. The best way to get from one to the other was by the River Thames. Linking them, too, was the river bank — the 'strand'. Its proximity to the Thames, with its relatively clean air and easy access for river traffic, made this a favourite site for noblemen's palaces. The building of the Victoria Embankment in the 1860s divorced the Strand from the Thames, but in the Embankment Gardens you can still see what was once the landing stage (known as York Steps).

The Strand and its locality developed in a haphazard way until 1905, when a major road-building scheme widened it and created the great crescent of Aldwych, leading into Kingsway. Continuing the tradition of large-scale accommodation begun by the noblemen's palaces, a number of substantial hotels appeared in the area. The doyen of them is the Savoy, which incorporates the Savoy Theatre where Gilbert and Sullivan operettas were first produced. (Hence their name, 'the Savoy Operas'.) The north-west side of Aldwych includes the Waldorf Hotel and the Strand and Aldwych theatres. Opposite, on the island, is India House, built with appropriate decorations in 1928 and now the office of the High Commissioner for India. A little further away is the Classical bulk of Bush House (1931), headquarters of the BBC's Overseas Service.

Strand and Aldwych

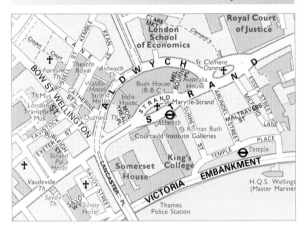

A curiosity just to the south of Aldwych is the so-called Roman bath. It can be seen by peering through the window of 5 Strand Lane, an alleyway entered through an archway on the west side of Surrey Street. The bath, which looks Roman but is not, is fed by a nearby spring. It may be of Tudor date.

***The Descent from the Cross** by Rubens is one of the masterpieces from the Lee Collection, now in the keeping of the Courtauld Institute at Somerset House.*

Somerset House and the Courtauld Institute

STRAND, WC2
⊖ ALDWYCH
⊖ TEMPLE
ATLAS REF 172 c1

Somerset House was the very last of the great Strand palaces to be built. It stands on the site of what was the palace of Edward Seymour, Duke of Somerset, Lord Protector of England during the reign of Edward VI (1547–53). After Somerset's execution in 1552 his palace passed to the Crown, thereby beginning the unfortunate tradition of it being occupied by government offices. The present Classical building, the work of Sir William Chambers, was built between 1776 and 1786. Along the river frontage there is an immense terrace which gives a dramatic indication of how the Strand palaces must have looked when the River Thames flowed

right up to them, before the building of the Embankment.

In 1990, the Courtauld Institute for the teaching of art history moved into part of the building facing the Strand. Apart from providing a suitable home for this great art collection, the move opened up part of Somerset House not previously accessible to the general public, and the Courtauld Institute is therefore well worth visiting on this account alone.

The Courtauld Institute is part of the University of London. The core of the collection was bequeathed by a wealthy textile manufacturer, Sir Samuel Courtauld, in 1931, and by Lord Lee of Fareham. The Courtauld bequest forms one of Europe's most important collections of Impressionist and Post-Impressionist paintings, including such famous works as Manet's *Bar at the Folies-Bergère*, Van Gogh's *Self Portrait* and works by such artists as Pissarro, Degas and Gauguin. The **Lee collection** tends more to the traditional, with works by Botticelli, Cranach, Bellini and Rubens. In 1981 the Prince's Gate collection further enriched the gallery with modern and Classical works.

Open Mon–Sat 10.00am– 6.00pm, Sun 2.00pm–6.00pm. Admission fee.

St Clement Danes

STRAND, WC2
⊖ TEMPLE
⊖ ALDWYCH
ATLAS REF 172 C1
Like two graceful galleons sailing in line ahead, the two beautiful little churches of St Clement Danes and St Mary-le-Strand mark the junction between Strand and Fleet Street.

An unforgettable photograph of the Blitz of 1941 shows the tower of St Clement Danes like a vast torch, with smoke and flame spouting from the embrasures. It seemed impossible that the gutted church could ever live again, but in the 1950s it was brilliantly restored by W A S Lloyd and appropriately became the memorial church of the Royal Air Force (RAF), commemorating the 125,000 service members who were killed in the Second World War. Over 700 badges of RAF units have been cut from Welsh slate and inserted into the floor. The American Shrine under the north gallery commemorates the 19,000 members of the

United States of America Air Force (USAAF) who died in Europe. The ancient crypt, once a burial place, has been turned into a chapel.

The church is said to owe its name to a settlement of Danes in the area before 1066. The church was not touched by the Great Fire of London in 1666, but it became ruinous and was rebuilt by Sir Christopher Wren in 1680. Its bells still play the opening bars of the old nursery rhyme *Oranges and Lemons*, to the delight of children. The steeple was added by James Gibbs, the English architect, in 1719. It has a family resemblance to that of its neighbour, St Mary-le-Strand.

St Mary-le-Strand

STRAND, WC2
⊖ ALDWYCH
ATLAS REF 172 C1
Built by Gibbs between 1714 and 1717, St Mary-le-Strand was the first of 12 churches erected in the reign of Queen Anne to provide for London's expanding population. Originally it was intended to place a statue of Queen Anne on a 250ft (76m) high column in front of the church. She died in 1714, before the work was completed, and in order not to give offence to the Hanoverian dynasty which succeeded her, the statue was erected at Queen Anne's Gate, St James's Park.

The approach to the church is through a tiny garden forecourt up to a handsome porch. Gibbs was evidently much influenced by a visit to Rome in 1703, for the interior of the church, and the ceiling in particular, is strongly reminiscent of Renaissance Rome. The parish has been combined with St Clement's and St Mary-le-Strand is now used for services, concerts and exhibitions. In the churchyard on the east side is a statue of the 18th-century man of letters, Dr Samuel Johnson, gazing down at his beloved Fleet Street.

Royal Courts of Justice

STRAND, WC2
⊖ TEMPLE
⊖ ALDWYCH
ATLAS REF 172 C2
Unwary foreign visitors have been known to mistake this remarkable building for St Paul's Cathedral, so determinedly ecclesiastical is its appearance. This is not surprising, for one of

its architects, Sir Arthur Blomfield, specialised in church architecture. Begun in 1874 by G E Street, it was completed in 1881 and is a fine example of Victorian Gothic architecture. The most outstanding feature inside is the immense Central Hall.

Better known simply as the Law Courts, the Royal Courts of Justice house the Supreme Court of Justice for England and Wales, which hears important civil, rather than criminal, law cases.

Galleries open Mon–Fri 10.30am–1.00pm and 2.00pm– 4.00pm.

Top: the tower and soaring wedding-cake spire of St Clement Danes, which may have begun life as the church of Danish settlers in London in Anglo-Saxon times. In the foreground is a memorial to Gladstone by Sir Hamo Thornycroft.
Above: eagles on the pews. The church was magnificently restored after severe damage in the Blitz, as the central church of the Royal Air Force.

⊖ TEMPLE
⊖ BLACKFRIARS

Fleet Street and Temple

ATLAS REF 173 D1/2

◆ EC4 ◆

Until 1878 you knew exactly the moment when you were entering the City of London because you had to pass through Temple Bar, the main gate to the west. In the Middle Ages this major gate in the city wall would have been decorated with traitors' heads. In 1672 Sir Christopher Wren built an elegant version of the gate, which was taken down in Victorian times to improve traffic movement. (It is now in Theobald's Park, Hertfordshire.) In its place, the present Temple Bar Memorial was erected in 1880. On state occasions, the coach conveying the monarch halts at this memorial and is met by the Lord Mayor of London. The Lord Mayor offers the great Sword of State: this is touched by the monarch as a gesture of acceptance, and the sword is thereafter borne ahead, as an indication that the City is now responsible for the protection of the monarch.

In other words, the City of London still exists as a distinctive entity, and you are aware of this as soon as you enter Fleet Street. The policemen's helmets are shaped like Roman helmets. The Sword of St Paul, the City's badge, is evident everywhere, the streets are narrow — and there are few pedestrian crossings. The City is a law unto itself.

Fleet Street and Temple

[Map showing Fleet Street and Temple area, including Royal Court of Justice, Public Record Office, Dr Johnson's House, Chancery Lane, Fetter Lane, Fleet Street, Shoe Lane, Ludgate Circus, St Brides, Bride Lane, New Bridge St, Blackfriars, Prince Henry's Room, Temple Church, Inns of Court and Chancery, Crown Office Row, Inner Temple, Middle Temple Hall, Middle Temple, Temple, Victoria Embankment, H.M.S. President]

Fleet Street EC4

⊖ ALDWYCH
⊖ BLACKFRIARS
⊖ TEMPLE

ATLAS REF 173 D2

Until the 1980s this was London's 'street of ink'; the offices of every major newspaper could be found either on it, or a few yards away. With the advent of new technology times have changed, but some of the buildings in which news was made, as well as reported, can still be identified.

On the north side is the Classical front of what used to be the *Daily Telegraph*'s offices, built in 1930. A little further along is the brash, black-glass front of Lord Beaverbrook's *Daily Express*, utterly different in feeling though built only a year later. On the other side of the road is **Reuter's** office, built by Edwin Lutyens in 1935. And for a last touch of the romance of Fleet Street continue on to **Ludgate Circus** where on the last building on the north side you can see a plaque to the early 20th-century crime novelist Edgar Wallace, who used to sell newspapers on that spot.

*A bust of Lord Northcliffe can be seen outside the Fleet Street Church of St Dunstan in the West. Northcliffe was the principal creator of popular tabloid journalism in Britain and is one of the archetypal figures of Fleet Street. He founded both the **Daily Mail** and the **Daily Mirror**.*

The circular nave of Temple Church — London's only round church — was completed in 1185. The rectangular chancel was added later.

Temple EC4

⊖ TEMPLE
ATLAS REF 173 D1

Much of London's fascination lies in the unexpected courtyards, alleys and squares that lie off its main thoroughfares. Near **Temple Bar Memorial** a modest archway on the south side of Fleet Street leads into another world. **Inner** and **Middle Temple**, as the area is known, is at the very core of lawyers' London, but the public is free to enjoy the quiet courtyards and lanes. At the heart of the Inner Temple is **Temple Church**, built by the Knights Templar and consecrated on 10 February 1185. It is one of only five circular churches in England and one of London's most unusual medieval structures. Astonishingly, the church survived both the Great Fire of 1666 and the even more destructive Blitz of 1941. The world-famous effigies of knights in Purbeck marble were badly damaged in the war but have been restored and can be seen in the floor of the nave, where they have lain for seven centuries.

In **Middle Temple Hall**, Shakespeare's *Twelfth Night* was first performed in 1602. **Fountain Court** is described by Charles Dickens in *Martin Chuzzlewit*, and it is claimed that the picking of white and red roses in **Temple Gardens** gave the name to the Wars of the Roses.

Middle Temple Hall open Mon–Sat 10.30am–11.30am and 3.00pm–4.00pm. Closed in August.

St Bride's Church

FLEET STREET, EC4
⊖ BLACKFRIARS
ATLAS REF 173 D2

Even among the office blocks of the City, St Bride's can be distinguished from a distance because of its delightful 'wedding cake' spire. Although the main part of the church was built by Sir Christopher Wren between 1670 and 1684, the spire was not added until 1701. It survived the Blitz, although the rest of the church was gutted. The restoration in 1957 closely followed Wren's design.

The Blitz opened up one of the most fascinating sites in the City, the crypt of the church. This has now become a museum, displaying the ruins of previous buildings on the site. The earliest

is a Roman pavement, and nearby are the foundations of a Saxon church, possibly the first building dedicated to the worship of Christ in the City.

In the alleyway beside the church is the **Bell Tavern**, originally built by Wren to accommodate his workers. In the doorstep at the Fleet Street entrance there is a crossed knife and fork, of early 19th-century pattern.

Ye Olde Cheshire Cheese

WINE OFFICE COURT, EC4
⊖ BLACKFRIARS
ATLAS REF 173 D2

Tucked off the north side of Fleet Street in an alleyway is Ye Olde Cheshire Cheese, probably the most famous pub in London and for centuries the haunt of men of letters, from the 18th-century Dr Samuel Johnson to the novelist G K Chesterton. Even teetotallers enjoy this snug, wood-panelled building which has survived fire, air raids and developers. A famous steak-and-kidney pie is served here.

Dr Johnson's House

17 GOUGH SQUARE, EC4
⊖ BLACKFRIARS
ATLAS REF 173 D2

From Fleet Street, Wine Office Court leads into a maze of alleyways, many rebuilt since the Second World War. Gough Square has largely survived, and with it the 17th-century building where Dr Samuel Johnson lived from 1748 to 1759. Here he compiled his great *Dictionary*, with the help of six assistants. Even without the attraction of Johnson the house is well worth visiting, as it is a remarkably well-preserved example of an 18th-century City residence.

Open Mon–Sat, May–Sep 11.00am–5.30pm, Oct–Apr 11.00am–5.00pm. Admission fee.

Public Records Office

CHANCERY LANE, WC2
⊖ CHANCERY LANE
ATLAS REF 172 C2

The records of the nation, from the Norman Conquest onwards, were originally held in the Tower of London. In 1851 they were transferred to this elaborate building. Most of the public records were moved to Kew in 1977 and part of the office is now a museum. On display are a number of outstanding documents, including the original Domesday Book, the great survey of England compiled for William the Conqueror in 1086.

Open Mon–Fri 10.00am– 5.00pm.

*A first edition of Dr Johnson's famous **Dictionary** can be seen in the house where he compiled the great work, in Gough Square. It is conveniently close to Johnson's favourite tavern, Ye Olde Cheshire Cheese.*

♁ ST PAUL'S
♁ BLACKFRIARS
🚌 6, 9, 11, 15

St Paul's Cathedral

ATLAS REF 173 E2

◆ EC4 ◆

St Paul's

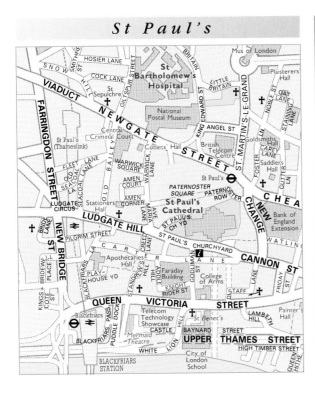

The St Paul's area of London was almost totally rebuilt after the Great Fire of 1666. Almost 300 years later, St Paul's Cathedral alone survived the devastation of the Blitz. It became a symbol of hope to beleaguered Londoners.

Just five days before the Great Fire of London broke out, in August 1666, a commission met to consider Sir Christopher Wren's plan to repair old St Paul's Cathedral. Wren was reluctant to undertake the work, thinking the medieval building too far gone for repair, and he was probably relieved when the Great Fire destroyed most of the building. He reported that 'What time and weather had left entire in the old . . . the late Calamities of the Fire hath so weakened and defaced that it now appears like some Antique ruin of 2,000 years' continuance'. Reluctantly, the commissioners agreed that it would be necessary to rebuild the cathedral completely, and the old church was demolished. It is said that a workman, instructed to place a stone to mark the central point of the new building, picked up a block marked *Resurgam* ('I shall arise'), which Wren took as an omen. Work began in 1675 when Wren was 43 years old; in 1710, as an old man of 78, he was finally able to sit in the completed cathedral.

Wren not only designed St Paul's, he also drew up an elaborate plan for the rebuilding of the entire City of London, which would have given the cathedral a worthy approach. His plan was never adopted, and gradually a series of mean buildings began to hem in his great construction. Miraculously, the cathedral survived air raids during the Second World War, one of the most spectacular wartime photographs showing the great dome wreathed in smoke and flame. St Paul's survived largely through the

St Paul's Cathedral, from the south-east. In the tower at the far left is Britain's heaviest hanging bell, Great Paul, weighing almost 17 tons (17,340kg).

devoted guardianship of its custodians (a tablet recognising their work can be seen in the west entrance), although most of the buildings surrounding it were destroyed. The area was rebuilt after the Second World War, and though it had the advantage of opening up a series of vistas around the cathedral, most of the architecture was in the dreary style of the 1960s. In 1990 plans were unveiled for a redevelopment of the locality, to give St Paul's the setting it deserved.

St Paul's is the cathedral church of the City of London, and although coronations take place in Westminster Abbey, most great ceremonies of state take place in St Paul's. It has witnessed many great national events over the centuries, including the Diamond Jubilee of Queen Victoria in 1897 and the marriage of Prince Charles to Lady Diana Spencer in 1981.

The main entrance to the cathedral is through the **west front**. The overall impression conveyed by the great interior is of height, light and a kind of intellectual austerity. There are relatively few monuments. The ones that do exist are to important national heroes, predominantly military figures. Immediately to the left inside the entrance is a monument to Lord Kitchener, the First World War commander who was drowned in 1916 on his way to Russia. The

most outstanding statue is of Arthur Wellesley, Duke of Wellington, (1769–1852), designed by Alfred Stevens in 1856. Horatio, Lord Nelson and Sir Christopher Wren are both buried in the crypt, Nelson in the cask of spirits which preserved his body after the Battle of Trafalgar. Both have memorials in the **nave**; the one to Nelson is in the south transept, while Wren's, consisting of the famous phrase *Lector, si monumentum requiris, circumspice* ('Reader, if you seek his monument, look around you') is in the pavement below the dome. In the **south choir aisle** there is an unusual monument to the metaphysical poet and preacher John Donne (1573–1631), the only one to survive from the medieval cathedral, showing him wrapped in his shroud. The paintings in the 365ft (111m) high **dome**, which has been described as one of the most beautiful in the world, are by Sir James Thornhill and depict scenes in the life of St Paul.

There are several fascinating areas of the cathedral open to the public on payment of a fee. The **crypt**, whose entrance is in the south transept, has memorials to artists and men of science. The bay containing Wren's tomb is known as **Painters' Corner**, owing to the many

famous artists buried there. In the south aisle of the nave is the entrance to the upper parts of the church, including the **library** and the famous **Whispering Gallery**. The latter forms a circle of such perfect proportions around the base of the dome that by placing your ear against the wall, you can hear a whisper from many yards away as it travels around the circumference. Steps lead up to the ball at the very top of the dome. While the view from here is spectacular, the approach is even more dramatic, by a series of iron staircases winding up within the inner and outer skin of the dome, giving a vivid picture of the sheer size of Wren's stupendous construction.

Immediately to the north of the cathedral is **Paternoster Row**. For centuries this was a centre of the book trade until, in the air raids of 1941, 5 million books went up in flames. To the west of the cathedral is a charming little garden with a replica of **St Paul's Cross**, the site of many a stirring sermon in the Middle Ages.

Entrance to the cathedral is restricted during services. Crypt and Whispering Gallery open Mon–Fri 10.00am–4.15pm, Sat 11.00am–4.15pm. Admission fees.

Looking up into the immense Baroque dome, which is 218ft (66m) above the floor. The famous Whispering Gallery runs around the base of the dome and there are more galleries higher up.

St Paul's Area

Justice with her sword and scales stands atop the Old Bailey, the Central Criminal Court where many famous trials have been held. The figure is 212ft (65m) above street level, London's highest outdoor statue. The building is on the site of the old Newgate Prison.

A set of stamps intended to mark the celebration of 800 years of Lord Mayors of London: presentation visuals by Jeffery Matthews, from April 1988. These actual size drawings were submitted showing the idea of 'civic regalia', which was subsequently discarded. Linked by the mayoral chain are treasures of the City of London.

St Martin Ludgate

LUDGATE HILL, EC4
⊖ BLACKFRIARS
⊖ ST PAUL'S
ATLAS REF 173 D2

Ludgate was one of six gates once leading into the City of London. The first recorded church on this site, built about 1174 against the city wall, was totally destroyed by the Great Fire in 1666. It was rebuilt by Sir Christopher Wren between 1677 and 1687. Having survived the air raids of 1941, it is today an excellent example of Wren's ingenuity. The furnishings are mostly original and include an unusual churchwarden's double chair, dating from around 1690.

Central Criminal Court

OLD BAILEY, EC4
⊖ ST PAUL'S
ATLAS REF 173 D2

Named after the street in which it is located, the Old Bailey deals with crimes committed in the Greater London area and stands partly on the site of what was once the notorious Newgate Prison. In the 17th and 18th centuries prisoners condemned to execution began their long journey to Tyburn from Newgate city gate to the north, accompanied by the tolling bell of St Sepulchre in Newgate Street.

Built in 1902, the Old Bailey's most familiar feature is its statue of Justice high up on the dome, holding a sword and scales but not, as is popularly supposed, blindfolded.

Central Criminal Court judges traditionally carry posies on the first two days of sessions, a custom dating back to the time when the stench of the packed courtroom might have overwhelmed them.

Open Mon–Fri 10.30am– 1.00pm and 2.00pm–4.00pm.

National Postal Museum

KING EDWARD BUILDING, KING EDWARD STREET, EC1
⊖ ST PAUL'S
ATLAS REF 173 E2

The National Postal Museum is situated in the 'new' addition to the King Edward Street post office (built in 1910), undoubtedly the most luxurious post office in the country today, with its reminders of Edwardian opulence. Founded in 1966, the museum is a magnet to philatelists, particularly those specialising in British postal history.

Open Mon–Thu 10.00am– 4.30pm, Fri 10.00am–4.00pm.

Museum of London

LONDON WALL, EC2
⊖ BARBICAN
⊖ ST PAUL'S
ATLAS REF 173 E2

All of London's great museums have benefitted from a revolution in museum display, with its abandonment of static, overcrowded cases and shelves in favour of lively displays, reminiscent of shop window-dressing. The Museum of London is a stunning example of these innovative ideas.

A museum devoted to London's history was first established in 1826, but it never occupied a building designed specifically for its purposes, being housed in the Guildhall. Even when the Museum of London was established in 1911, exhibits were displayed in Kensington Palace. Until its present building was opened in 1976, not only were the museum's artefacts housed in different places, they tended to migrate rather confusingly from Kensington Palace to Lancaster House, and from the Guildhall to the Royal Exchange. The present building, constructed on an elevated walkway, has enabled the many exhibits of the museum to be gathered together under one roof and linked thematically for the first time.

The museum shows the growth of London from a riverside settlement to the

conurbation of today. The display starts with **geological and geographical models**, followed by exhibits arranged in chronological order. These range from Roman survivals (including a ladder found in a well and part of a girl's leather underwear) to a Second World War air-raid shelter. There is a dazzling display of **Elizabethan jewellery** and what appears to be the entire stock of a 17th-century goldsmith's, found in a cellar at Cheapside. The splendid **Lord Mayor's Coach**, made in the 18th century, enjoys pride of place in its own display. Perhaps the most evocative exhibit is a model of the Great Fire of London, showing the progress of the fire across the City, to the accompaniment of crackling flames and the cries of citizens.

Open Tue–Sat 10.00am– 6.00pm, Sun 2.00pm–6.00pm.

Roman Wall Remains

LONDON WALL, EC2
⊖ BARBICAN
⊖ ST PAUL'S
ATLAS REF 173 E2
Nearly 2,000 years after the Romans built their city wall, London's main traffic arteries follow its course, even where it has disappeared entirely. Just below the Museum of London is an impressive segment of the wall, with a Roman base and a medieval upper section. Behind it, an attractive shallow moat has been created (in an area that would once have been outside the city boundary), and there is a small garden in front. Below the road, underground, are the foundations of the Roman fort.

Open first Tue in each month 10.30am–12.00noon, and third Fri in month 2.30pm–4.00pm. Ask at the Museum of London for the gate to be opened.

The Barbican Centre

SILK STREET, EC1
⊖ BARBICAN
⊖ MOORGATE
ATLAS REF 173 E2/3
The Barbican takes its name from a fortified gate that was part of London's medieval defences. During the Second World War, this area was heavily damaged by air raids; it subsequently became the site of an ambitious, and much-criticised piece of post-war reconstruction. The plan was to create three zones —

commercial, residential and cultural — and so bring back life to what had become a badly run-down area. The new commercial and residential zones were successful (a very attractive part of the development is near St Giles Cripplegate, with a paved piazza and moat), but the Barbican Centre, and its surrounding cultural zone, is still a subject of controversy. Begun in 1971 and completed in 1982, the Barbican includes a concert hall seating over 2,000, two theatres, three cinemas, a host of restaurants, conference rooms, and an art gallery. Although contributing richly to London's cultural life, the uncompromising nature of the Barbican's architecture has earned it many critics.

Open Mon–Sat 9.00am– 11.00pm, Sun and Bank Holidays 12.00noon–11.00pm.

The College of Arms

QUEEN VICTORIA STREET, EC4
⊖ BLACKFRIARS
ATLAS REF 173 E1
This charming, 17th-century building stands on a site that has

been occupied by the College of Arms since 1555. The College of Arms regulates the conferment of armorial bearings and pedigrees in Britain (except Scotland) and the Commonwealth. Sometimes called the Heralds' Office, its officers have resounding titles such as Rouge Dragon Pursuivant. They assist the Earl Marshal, an office hereditary to the Duke of Norfolk since 1672, in arranging state ceremonies such as coronations.

In general, only those members of the public with specific queries relating to heraldry can gain access to the college.

Telecom Technology Showcase

QUEEN VICTORIA STREET, EC4
⊖ BLACKFRIARS
ATLAS REF 173 E1
Appropriately placed in a modern block, the Telecom Technology Showcase displays telecommunications instruments and other exhibits, from early telegraphs to modern satellites.
Open Mon–Fri 10.00am– 5.00pm.

This handsomely ornamented horse-drawn fire engine of 1862 stands in the Museum of London's 19th-century gallery. The Metropolitan Fire Brigade was formed three years later and modernised the capital's fire-fighting system, though it was not until 1921 that the last horse-drawn appliances went out of service.

The City

ATLAS REF 173 E1/2, F1/2

◆ **EC1, EC4** ◆

The City

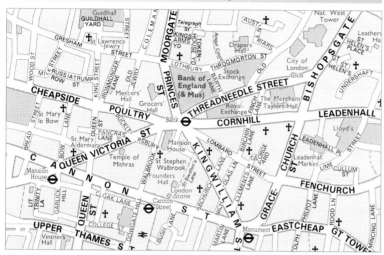

The Square Mile of the City was once bounded by walls, with gates at Ludgate, Newgate, Aldersgate, Cripplegate, Bishopsgate and Aldgate. Despite the zeal of developers, this part of London still has its own unique geography — one of nooks and crannies.

Mile' of our time, which is one of the leading financial centres of the world.

The massive redevelopment of this area in post-war years and improved archaeological techniques have unveiled a wealth of new detail about London's history before the Norman Conquest in 1066. The Romans built their city on two low, scrub-covered hills which were divided by a narrow stream, the Walbrook, and separated from the hinterland by a wider stream, the Fleet. Both have subterranean courses which can be followed today; the Fleet runs beneath Farringdon Street, and the Walbrook below the lane of that name, which runs south from the Mansion House.

The city of *Londinium* was walled about the year AD200. Although only fragments survive, the course of the wall can be traced to the west along New Bridge Street and Farringdon Street, to the north by Houndsditch, and to the east by the Minories. A section of the river wall was uncovered in the Tower of London in 1979 and is now on view.

The Romans built a garrison fort in the north-west corner of the wall, on what is now the Barbican. Just east of the Walbrook, the Roman governor's immense palace lay on the site of what is now Cannon Street station.

Set in the wall of a bank in Cannon Street, immediately opposite the railway station, is an iron grill. Behind the grill is a large lump of stone. Known as London Stone, it is arguably considered to be the *millarium* of the Roman city — the point from which distances were marked. Here you are standing at the very heart of Roman *Londinium*, the famous 'Square

Temple of Mithras

QUEEN VICTORIA STREET, EC4
⊖ MANSION HOUSE
⊖ CANNON STREET
ATLAS REF 173 E1

This was one of the great finds of post-war redevelopment. Archaeologists suspected that a Roman temple possibly lay hereabouts when a plaque

dedicated to the god of light, Mithras, was found in Walbrook in 1889. In 1954 excavations for an immense new office block, Bucklersbury House, uncovered not only the foundations of the temple but also some exquisite statuary, including a head of Mithras which is now in the Museum of London. The temple was removed, stone by stone, and

reassembled in its original form just outside the office block, where it is now on permanent view to the public.

The temple was used at least until AD350, and bears a strong resemblance to the structure of an early Christian church, with its entrance to the east, nave and raised sanctuary terminating in a triple apse.

Right: Mithras, the Persian god of light, was a popular deity with Roman soldiers and his cult was a powerful rival to Christianity. The remains of this second-century temple dedicated to him were discovered in London in 1889.

Mansion House

WALBROOK, EC4
⊖ BANK
⊖ MANSION HOUSE
ATLAS REF 173 F1

The Romans placed their ceremonial buildings along the bank of the Walbrook. Centuries later, Londoners unconsciously followed suit when the official residence of the Lord Mayor was built. (The stream itself had long since disappeared underground.) The Mansion House, designed in Palladian style by George Dance the Elder, was built between 1739 and 1753. For a building with such an important function, the architecture is curiously reticent. The interior is, however, splendidly opulent, with a superb collection of paintings of London. The focal point is the great **Egyptian Hall**, where every year the Ceremony of the Knollys Rose is held. In the 14th century, the wife of Sir Richard Knollys, a friend of Edward the Black Prince, was fined a red rose (to be paid annually) for an illegal construction. The revived ceremony takes place around Midsummer's Day (24 June) when the Lord Mayor is presented with a single red rose gathered that day in Seething Lane.

The Guildhall

ALDERMANBURY, EC2
⊖ BANK
⊖ ST PAUL'S
ATLAS REF 173 E2

Unlike the ancient guildhalls in most of our historic cities, this is still used as an administrative centre. Astonishingly, it survived the two great catastrophes in London's history, the Great Fire of 1666 and the Blitz, though it was badly damaged by both. Air raids in the Second World War totally destroyed its roof, but the medieval walls were left standing and since then a dignified square has been created in front of the building.

The Guildhall was built between 1411 and 1425, although it was restored after the Great Fire and in the 1860s. The **Great Hall** is a spectacular chamber, more than 150ft (46m) long and 89ft (27m) high. In the past it was used for state trials, notably those of Lady Jane Grey in 1553 (recorded by an inscription) and Archbishop Thomas Cranmer in 1556. Today it is the scene of major receptions and banquets, such as

the Lord Mayor's Banquet on the second Saturday in November each year, when the Prime Minister traditionally gives an important speech.

The banners of the 12 major city livery companies hang from the splendid ceiling, rebuilt by Sir Giles Gilbert Scott in the 1950s. On the balcony at the west end are statues of the two mythical giants, Gog and Magog. These figures were made to replace ones originally used in civic pageants in the 15th century. The statues around the walls commemorate major political figures; they include one of Sir Winston Churchill, by Oscar Nemon.

Open Mon–Fri 10.00am–5.00pm, Sat 10.00am–4.00pm.

The Monument

MONUMENT STREET, EC3
⊖ MONUMENT
ATLAS REF 173 F1

Frequently described as the tallest isolated column in the world, the Monument was designed by Robert Hooke, a colleague of Sir Christopher Wren's, and erected in 1671 to commemorate the Great Fire of London. It is 202ft (61m) high and surmounted by an urn and a gilded ball of flames. A climb up 311 spiral steps provides fine views.

Open Apr–Sep, Mon–Fri 9.00am–5.40pm, Sat and Sun 2.00pm–5.40pm; Oct–Mar, Mon–Sat 9.00am–3.40pm. Admission fee.

The banners hanging in the Guildhall are those of the 12 leading livery companies of the City of London. It was from the Guildhall that the City was governed.

The City

The commanding portico of the Royal Exchange, designed by Sir William Tite, has sculptures by Richard Westmacott in the tympanum. In front of the building is a war memorial to London regiments, designed by Sir Aston Webb.

Bank of England Museum

BARTHOLOMEW LANE, EC2
⊖ BANK
ATLAS REF 173 F2
The museum charts the history of the Bank of England from its foundation by Royal Charter in 1694 to today. On display are gold bars, dating from Roman times, as well as the high technology used in modern transactions and a unique collection of bank notes. A video tells the story of behind-the-scenes action in the bank.
Open Easter–end Sep, Mon–Fri 10.00am–5.00pm, Sun 11.00am–5.00pm.

Royal Exchange

CORNHILL, EC3
⊖ BANK
ATLAS REF 173 F2
The two previous buildings on this site were both destroyed by fire in 1666 and 1838. The present building was opened by Queen Victoria in 1844. The tympanum over the vast Classical portico represents allegorical figures associated with commerce. The golden grasshopper on the tower to the east is probably from the first Royal Exchange

and was the badge of its founder, Sir Thomas Gresham. Today the building is the home of the London International Financial Futures Exchange.

Leadenhall Market

GRACECHURCH STREET, EC3
⊖ FENCHURCH STREET
⊖ BANK
ATLAS REF 173 F1
The City is not entirely devoted to exchanging pieces of paper. Here, in a flamboyant building erected in 1881, is a provisions market that has been in existence since at least the 14th century. This is probably the geographical centre of Roman London; in 1881 the foundations of a major basilica, or town hall, were discovered on the site.
Open Mon–Fri 9.00am–5.00pm.

Lloyd's

LIME STREET, EC3
⊖ BANK
ATLAS REF 178 A3
This remarkable glass construction by Richard Rogers is outstanding. Lloyd's association of insurance underwriters developed from meetings of merchants in a coffee-house kept by Edward Lloyd in the

1680s. Initially their interest was in shipping — *Lloyd's List,* a shipping register founded in 1734, is still the bible of the shipping world. Gradually, Lloyd's extended its activities and today covers virtually all forms of insurance.
The heart of the building is a large chamber called simply The Room, where underwriters gather to trade. On the caller's rostrum is the famous **Lutine Bell,** salvaged from a ship that sank in 1799 while carrying a cargo of gold insured by Lloyd's. Two strokes of the bell signify good news, one stroke bad.
Visitors are admitted to the viewing gallery by appointment.

Stock Exchange

OLD BROAD STREET, EC2
⊖ BANK
ATLAS REF 173 F2
The Stock Exchange was founded in 1773 and moved into a permanent home on this site in 1802. The building survived Second World War air raids, but was demolished in the 1960s to make way for the present immense and handsome structure. A visitors' gallery has been incorporated into the building.
Open Mon–Fri 9.45am–5.00pm.

Wren Churches

At 2 o'clock on the morning of Sunday 2 September 1666, a fire broke out in Pudding Lane, near what is now Monument. By the time the fire ended three days later, four-fifths of the City of London lay in ashes, including 88 churches, most of them many centuries old. Sir Christopher Wren and his assistant, Nicholas Hawksmoor, were commissioned to rebuild 55 of them.

Wren churches tend to be small and intimate. Wren disliked the Gothic style of architecture; as a result, his churches are coolly intellectual and testify to his view that proportion is far more important than ornament. At the same time, Wren was often faced with the problem of fitting a new church onto an existing, frequently irregular site. Most of his churches were damaged in the Second World War (in many cases the towers alone surviving) and their post-war restoration is a tribute to the technical skill of modern architects.

Each church has something to offer the visitor. The five featured here are among the most important structures, either architecturally or historically. See also the entries for St Bride's (page 103), St Clement Danes (page 101) and St James's, Piccadilly (page 68).

The delectable spire and tower of St Mary le Bow rise 217ft (66m). Wren's church, modelled on one in Rome, was rebuilt after the Blitz. Curfew bells were once rung here, which may account for the tradition that the true Cockney is born within earshot of St Mary le Bow's bells.

St Stephen

WALBROOK, EC2
⊖ BANK
ATLAS REF 173 F1
Commonly regarded as one of Wren's masterpieces, this church displays the architect's ingenuity in adapting to an awkward site. The 12 steps which lead up to the lobby follow the line of the old Walbrook stream. The interior is a simple rectangle made dramatic by a cluster of 16 Corinthian columns. The dome was probably a prototype for the vast dome of St Paul's.

St Mary le Bow

CHEAPSIDE, EC2
⊖ BANK
ATLAS REF 173 E2
Also known as Bow Church, this is the home of Bow Bells, within the sound of which you must be born to be a 'Cockney'. The Norman crypt survived both the Great Fire and the Blitz. So did the great tower, topped by the most superb of Wren's steeples

— one of the reasons why this was the most expensive of his City churches.

St Lawrence Jewry

GRESHAM STREET, EC2
⊖ BANK
⊖ ST PAUL'S
ATLAS REF 173 E2
St Lawrence Jewry was totally gutted by fire in 1940, and has been brilliantly restored since. The steeple is actually a fibreglass copy of the original. The church takes its name from the fact that this was the area occupied by the Jews until their expulsion from England by Edward I in 1290. Set in the forecourt of the Guildhall, it is London City Corporation's official place of worship, as shown by the dignified furnishings of the interior. The east front gives on to the approach to the Guildhall. It is based on one of Wren's designs for St Paul's, and is decorated with Corinthian columns and swags.

St Benet

PAUL'S WHARF, ST BENET'S HILL, UPPER THAMES STREET, EC4
⊖ BLACKFRIARS
ATLAS REF 173 E1
Although cut off by a major traffic artery, this elegant little brick church still retains its dignity. It is now the Metropolitan Welsh Church, in which services are conducted in Welsh. Inigo Jones was buried here in 1652.

St Mary Aldermary

QUEEN VICTORIA STREET, EC4
⊖ MANSION HOUSE
ATLAS REF 173 E1
St Mary Aldermary is one of Wren's few Gothic buildings. He was obliged to adopt the Gothic style because the bequest which provided money for his rebuilding programme stipulated that the church should be a copy of the previous building. It was heavily restored by the Victorians.

The charming Church of St Benet, Paul's Wharf, was built by Wren in dark red brick, with stone garlands above the windows.

☉ TOWER HILL
🚌 15, 25
🚢 WESTMINSTER,
CHARING CROSS
GREENWICH AND
HMS *BELFAST*

The Tower of London

ATLAS REF 178 A3

◆ EC3 ◆

The Tower of London is unique. Founded nine centuries ago, it is still officially a fortress palace. For more than 400 years, from the time of the Norman Conquest in 1066 until the reign of King Henry VIII (1509–47), it was the principal fortress of the monarch. Since then it has been, at various times, a storehouse for weapons, public records, and Crown Jewels.

The Constable of the Tower — usually a retired, high-ranking serviceman — still has the privilege of direct access to the monarch. The Yeomen Warders of the Tower are former Warrant Officers of the Army or Royal Air Force, and, dressed in their colourful uniforms, they are formidably competent custodians. (Another name for the Yeoman Warders, 'Beefeaters', means exactly what it says and was originally coined as a derogatory term.)

The oldest part of the Tower of London is the White Tower, begun about 10 years after the Norman Conquest and completed by 1100. For more than 250 years afterwards it was the only major building on the site, which is why the whole complex is called the Tower of London today, rather than the 'Castle of London'. The Normans incorporated some parts of the Roman city wall into the defences on the east side (the course of the wall can still be traced), but it was not until the reign of King Edward I in the 13th century that the huge surrounding wall and turrets were built, and the Tower began to look as it does today. The fortress was far too strong ever to be successfully attacked.

There are 15 towers in all, apart from the great central keep. Each tower has its own individual name and history. Contrary to popular imagination, the Tower has never contained dungeons or cells for prisoners; felons of the past were simply allocated any convenient and reasonably secure quarters. Surveillance appears to have been somewhat haphazard, for there were a number of escapes. Conditions in the Tower were by no means inhumane — the Governor received a daily allowance for poor prisoners, while the aristocracy was permitted its furniture and servants.

In medieval days the Tower of London was, in effect, a city within the City, with a resident population and its own traditions, set apart from the rest of London by two walls and a moat. (This was once water-filled, but is now dry.) Between the two wall circuits are the casemates, in which the lodgings of the Yeomen Warders are situated. Over the years, more and more of the Tower has been made accessible to the public, and today visitors can enter at least three-quarters of the complex. The main sights, from the entrance through the Byward Tower, are described below.

Bell Tower. This, the first tower of the inner circuit, can only be entered via the Governor's lodgings. It has housed some important prisoners in the past, including famous 16th-century religious dissenters such as Sir Thomas More and Bishop John Fisher. (*Not open to the public.*)

Bloody Tower. The entrance to the inner ward is through a gate in this tower. By tradition, the Bloody Tower was the setting for the murder of the two young Princes in the Tower, Edward V and his brother Richard, in 1483. Many believe that their uncle, Richard, Duke of Gloucester (later King Richard III) was the perpetrator of the crime. Today, the Bloody Tower is furnished as it might have been when the great Elizabethan courtier, explorer and writer, Sir Walter Raleigh, was imprisoned here in the early 17th century.

The Wakefield Tower. Built by King Henry III in the 13th century as part of a private lodging (of which only the tower survives), Wakefield Tower has a blocked-up doorway, marking the king's private water-gate.

Traitor's Gate. Despite its sinister name, this was simply used as the main entrance to the Tower from the Thames in medieval days. Many famous prisoners landed here, including Princess Elizabeth (later Queen Elizabeth I), who was imprisoned for a time by her Catholic sister, Queen Mary.

The White Tower. So-called because it was white-washed in the 13th century, the White Tower is the nucleus of the Tower of London and is used as a museum of arms and armour. Access to the upper floors is by spiral staircases ('vices') built within the thickness of the walls. The **Chapel of St John** is a perfect example of Norman ecclesiastical architecture.

In 1664 the skeletons of two young boys were discovered just to the south of the White Tower. By order of King Charles II they were interred in Westminster Abbey. They are thought to be the murdered Princes in the Tower.

Queen's House. This is the pretty, half-timbered Tudor building in the inner ward, to the right of the Bloody Tower. It has always been used as the Governor's lodgings, and both Queen Anne Boleyn (second wife of Henry VIII) and Lady Jane Grey (who reigned for nine

Tower Hill

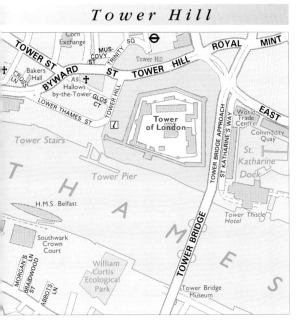

Most of the political prisoners who were executed at the Tower were not dispatched inside the fortress itself, but on Tower Hill, watched by excited crowds who came to enjoy the spectacle. Among those who lost their heads there were Sir Thomas More and Thomas Cromwell in the 16th century, the Earl of Strafford, Archbishop Laud and the Duke of Monmouth in the 17th, and the 80-year-old Simon, Lord Lovat, a Jacobite, in the 18th. The last to lose their lives there were two prostitutes and a soldier. They were hanged on Tower Green in 1780 for their part in the Gordon Riots.

days before the accession of her Catholic cousin, Mary Tudor, in 1553) lodged here before execution. Following the discovery of the Gunpowder Plot in 1605, the chief conspirator, Guy Fawkes, was tried in an upper room in this building. (*Not open to the public.*)

Beauchamp Tower. In this tower there are dozens of inscriptions incised into the walls by former prisoners. Among them is the name IANE, probably the work of Lord Guildford Dudley, husband of Lady Jane Grey.

Tower Green. Only seven people were ever executed on Tower Green, the small square within the inner ward of the Tower. Four of these executions were at the command of King Henry VIII. Political prisoners were usually beheaded on Tower Hill, while common felons were hanged at Tyburn.

Chapel of St Peter ad Vincula. In 1870 the uneven floor of the nave was raised, to reveal a horde of human remains. Among the skeletons were those of two of Henry VIII's wives, Anne Boleyn and Catherine Howard. A brass plate identifying 34 of the corpses can be seen in the south wall of the chapel.

The Crown Jewels. In the 17th century, an audacious attempt was made to steal some of the Crown Jewels when they were housed in the Martin Tower. (Oddly enough, King Charles II later granted a pension to the would-be thief!) Today the Crown Jewels are displayed in a custom-built strongroom below Waterloo Barracks, on the north side of the Tower. Onlookers are often surprised that no medieval crowns appear to be among the collection. The reason is simple; during the Commonwealth in the 17th century, much regalia was sold to raise funds. Most of the jewels on display were either made especially for the coronation of King Charles II in 1660, or acquired subsequently.

Ceremony of the Keys. Every night, at 9.45pm, this ceremony takes place in the Tower — a tradition that has continued unbroken for centuries. It lasts exactly 15 minutes, during which time the keys are paraded by the Yeomen Warders in an elaborate ritual.

Open Mar–Oct, Mon–Sat 9.30am–5.00pm, Sun 2.00pm–5.00pm; Nov–Feb, Mon–Sat 9.30am–4.00pm. Admission fee. The public is admitted to Sunday morning services in the Chapel of St Peter ad Vincula throughout the year. Free tickets for the Ceremony of the Keys are available on application from the Governor.

A fisherman tries his luck. In the background is the White Tower, the central keep of the Tower of London. Built for William the Conqueror and his successor, William Rufus, it has commanded the river for nine centuries. The walls are up to 15ft (4.5m) thick.

Tower of London Area

Tower Hill EC3

⊖ TOWER HILL
ATLAS REF 178 F3

The massive air raids of the Second World War cleared the Tower Hill area of many commercial buildings which had sprung up over the years. Apart from the major traffic highway which bisects the area, Tower Hill's dimensions are much the same today as they were in the 16th century. Just outside Tower Hill underground station there is an impressive section of Roman city wall, with a small garden beside it. At the far end of the underpass opposite the underground station there is the foundation of the postern gate which once led into the City.

Over the centuries, Tower Hill has been the site of many executions; the place where hundreds went to their deaths between the 14th and 18th centuries is marked by a rectangle of brick paving in what is now Trinity Square. During an execution here, that of Simon, Lord Lovat in 1747, a stand holding the spectators collapsed, killing 12 of them.

All Hallows-by-the-Tower

BYWARD STREET, EC3
⊖ TOWER HILL
ATLAS REF 178 A3

Every three years this little church and its mighty neighbour, the Tower, have a 'confrontation' during the beating of the bounds on Ascension Day. It is a light-hearted affair today, but is sprang out of the frequently bitter relationship between the Crown, which controlled the Tower, and the City.

The church is at least three centuries older than the Tower and its site is of great antiquity. Incendiary bombs gutted it in 1940, revealing a Saxon arch of the 7th century. Other Saxon finds uncovered at this time included a shaft, inscribed with the name, *Werhenworrth*, and part of a stone cross. These represent a large proportion of the few pre-Norman ecclesiastical remains discovered in London.

The history of the site goes back even further, for the remains of a Roman pavement are in the **crypt**, and ashes have been discovered below the church, possibly dating from Boudicca's sack of London.

Past priests of this church have attended prisoners of the Tower on their way to execution at Tower Hill. The **graveyard** has also temporarily harboured many headless bodies, including that of Archbishop William Laud, executed by Cromwell's Long Parliament in 1645 for his persecution of Puritans.

Other famous names associated with this church include William Penn (1644–1718), the founder of the American state of Pennsylvania, who was baptised here, and John Quincy Adams, 6th President of the United States, who married here in 1797.

All Hallows has strong maritime connections, due to its proximity to the port nearby. Among its furnishings are an ivory crucifix from one of the ships of the Spanish Armada, and various ship models, including one of the 19th-century merchant clipper, *Cutty Sark* (the real ship can be seen at Greenwich). There is also a superbly carved **font cover** of 1682 by Grinling Gibbons, which was removed from the church during the Second World War.

This is the church of the Toc H Movement, founded by the Rev. Tubby Clayton after the First World War to fight loneliness and hatred and to encourage Christian comradeship.

In the churchyard to the north there was once a **royal chapel**, founded by Richard the Lion Heart in the 12th century. It was destroyed during the Dissolution in the 1530s and is now largely forgotten, except in the name of Chapel Alley.

Tower Bridge E1

⊖ TOWER HILL
ATLAS REF 178 A2

First of the Thames bridges upstream, this landmark adjacent to the Tower of London was built between 1886 and 1894. It is both aesthetically and technically outstanding. The bridge itself measures some 200ft (61m) between the Gothic towers on either side, which have made it the very symbol of London. The two walkways connecting the towers are 142ft (43m) above high-tide level, while the bascules of the central road-span

Yeoman Warders of the Tower, or 'Beefeaters', in Tudor uniform, and the choirboys of the Church of All Hallows during the ceremony of beating the bounds. The boys thwack the parish boundary stones with willow rods.

weigh 1,000 tons (1,020 tonnes) each. They can be raised within minutes to allow the passage of shipping.

The glass-enclosed walkway in the north tower has superb views of Butler's Wharf downstream, with HMS *Belfast* to the west and St Katharine's Dock on the north bank. **Tower Bridge Museum**, to the south, contains the original steam-driven machinery that was used in Victorian times to lift the bridge. There are also exhibitions in the north-west and south towers. Tower Bridge is now illuminated at night, making it a splendid sight.

Open Apr–Oct, Mon–Sat 10.00am–5.45pm; Nov–Mar, Mon–Sat 10.00am–4.00pm. Admission fee.

St Katharine Dock E1

⊖ TOWER HILL
⊖ ALDGATE

ATLAS REF 178 B2/3

Opened in 1973 in its present, renovated form, the new harbour at St Katharine Dock was the first to be redeveloped at the end of the Docklands era. Next to the Tower of London, St Katharine Dock was constructed by the great engineer, Thomas Telford, in the 1820s and was for many years the leading dock in the Pool of London, with the advantage of being the closest to the City.

Today, the area enjoys new life as a residential and trade centre and as a yachting marina. Thames sailing barges and luxury yachts

moor here, and in **Ivory House**, built by Telford, visitors can see 19th-century industrial apartments and shops.

The **Dickens Inn** is a good example of the renovation that has taken place here. An 18th-century, wooden-framed brewery, it was discovered incorporated into a warehouse of later date. Moved to its present site during the redevelopment of the area and now turned into a public house, it is a pleasant place to meet locals.

There are several apartment blocks between the docks and the river, where the Thames estuary lightship, *Nore*, and the steam tug, *Challenge*, are moored.

Tower Bridge, floodlit at night. Its massive towers were built on steel frames to support the weight of the formidable bascules, which rise to let ships through. In 1952 a bus caught on the bridge jumped the gap between the bascules as they were rising.

⊖ WATERLOO

The South Bank

ATLAS REF 176 c4

◆ SE1 ◆

When people talk of 'the South Bank' in London they are not generally referring to a whole stretch of riverbank on the southern side of the Thames, but to a specific area between the southern ends of Hungerford and Waterloo bridges. This is the home of the South Bank Centre, where concert halls, theatres and galleries stand on a site rehabilitated, after years of neglect, for the 1951 Festival of Britain.

The South Bank

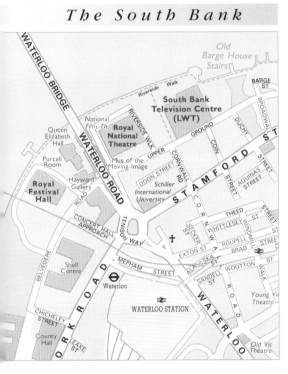

London has been accused of turning its back on the Thames and failing to enjoy its river in the way that such cities as Paris, Rome and Florence enjoy theirs. Too often the Thames is seen as a barrier rather than as an artery of communication. For the architectural writer Ian Nairn in 1966, the South Bank was 'the key to London' which had 'never been fully realised'. Some find the acres of concrete on the South Bank bleak and unwelcoming. However, it does acknowledge the potential of the river and its buildings contain galleries and terraces with magnificent views.

The South Bank Exhibition was intended to contribute to the 1951 Festival of Britain by telling the story of the land

and the people of Britain. It was part of a well-meaning attempt to cheer the nation up after the austerities of war, and a futuristic fun-fair atmosphere was created with the help of water-sculptures, murals and memorable oddities such as the Skylon, a huge, cigar-shaped 'vertical feature' which floated above the site and could be illuminated at night. Numerous pavilions were specially built, but the Royal Festival Hall was the only building intended to be permanent. Everything else was swept away, with the promise that the site would be dedicated to cultural activity in future. A foundation stone was laid for a National Film Theatre and there was talk (which never came to anything) of a new national opera house, too.

Today the site on the South Bank is the largest centre for the arts in the world. Within a short distance of one another are the Royal Festival Hall, the Queen Elizabeth Hall, the Purcell Room, the Hayward Gallery, the Royal National Theatre, the National Film Theatre and the Museum of the Moving Image. There is enough going on here to keep most visitors occupied for months. If it all becomes overpowering, try going on a gentle walk along the river towards Westminster Bridge — quotations from poems have been inscribed on some of the paving stones along the route.

Two good ways to approach the South Bank Centre are from Hungerford Footbridge, or from Waterloo Bridge. There are steps up to Waterloo Bridge from Victoria Embankment on the northern side of the river, and there is also access at a higher level from the Strand.

Unheard inside, trains rumble and clatter past the Royal Festival Hall on Hungerford Bridge. Next to it there once stood the Lion Brewery, with its magnificent statue of a lion, specially made for it in the artificial Coade stone factory where County Hall is today. The brewery is no more, but the lion gazes majestically across Westminster Bridge from its perch outside County Hall.

Blazing with light along the river front, the Royal Festival Hall dominates the South Bank.

Royal Festival Hall

SOUTH BANK, SE1
⊖ WATERLOO
⊖ EMBANKMENT
ATLAS REF 176 C4

When plans for the Festival of Britain were announced in 1948, they included the construction of a new, permanent concert hall. The foundation stone of the Royal Festival Hall was laid the following year and the building, designed by Robert Matthew and Leslie Martin, opened in May 1951, with seating for 2,900 people. Modifications have since taken place, but today the Royal Festival Hall is regarded as a classic of its era. It has recently been listed as a building of special architectural and historical interest.

Those who praise the Royal Festival Hall comment on its elegance and its successful approach in moving large audiences, without creating problems of congestion. There is a sense of space about the public areas, and an ingenious network of stairways and landings results in a building which is expansive without lacking human scale. Good-quality materials were used for its construction and interior design, and the woodwork is characteristic of the 1950s.

The **concert hall** benefitted from the latest acoustic design techniques, but people have argued over how successful it actually is as an auditorium. Again, high-quality materials are in evidence and seating space is generous, with great care taken to ensure uncluttered views of the stage area.

Today the Royal Festival Hall houses much more than just a concert hall. It has a bookshop and restaurants, and since 1988 it has been the home of the Arts Council's **Poetry Library**. Visitors can make use of a comprehensive archive of poetry and attend readings and other literary events in a small studio area, known as the Voice Box. Elsewhere, there are free temporary art exhibitions and a number of free foyer events.

Open daily from 10.00am until the end of evening performances. Temporary art exhibitions open daily, 10.00am–10.00pm. Foyer events daily, 12.30pm–2.00pm. Jazz every Fri, 5.15pm–6.45pm. Poetry Library open daily, 11.00am–8.00pm. Closed on Christmas Day (from 3.00pm) and Boxing Day (until 11.00am).

The Purcell Room and Queen Elizabeth Hall

SOUTH BANK, SE1
⊖ WATERLOO
⊖ EMBANKMENT
ATLAS REF 176 C4

Work on these two smaller concert halls, adjacent to the Royal Festival Hall, began in 1965 and they opened in 1967. The Queen Elizabeth Hall was designed to seat 900 people and its stage has recently been adapted for the performance of full-scale operas and musicals. The Purcell Room, with 370 seats, hosts chamber concerts and performances by solo artists.

The Hayward Gallery

SOUTH BANK, SE1
⊖ WATERLOO
⊖ EMBANKMENT
ATLAS REF 176 C4

The Hayward Gallery was designed by London County Council's Architects' Department. There is an art bookshop and a café here, and the gallery space can work very well. The building is named after Sir Isaac Hayward, the leader of Greater London County Council when the gallery opened in 1968.

Open daily, 10.00am–6.00pm (10.00am–8.00pm on Tue and Wed). Admission fee to exhibitions.

*The Hayward Gallery has objects of beauty inside, in the form of temporary exhibitions. This Russian painting was in **The Twilight of the Tsars** exhibition.*

The South Bank

Museum of the Moving Image

SOUTH BANK, SE1
⊖ WATERLOO
⊖ EMBANKMENT
ATLAS REF 176 c4

The most recent arrival on the South Bank, the Museum of the Moving Image opened in 1988. It tells the story of the moving image from Javanese shadow puppets — dating back to at least 2,000BC — to the very latest film and television special effects. Posters and props, stills and clips from hundreds of films and television programmes are used to illustrate the evolution of the moving image, and visitors are encouraged to enter into the spirit of it all — taking turns at reading the news as though for a television broadcast, or allowing themselves to be interviewed on screen. The sense of illusion is encouraged by a staff of actor-guides who sometimes ask the public to take part in off-the-cuff improvisations. One exhibit uses film to give visitors the impression that they are actually flying above London and looking down below.

Crammed into an awkward space beside Waterloo Bridge, the lively Museum of the Moving Image welcomes the visitor to the neon-glitter world of films and television.

As well as housing a large permanent exhibition, the museum has a number of temporary displays and its own cinema.

Open Tue–Sat 10.00am–8.00pm, Sun and Bank Holidays 10.00am–6.00pm (Oct–May), 10.00am–8.00pm (Jun–Sep). Admission fee.

The Royal National Theatre

SOUTH BANK, SE1
⊖ WATERLOO
⊖ EMBANKMENT
ATLAS REF 176 c4

Built between 1967 and 1976, the Royal National Theatre houses three separate performance areas: the **Olivier theatre**, said to have been inspired by the ancient Greek theatre at Epidaurus and seating 1,200 people around a circular open stage; the **Lyttelton**, a smaller theatre seating 900 in front of a proscenium arch; and the **Cottesloe**, a studio where seating can be removed so that audience and actors mingle freely.

Designed by Sir Denys Lasdun

and Partners, the building has large public foyers where there are free musical performances in the early evening. There are also usually several free exhibitions in the various galleries. Restaurants, bars and bookshops mean that the building has something to offer at almost every time of day or night. In summer, eating and entertainment spread onto the terraces outside. Those who want to go backstage to understand how this highly complex building works can take comprehensive and thoroughly informative guided tours.

Open Mon–Sat from 10.00am onwards.

The National Film Theatre

SOUTH BANK, SE1
⊖ WATERLOO
⊖ EMBANKMENT
ATLAS REF 176 c4

Like the Museum of the Moving Image, the National Film Theatre (NFT) is part of the British Film Institute. It has two cinemas and in the evenings it also takes over the Museum of the Moving Image cinema. Using all three, the NFT

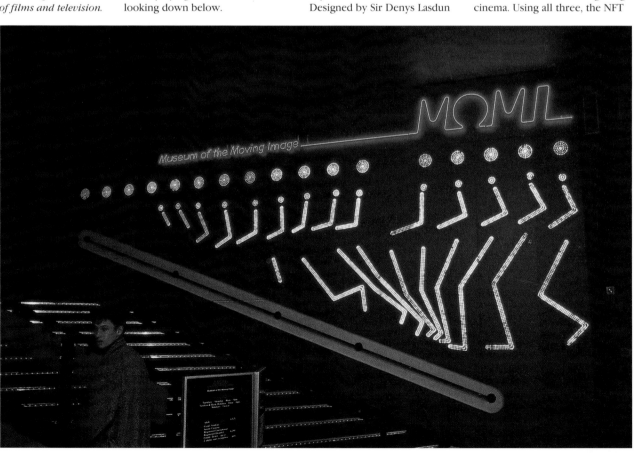

screens around 2,000 films each year. Everything can be seen here, from early silent films with piano accompaniments to the latest releases. There is a small charge for day membership and facilities include a snack bar and restaurant.

Box office open daily, 11.30am–8.30pm.

Waterloo Station

YORK ROAD, SE1
⊖ WATERLOO
ATLAS REF 176 C4

With 21 platforms, Waterloo is one of London's largest stations, but it stands on an awkward site which detracts from its character. After the formation of the London and South-Western Railway in 1845, existing railway lines were extended from an earlier terminus at Nine Elms and a new Waterloo Bridge terminus was completed in 1848. This became increasingly congested over the next 50 years and by the end of the century another new station was considered necessary. Work began in 1907 to designs by J R Scott and the station building as we know it today was finally opened in 1922. There is a grand Edwardian façade, which is difficult to see outside because of the constraints of the site. Inside, the vast concourse accommodates a number of shops and places to eat.

The Old Vic Theatre

WATERLOO ROAD, SE1
⊖ WATERLOO
ATLAS REF 177 D3

Britain had a National Theatre Company before it had a National Theatre building, and many of that company's most memorable productions were staged at the Old Vic, a short walk down Waterloo Road from the station.

A theatre opened as a 'house of melodrama' on this site in 1818 and was called the Royal Coburg. Some of the building material came from the old Savoy Palace, then being demolished on the opposite bank of the Thames. The theatre's name was changed to the Royal Victoria in 1833, in compliment to the youthful princess who would ascend the throne four years later. In 1881 it was given a new interior and converted into a temperance music hall, where working-class audiences could enjoy an evening's improving entertainment free of the temptation of drink.

The Royal Victoria Coffee Music Hall, as it was now called, was run by a social reformer and London County Councillor named Emma Cons. To assist her she called in her niece, the redoubtable Lilian Baylis, a professional violin player and teacher by training, who took over sole management when her aunt died in 1912. She energetically raised the theatre's standards, putting on operas, ballets and all the plays of Shakespeare at popular prices. The Old Vic, as it was now affectionately known, became the London 'home of Shakespeare', and by the time Miss Baylis died in 1937 it was one of the leading playhouses in the capital.

Badly damaged by bombing in the Second World War, the Old Vic was reopened in 1950 and in 1963 it became the temporary home of the new National Theatre Company, under Sir Laurence Olivier. The first production was *Hamlet*, with Peter O'Toole.

In the 1980s, under the dedicated ownership of Ed

Mirvish, the theatre was thoroughly refurbished and restored to a condition of late-Victorian splendour. A listed building, it is regarded by historians today as one of London's most precious theatrical possessions, with ornate balconies and rich plaster decoration.

Box office open Mon–Sat 10.00am–8.00pm.

Stamford Street SE1

⊖ WATERLOO
ATLAS REF 177 D4

Connecting Waterloo with the southern approach to Blackfriars Bridge, Stamford Street was originally built across marshes. Along one side is what is known as the Coin Street development of houses, shops and a riverside park. This was constructed after a hard-fought battle in the 1980s between local people and developers.

A striking feature here is the **Oxo Tower**. This was ingeniously constructed in 1928 to get round a prohibition on outdoor advertising.

The Old Vic in its handsome 19th-century building has a history of top-class stage productions at affordable prices.

⊖ LAMBETH NORTH

Lambeth

ATLAS REF 176 C3

◆ SE1 ◆

Lambeth

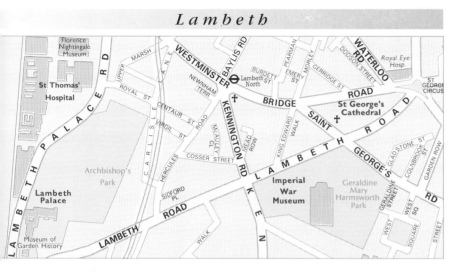

Archbishops of Canterbury created a settlement on the south bank of the Thames, west of Southwark. A few traces of the former village centre have survived, in such street names as Lambeth High Street and Black Prince Road. The latter commemorates the fact that Edward the Black Prince owned the Manor of Kennington here in the 14th century. Substantial sections of it still belong to the Prince of Wales, as part of the Duchy of Cornwall estate.

Until the 18th century Lambeth consisted largely of fields and marshes. The name is thought to mean 'muddy harbour'. It was a favourite place for sportsmen shooting duck, and a ferry transported horses across the Thames to Westminster (hence the name Horseferry Road on the north side of the river). The building of Westminster Bridge in 1750 opened up the area to development and Lambeth today is a higgledy-piggledy but fascinating consequence of the often turbulent social changes of the last two centuries.

Resting peacefully in the churchyard of St Mary at Lambeth (now the Museum of Garden History) is the notorious Captain Bligh of the **Bounty**. *After the mutiny aboard his ship in 1787, Bligh steered a longboat and 18 loyal hands to safety in the Dutch East Indies after a 3,500 mile (5,631 km) voyage across the Pacific, an epic feat of navigation.*

Building their London palace across the river from the Royal Palace of Westminster and Westminster Abbey, the

Imperial War Museum

LAMBETH ROAD, SE1
⊖ LAMBETH NORTH
⊖ ELEPHANT & CASTLE
ATLAS REF 177 D3

This superbly conceived museum of warfare recalls the conflicts of, primarily, the First and Second World Wars. The displays are a thrilling demonstration of technology harnessed to destruction, but set in the context of military and civilian suffering.

Inside the entrance, the principal exhibition hall is a cathedral of destruction. Tanks of First and Second World War vintage point menacingly at you, interspersed with elegant armaments ranging from a First World War trench periscope to a V2 rocket. Hanging overhead are planes from both wars, from early biplanes such as the Sopwith Camel to Second World War machines, such as the Spitfire and the Focke Wulf 190.

The main **First and Second World War galleries** are on the lower ground floor. A warren of galleries illustrates different aspects of each conflict — on land, at sea and in the air. The exhibits are so colourful, so neatly displayed and explained, that it takes the historic films shown on monitor screens to put them all in context.

Right: from biplane to rocket. A view of the main exhibition hall of the Imperial War Museum, which charts the history of modern British warfare on land, by sea and in the air.

In 'The Trench War' you walk through a First World War trench at night, passing dugouts and hearing the sound of battle from beyond the barbed wire. The 'Blitz Experience' sits you in an East End air raid shelter where the shock of a near miss is, literally, a severe jolt. Even more alarming is 'Operation Jericho', re-enacting the 1944 Mosquito bomber raid on Amiens prison in France to release French Resistance prisoners who were under threat of execution. General Montgomery's North Africa and Normandy caravans are a gentler curiosity.

The museum was completely rebuilt and reorganised internally in the 1980s. The collection of Victoria and George Crosses is especially moving. Its art galleries constitute the second-largest collection of British 20th-century art — with sculptures as well as paintings and sketches. There is a fine head of Sir Winston Churchill by Sir Jacob Epstein. There are pictures from the First World War by Paul Nash, Sir William Orpen, Stanley Spencer and others, and from the Second World War by Edward Burra, Henry Moore, Graham Sutherland, John Piper and many more. The cinema offers a weekend programme of documentary and feature films, and the bookshop has a wide range of literature.

The building itself used to be part of the Bethlem Royal Hospital, an asylum ('Bedlam') for the insane. Built in 1812, it was later briefly the home of Lord Northcliffe, the press baron, before it was taken over by the Imperial War Museum in 1936.
Open daily 10.00am–6.00pm. Admission fee.

St George's Cathedral

ST GEORGE'S ROAD, SE1
⊖ LAMBETH NORTH
ATLAS REF 177 D3
Designed by AW Pugin in the 1840s as the Roman Catholic cathedral of South London, the Victorian Gothic church was badly damaged by Second World War bombing. Rebuilt in the 1950s, it remains a plain edifice, inside and out. The **Lady Chapel** was added in 1963.

At the crossroads here is an obelisk which commemorates the successful campaign of a Lord Mayor of London to introduce the reporting of proceedings in Parliament in the 1770s. This imposing object was formerly

located a short distance away at **St George's Circus**, where the roads from Waterloo Bridge, Blackfriars Bridge and Lambeth Bridge meet. This area, nowadays nondescript, was once an open space called St George's Fields, where soldiers drilled, criminals were hanged, Londoners took the air and large crowds of protestors would gather.

Florence Nightingale Museum

ST THOMAS'S HOSPITAL, LAMBETH PALACE ROAD, SE1
⊖ LAMBETH NORTH
⊖ WATERLOO
ATLAS REF 176 C3
The Italianate river front facing the Houses of Parliament across the Thames was created in the 19th century, when new premises were built here for the ancient hospital of St Thomas's, Southwark. Florence Nightingale's experience of Parisian hospitals inspired this early British example of hygienic hospital design.

The Florence Nightingale Museum is housed in the hospital's post-war buildings, beside Westminster Bridge and overlooking the Albert Embankment. It is named after the great nurse who founded the world's first school of nursing at old St Thomas's Hospital in 1860. Personal mementoes evoke the horrors of the Crimean War (1853–56), in which Florence Nightingale first made her reputation as 'the Lady with the Lamp'. Her work for medical and humanitarian causes in later life is also depicted. Less well-known than her pioneering work to redesign hospitals, barracks and prisons, and her reforms of nursing and midwifery practices, are her efforts on behalf of India.
Museum open Tue–Sun 10.00am–4.00pm. Admission fee.

Lambeth Palace

LAMBETH PALACE ROAD, SE1
⊖ LAMBETH NORTH
ATLAS REF 176 C2
The palace, which is the London home of the Archbishop of Canterbury, is a charming spectacle on the south bank of the river. The first archbishop to live here was Stephen Langton in the early 13th century. In 1547 Thomas Cranmer wrote the English Prayer Book here, but also caused great controversy by eating meat during Lent in the Great Hall. The handsome Tudor

gatehouse in red brick dates from the 1490s, and Gothic-style buildings were added in the 1820s and 1830s.

Museum of Garden History

LAMBETH PALACE ROAD, SE1
⊖ LAMBETH NORTH
ATLAS REF 176 C2
Britain's first museum of gardening history has been created here in the former parish church of St Mary at Lambeth, next door to Lambeth Palace, by the Tradescant Trust. (The church was closed in the 1970s.) The trust takes its name from two John Tradescants, father and son, who were gardeners to King Charles I in the 17th century and propagated many exotic plants in their garden at Lambeth. Their tomb can be seen in the churchyard, which has been planted with shrubs and plants of the kind they grew.
Open Mar–Nov, Mon–Fri 11.00am–3.00pm, Sun 10.30am–5.00pm. Admission fee.

This stained-glass window in St George's Roman Catholic Cathedral shows Christ healing the sick. It was installed to commemorate the visit of Pope John Paul II in 1982.

⊖ LONDON BRIDGE

Southwark and The Borough

ATLAS REF 177 E3/4, F3/4

◆ SE1 ◆

Southwark's importance stemmed directly from its geographical position at the southern end of London Bridge (hence the name, 'South Work'). In medieval times it was the gateway to London from the south and the busy traffic between London and the Continent passed through it along the Old Kent Road. The heart of the area is still familiarly known as 'The Borough'.

Southwark/The Borough

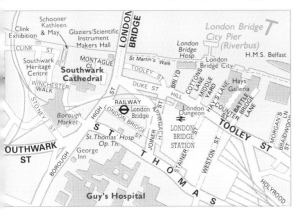

Southwark has a lively history. It was a flourishing port for centuries and was famed for its inns and brothels. Chaucer's pilgrims in *The Canterbury Tales* started their journey to Canterbury at the Tabard Inn in Southwark, which was demolished in the 1870s. The area was also a place of entertainment and was home to several Elizabethan and Jacobean theatres: the Rose, the Swan, the Globe — where Shakespeare acted and where many of his plays

John Harvard was born in a house in Borough High Street in 1607 and christened in Southwark Cathedral. His father, Robert Harvard, was a prosperous butcher and the family lived for a time in Tooley Street. John inherited the Queen's Head Inn from his mother. The sale of it raised money that went to found Harvard University, after John had emigrated to New England. Harvard Chapel in Southwark Cathedral is maintained by the university in his memory.

were produced — and the Hope. It was also famous for its hospitals, such as Guy's and St Thomas's, and for its prisons, which included the notorious Clink (hence the expression 'in the clink') and the Marshalsea, the debtors' prison in which Charles Dickens's father was incarcerated and which is vividly described by him in *Little Dorrit*.

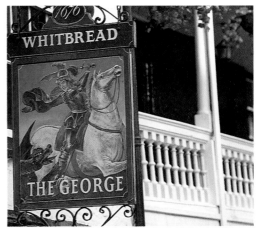

Owned by the National Trust, the splendid old George Inn preserves the aura of bygone coaching days.

London Dungeon

28/34 TOOLEY STREET, SE1
⊖ LONDON BRIDGE
ATLAS REF 177 F4

The arches underneath London Bridge railway station provide an atmospheric setting for a blood-and-thunder bringing-to-life of the horrors of past ages, as the rumble of trains overhead mingles with blood-curdling shrieks and screams of agony.

With the slogan 'Abandon hope, all ye who enter here', and set in a 'vast slimy darkness', the London Dungeon is one of the most successful attractions in the capital. The management gives a solemn warning that the dungeon is not recommended for those of a squeamish or nervous disposition, or to unaccompanied children.

A sign outside the French Revolution section, (the 'Theatre of the Guillotine', where visitors are condemned to death by the Tribunal and taken away to St Lazare prison by guards),

promises 'Next execution 11.15am'. Elsewhere a series of life-size tableaux graphically

depicts torture and death in gruesome, disagreeable and painstakingly accurate detail.

Right: stirring the pot. Boiling alive is one of the methods of execution displayed in the London Dungeon, one of the capital's most successful attractions.

The sufferings of Protestant martyrs burned at the stake during the reign of Mary Tudor in the 16th century vie with a full-frontal hanging, drawing and quartering, and the beheading of Simon, Lord Lovat in 1747. The 'speaking head' of Anne Boleyn explains how she was wrongly accused, while the executioner thoughtfully prepares to take her head off her shoulders.

There is a working model rack, an instrument of torture known as the Scavenger's Daughter, and grimly vivid scenes of branding, flogging and boiling alive, a grotesquely horrible punishment used in Tudor England. The martyrdom of St George, England's patron saint, apparently involved him being tied to a cross and torn with pointed irons, nailed to a table, gashed with sharp wheels and boiled in molten lead.

Other attractions include a reconstruction of the gallows at Tyburn, a feature on Newgate prison and a full-scale reconstruction of Pudding Lane, bringing the Great Fire of London vividly to life.

All this is greatly enjoyed by children, and by adults with sufficiently strong stomachs, and London Dungeon, which was founded in 1975, now draws more than 600,000 visitors a year. The arches above it support the longest railway viaduct in Britain. Built for the London and Greenwich line in 1836 and still used by trains, it runs for 3¾ miles (6km).

Open daily, Apr–Sep 10.00am–5.30pm, Oct–Mar 10.00am–4.30pm. Admission fee.

George Inn

77 BOROUGH HIGH STREET, SE1
⊖ BOROUGH
⊖ LONDON BRIDGE
ATLAS REF 177 F4
This is the only example of a galleried inn still to be seen in London. The original building on this site, which was frequented by Shakespeare, burned down in a disastrous fire which destroyed many buildings south of the Thames in 1676. Today the inn that can be seen by visitors is a 17th-century replica of the medieval hostelry, with galleries overlooking a central courtyard.

Dickens knew the George Inn well, and used it as a location in many of his books, including *Little Dorrit*. Scenes from Shakespeare and Dickens are enacted in the courtyard during the summer.

London Bridge City

COTTONS LANE,
TOOLEY STREET, SE1
⊖ LONDON BRIDGE
ATLAS REF 177 F4
Stretching along the river bank eastwards from London Bridge are the new and refurbished buildings of London Bridge City. The first part of this office-and-leisure complex was finished in 1987. It includes **Hay's Wharf**, originally begun in the 1650s and the oldest wharf in the Pool of London. Tea clippers from the East once tied up at Hay's Wharf, which was rebuilt in the 1930s. Also here is a new block called **Hay's Galleria**, formerly Hay's Dock, which has been infilled and roofed over with glass, Crystal Palace-style, to form a piazza with restaurants and wine bars. The view across the Thames from here, to the former Billingsgate Market and Customs House, with the Tower of London and Tower Bridge downstream, is one of the finest London has to offer.

HMS Belfast

MORGAN'S LANE,
TOOLEY STREET, SE1
⊖ LONDON BRIDGE
ATLAS REF 178 A2
This great Southampton-class cruiser is a floating tribute to some of the great naval battles of the Second World War. She was present at the Battle of North Cape in 1943, when the *Scharnhorst* was sunk, at the Normandy landings in 1944, and later saw action in the Korean War (1950–3). Today visitors can indulge their imaginations by boarding the ship and finding their way through hatches and up ladders, on to the navigation bridge and beside the main guns.

Open daily, Apr–Sep 10.00am–5.20pm, Oct–Mar 10.00am–4.00pm. Admission fee.

Design Museum

BUTLER'S WHARF,
SHAD THAMES, SE1
⊖ LONDON BRIDGE
ATLAS REF 178 B2
Just to the east of Tower Bridge is a street called Shad Thames, which squeezes its way between refurbished Victorian warehouses and gives a good sense of what the area was like a hundred years ago and more. It is often used as a setting for period films.

At Butler's Wharf is the Design Museum, an exhibition of everyday products illustrating why they look the way they do, and intended to encourage high standards in the design of consumer goods. Exhibits range from furniture, household appliances and toys to ceramics and graphics. There are temporary exhibitions, too. The museum is housed in a 19th-century warehouse and was opened by the Conran Foundation in 1989. There is a restaurant and a riverfront café-bar.

Open Tue–Sun 11.30am– 6.30pm. Admission fee.

*The last surviving Royal Navy battleship of the Second World War, HMS **Belfast** was turned into a floating museum in 1971, and is now moored near Tower Bridge. She carried a crew of 800 men and her heavy guns had a range of 14 miles (22km).*

Southwark and The Borough

The handsome **tower** stands 160ft (48.7m) high. The upper stages were added in the 16th century. The arches immediately inside the south door, through which you enter the cathedral, date from the Middle Ages. The **nave** is an 1890s restoration by Sir Arthur Blomfield, and the Victorian font is by G F Bodley, who also designed the bishop's throne. There is also a splendid **altar screen**, dating from 1520, with statues added in 1912. The altarpiece itself is by Sir Ninian Comper and dates from 1929. There are some fine carved and painted bosses to be seen, originally from the 15th-century roof.

The cathedral is particularly rich in impressive monuments, including one to the 15th-century poet **John Gower**, a friend of Chaucer. He rests under a canopy, his hands folded, with his head pillowed on three of his own books. There are also interesting memorials to Bishop Lancelot Andrewes of Winchester, who died in 1626, one of the principal creators of the Authorised Version of the bible, and of a 17th-century pill-doctor called Lockyer. 'His virtues and his PILLS are so well known,' says the inscription, 'that envy can't confine them under stone.'

Tablets in the floor commemorate William Shakespeare's younger brother, Edmund, and two 17th-century playwrights, John Fletcher and Philip Massinger. The monument to Shakespeare himself is much more recent, dating from 1912, with an effigy of the Bard and an enjoyable stained-glass window by Christopher Webb showing characters from the plays. Shakespeare lived in Southwark from 1599 to 1611 and was a partner in the Globe theatre.

The **Harvard Chapel** of 1907 is a memorial to another famous resident, John Harvard, founder of Harvard University in America, who was born in Southwark and baptised in the church in 1607. There is also a tablet to the famous American lyric-writer Oscar Hammerstein (1895–1960), of Rodgers and Hammerstein fame.

Open daily, 10.00am–6.00pm.

The tomb of John Gower in Southwark Cathedral, bright with colour. The poet, who died in 1408, is shown lying peacefully with his head pillowed on three of his own books, written in three different languages — French, Latin and English.

Southwark Cathedral

BOROUGH HIGH STREET, SE1
⊖ LONDON BRIDGE
ATLAS REF 177 F4

The cathedral is widely regarded as London's most impressive church in the Gothic style after Westminster Abbey, and one of its most important medieval buildings. The first church on the spot, close to the Thames, was built for a convent early in the 7th century. Later there was an Augustinian priory here, which built the medieval church (substantial parts still survive). In 1540, with the Dissolution of the Monasteries, the priory was closed down and the parishioners of Southwark took the priory church over as their parish church. In 1905 it became the cathedral of the new diocese of Southwark, which includes most of South London.

The dedication to St Saviour and St Mary Overie is unusual. St Saviour is Christ under another guise and St Mary is the Virgin Mary, while Overie may mean 'over the water' — from the City. Or it may be a corruption meaning 'of the ferry'.

*The tall masts and rigging of the schooner **Kathleen & May**.*

The Kathleen & May

ST MARY OVERIE DOCK,
CATHEDRAL STREET, SE1
⊖ LONDON BRIDGE
ATLAS REF 177 F4
This 16th-century dock close to Southwark Cathedral has been the resting place since 1986 of the *Kathleen & May*, the last remaining three-masted topsail schooner. Built in 1900, she carried cargo round Britain's coasts. On board an exhibition shows how the crew of six lived and worked, and how the coastal trade used to function.

On the edge of the dock, the **Southwark Heritage Centre** has a good range of leaflets about the area. An excellent riverside trail leads past the dramatic modern buildings which have gone up along the Thames here in recent years.

Kathleen & May *open Apr–Oct, Mon–Fri 10.00am–5.00pm, Sat and Sun 11.00am–4.00pm; Nov–Mar, Mon–Fri 10.00am–4.00pm. Admission fee.*

The Clink Exhibition

CLINK STREET, SE1
⊖ LONDON BRIDGE
ATLAS REF 177 E4
Close by St Mary Overie Dock is the 14th-century rose window of the Great Hall of Winchester Palace, the London home of the Bishops of Winchester from the 12th century. The last bishop to live here was Lancelot Andrewes (1555–1626), and the building was largely destroyed by fire in 1814.

Southwark was in the diocese of Winchester for centuries and the palace presided over an area of some 70 acres (28.3ha) called 'the Liberty of the Clink', which was outside the City of London's jurisdiction. As a result, it was packed with taverns, bear-baiting and prize-fighting arenas, theatres

and 'stews', or brothels. The prostitutes, whose working hours and code of conduct were prescribed by the bishops, were known as 'Winchester geese'.

The Clink prison originally belonged to the bishops. It was burned down in 1780. The Clink Exhibition, in a warehouse basement in Clink Street, portrays the history of the 'stews' and life in the damp and squalid prison.

Open daily, 11.00am–5.00pm. Admission fee.

Shakespeare Globe Museum

1 BEAR GARDENS,
BANKSIDE, SE1
⊖ LONDON BRIDGE
⊖ BLACKFRIARS
ATLAS REF 177 E4
Bankside was the heart of London's theatre district in Elizabethan and Jacobean times. The site of the Rose theatre was uncovered in 1988, and a replica of the Globe theatre, where Shakespeare himself trod the stage and many of his plays were enacted, is due to be completed in 1993.

The Shakespeare Globe Museum at Bear Gardens (the name refers to bear-baiting with dogs), traces the history of the stage from Elizabethan times until the Commonwealth period, when the Puritans closed down theatres. The museum stands on the site of the Hope theatre.

Museum open Mon–Sat 10.00am–5.00pm, Sun 1.30pm–5.00pm. Admission fee.

St George the Martyr

BOROUGH HIGH STREET, SE1
⊖ BOROUGH
ATLAS REF 177 E3
This handsome Classical church was built in the 1730s on the site of a much older place of worship. It was damaged in the Blitz and restored in 1952. Dickens's *Little Dorrit* was christened in this church, and married in it as well. Marshalsea Road nearby preserves the memory of the notorious debtors' prison of that name, which was also used for political prisoners and was finally closed in the 1840s; imprisonment for debt was done away with in 1870.

Guy's Hospital

ST THOMAS STREET, SE1
⊖ LONDON BRIDGE
ATLAS REF 177 F4
The hospital, one of the most famous in the country, was founded in the 1720s by a

wealthy local financier named Thomas Guy, who started his career selling bibles and made a fortune out of financial speculation. Its 18th-century gateway, buildings and railings were damaged by bombing, but remain handsome, though dwarfed by the hospital's post-war tower blocks. There is a statue of Thomas Guy in the courtyard and a memorial to him in the chapel. Part of the 18th-century **London Bridge** is preserved in one of the quads.

St Thomas's Hospital Operating Theatre and Museum

9A ST THOMAS STREET, SE1
⊖ LONDON BRIDGE
ATLAS REF 177 F4
On the opposite side of St Thomas Street is the Church of St Thomas, which is now used as Southwark Cathedral's chapter house. Built in 1703, it was originally the chapel of old St Thomas's Hospital, which stood here until the 1860s when it was moved to Lambeth. An early 19th-century operating theatre, used only for women patients, was discovered in the attic in the 1950s, and is now fitted out as if ready for an operation. It is a semi-circular amphitheatre, with seats for students to watch and learn. In the middle are a stout operating table and a box of sawdust, which was used to soak up blood and could be pushed into position by the surgeon with his foot, as required. The theatre was last used in 1862.

Open Mon, Wed and Fri 12.30pm–4.00pm. Admission fee.

Like an audience at the playhouse or a congregation in church, the medical students at St Thomas's Hospital used to watch operations in this theatre. The box of sawdust soaked up the blood.

Greenwich

ATLAS REF 186

◆ SE10 ◆

Five miles below Tower Bridge the Thames gives way to Greenwich on the south shore. More than 2½ million visitors arrive here each year — many by riverboat — to visit the park with its stately historic buildings, or to stroll in search of Georgian houses, Victorian terraces and delightful little shops. Great architects of the past such as Inigo Jones, Sir Christopher Wren and Nicholas Hawksmoor have bequeathed some of their finest work to Greenwich. As a backdrop to the main buildings of the National Maritime Museum, Greenwich Park slopes uphill to Blackheath, where the Old Royal Observatory crowns the crest of the hill.

Looking down from the Old Royal Observatory today, it is easy to picture Greenwich's Tudor past, when Greenwich Palace, or Placentia, stood near the Queen's House. Here Prince Henry (later King Henry VIII) was born in 1491, and here, too, Queen Elizabeth I spent the happiest hours of her childhood. Shakespeare acted in the Great Hall; Sir Martin Frobisher, the great Elizabethan navigator, left England from here in search of the New World in the 1570s; and Sir Francis Drake sailed past in the *Golden Hind* on his return from circumnavigating the world in 1580. Greenwich Palace was completely rebuilt in Classical style in the mid-17th century, and as sail gave way to steam in the 19th, Greenwich grew from a riverside village into the sprawling borough that we know today.

Greenwich

The Old Royal Observatory

GREENWICH PARK,
ROMNEY ROAD, SE10
⇒ GREENWICH
ATLAS REF 186

'Within our park at Greenwich upon the highest ground' (as King Charles II decreed), stands the Old Royal Observatory, a part of the National Maritime Museum. This mellow, red-brick building has perfect proportions, and a fine octagonal room on the top floor. Wren's masterpiece, built in 1675 for John Flamsteed, the Astronomer Royal (after whom Flamsteed House is named), retains its ancient telescopes today. They include a 28in (71cm) refracting

telescope, one of the largest in the world. On top of one of the towers of **Flamsteed House** is a large red time ball, which slides

One of London's oddest walks takes you deep under the Thames from the Isle of Dogs to Greenwich. Lifts and stairs at each end descend to an echoing pedestrian tunnel, 1,217ft (371m) long and 11ft (3m) in diameter. It was constructed in 1902.

Right: Sir Christopher Wren designed the Old Royal Observatory at Greenwich, which was used until the 1950s. Telescopes and other instruments can be viewed inside today (top, right).

down each day at exactly 1.00pm to enable seamen on the Thames to set their clocks accurately.

The Old Royal Observatory is Britain's oldest government scientific institution and was originally designed to establish latitude and other guides to navigation by astronomy. Today it is a museum. Beside the Meridian Building runs **Longitude Zero** (the Greenwich Meridian), which visitors can bestride so that they have a foot in eastern and western hemispheres simultaneously. A 24-hour clock registers **Greenwich Mean Time** (GMT), on which all the clock time in the world is based.

Open summer, Mon–Sat 10.00am–6.00pm, Sun 2.00pm–6.00pm; winter, Mon–Sat 10.00am–5.00pm, Sun 2.00pm–5.00pm. Admission fee.

Greenwich Park

ROMNEY ROAD, SE10
⇌ GREENWICH
ATLAS REF 186
Greenwich Park was the first royal park to be enclosed, an event that took place in 1433. The great French architect, André Le Nôtre, laid out its paths and avenues in 1662, and many more have since been added. Visitors can wander as they please, and there is no shortage of walks.

The National Maritime Museum and Queen's House are situated at the northern side of the park, while a short walk southwards leads to the Old Royal Observatory and Blackheath.

Queen Elizabeth's Oak used to stand to the left of Blackheath Avenue, in the middle of the park. King Henry VIII is said to have danced around this tree with his second wife, Anne Boleyn, in the 16th century. Until it was blown down in a gale in July 1991, the hollow 20ft (6m) wide stump could still be seen. It once had a door and a window, and was used as a lock-up.

The Queen's House

GREENWICH PARK,
ROMNEY ROAD, SE10
⇌ GREENWICH
ATLAS REF 186
Situated between the wings of the National Maritime Museum, Queen's House has incomparable charm. This small palace, built near the site of Placentia, was begun by Inigo Jones for James I's queen, Anne of Denmark, in 1616. With the Banqueting House in Whitehall it ranks as the prototype of English Palladian architecture, and it was also the first home in England to be designed in Classical style.

Restored with great care in recent years at a cost of £5 million, Queen's House is now hung with 17th-century paintings and is furnished in a style befitting a miniature palace. First derided as a 'curious device', the house, with its extreme Classical simplicity, is today a memorial to the genius of its architect.

Open summer, Mon–Sat 10.00am–6.00pm, Sun 2.00pm–6.00pm; winter, Mon–Sat 10.00am–5.00pm, Sun 2.00pm–5.00pm. Closed for annual cleaning and maintenance, end Dec–end Jan. Admission fee.

National Maritime Museum

GREENWICH PARK,
ROMNEY ROAD, SE10
⇌ GREENWICH
ATLAS REF 186
Linked to the Queen's House by a double colonnade, this building — previously a boy's naval school — is now the largest maritime museum in the world. In it are 29 galleries of treasures, celebrating 'man's encounter with the sea'. Exhibits include not only examples of water transport, marine art and archaeology, but also models and artefacts, giving the social background to sailor's lives in the past.

Small ships of all kinds are on display in the **New Neptune Hall**, while gilded and elaborately carved barges can be admired in the **Barge Hall**. A glance into a Victorian river steamer evokes a scene in a painting by Tissot.

Among the most popular galleries are the two devoted to Horatio, Lord Nelson, one of Britain's greatest admirals. There is a dramatic simplicity in one exhibit; the jacket that he wore when he was shot at the Battle of Trafalgar in 1805. Visitors can still see the hole in the left shoulder where the fatal musket shot fired from a French ship entered Nelson's body.

Open summer, Mon–Sat 10.00am–6.00pm, Sun 2.00pm–6.00pm; winter, Mon–Sat 10.00am–5.00pm, Sun 2.00pm–5.00pm. Admission fee.

Ranger's House

CHESTERFIELD WALK, SE10
⇌ GREENWICH
ATLAS REF 186
Overlooking Blackheath and backing on to Greenwich Park, this was originally called Chesterfield House. It was the home of Philip, Earl of Chesterfield, who came to live here in 1748 and added the wings with circular bays. Now more generally known as the Ranger's House (it was the official residence of the Rangers of Greenwich Park after 1815), the building houses a collection of historic paintings and the **Dolmetsch collection** of musical instruments. The rooms are hung with portraits and the **Grand Salon** is used for concerts.

Open Good Fri/1 Apr (whichever is earlier)–30 Sep, daily, 10.00am–6.00pm; 1 Oct–Maundy Thu/31 Mar (whichever is earlier), daily, 10.00am–4.00pm.

Macartney House

CHESTERFIELD WALK, SE10
⇌ GREENWICH
ATLAS REF 186
A few yards away from the Ranger's House is Macartney House, bought in 1754 by General Edward Wolfe, the father of General James Wolfe. Wolfe the elder described it as 'the prettiest situated house in England'. From here General James Wolfe set out from England for Quebec, where he was killed in action in 1759.

The National Maritime Museum at Greenwich is now the country's premier museum of ships and the sea. It occupies wings added in 1816 to the Queen's House.

Greenwich and Docklands

Above: the splendour of Greenwich, seen across the Thames. In the centre is Queen's House, designed by Inigo Jones. The palatial buildings of the Royal Naval College in the foreground were designed by Sir Christopher Wren, who was instructed that the Queen's House must remain visible from the river.
*Right: the figurehead of the fast tea clipper **Cutty Sark**, which once breasted the waves to China.*

Royal Naval College

KING WILLIAM WALK, SE10
⇌ GREENWICH
ATLAS REF 180 C1

Two fine domed buildings with colonnades, a short distance from Greenwich Pier, are part of a group of 17th- and 18th-century distinction. Originally used as Greenwich Hospital (planned by Sir Christopher Wren to outshine Chelsea Hospital as a home for disabled and aged seamen), the buildings are now part of the Royal Naval College, which took over this complex in 1873.

Round the **Great Court**, facing the river, are twin domed buildings, symmetrically placed – the **chapel** and the **Painted Hall** (which has one of the few fine Baroque ceilings with murals in London). In its time, Greenwich Hospital was unduly grand for pensioners, who would probably have preferred better food and fewer restrictions. The present use of the buildings for naval studies seems more befitting the monumental architecture.

Chapel and Painted Hall open Fri–Wed 2.30pm–5.00pm. Admission fee.

Trafalgar Tavern

PARK ROW, SE10
⇌ GREENWICH
ATLAS REF 186

The Trafalgar Tavern, with its bow-fronted windows overlooking the river, was one of the inns famous for serving whitebait suppers, much enjoyed in the last century. Lord Palmerston and other Victorian ministers came here at the end of parliamentary sessions for special dinners of the fish, caught in Greenwich Reach. Among the other famous customers in the 19th century were the novelists Charles Dickens and William Makepeace Thackeray, and the cartoonist George Cruikshank.

The Cutty Sark *and* Gipsy Moth IV

GREENWICH PIER, SE10
⇌ GREENWICH
ATLAS REF 180 B1

In a dry dock by Greenwich Pier is *Cutty Sark*, one of the last and fastest tea clippers. Built in 1869, she has found her final rest here. No longer buffeted by the Roaring Forties, she houses an exhibition of ship's figureheads.

Nearby is *Gipsy Moth IV*, the 53ft (16m) ketch in which Francis Chichester sailed single-handed around the world in 1966–7. He was knighted by the Queen on his return.

Cutty Sark open, Eas–Sep, Mon–Sat 10.00am–5.30pm, Sun 12.00noon–5.30pm; Oct–Eas, Mon–Sat 10.00am–4.30pm, Sun 12.00noon–4.30pm. Admission fee. Gipsy Moth open, Eas–Sep, Mon–Sat 10.00am–5.30pm, Sun 12.00noon–5.30pm. Admission fee.

St Alfege's Church

GREENWICH CHURCH STREET, SE10
⇌ GREENWICH
ATLAS REF 186

One of Nicholas Hawksmoor's finest churches, St Alfege's as we see it today was built in 1714, replacing an earlier church of the 12th century. It stands on the site of the murder of Archbishop Alfege by the Danes in 1012.

The chief beauty of the church inside is its hanging expanse of ceiling, which can be viewed from the galleries (where there is also a royal pew). The tower was built by Hawksmoor's assistant, John James, in 1733, and is an early version of the 'pepperpot'. Henry VII was probably christened here. It is the burial place of Thomas Tallis, the 16th-century church musician, and General James Wolfe.

Open Apr–Oct, Tue–Fri 12.00noon–4.00pm, Nov–Mar, Thu–Sun 11.00am–3.00pm.

Docklands E1, E14, E16, SE16

⊖ TOWER HILL, THEN
DOCKLANDS LIGHT RAILWAY
ATLAS REF 179–80
Between Tower Bridge and
Woolwich — 7 miles (11.2km)
by river — an extraordinary
transformation has taken place
since 1981. A largely desolate area
fringing the Thames and covering
about 8½ sq miles (22 sq km) has
been regenerated. An overgrown
wilderness of disused docks and
crumbling warehouses has been
changed into a gleaming city of
the future. Really is should be
described as four cities, because
London's Docklands consist of
four zones. Three of them north
of the river (Wapping, the Isle of
Dogs, and the Royal Docks) are
linked; the fourth (Surrey Docks)
on the south side lies between
London Bridge and Deptford.

Each is formulating a personality
of its own — Wapping, up-market,
faintly 'yuppy'; Isle of Dogs,
stunning commercial buildings
dominated by the Canary Wharf
skyscraper; Royal Docks, out on
an eastern limb with individualistic
homes and commercial buildings
alongside miles of waterfront; and
Surrey Docks, flats and expensive
houses on the edge of a marina
and lakes.

The vast changes came about
when the once-proud Port of
London closed and a dynamic
plan was needed in the early
1980s to attract industry,
commerce and a new generation
of residents. In 1981 the London
Docklands Development
Corporation (LDDC) was formed
and it will probably maintain a
degree of supervision over the
areas until the end of the
century. Visitors can see a
remarkable combination of new
architecture (some splendid,
some distinctly idiosyncratic)
and enlightened planning,
alongside examples of both
speculation and praiseworthy
preservation of old buildings.

Canary Wharf

ISLE OF DOGS, E14
⊖ TOWER HILL, THEN
DOCKLANDS LIGHT RAILWAY:
CANARY WHARF
ATLAS REF 180 A4
The Canary Wharf complex, with
24 separate buildings covering
70 acres (28.3ha), is the most
controversial building in
Docklands. The Canary Wharf
Tower has 50 floors and at 800ft
(243.8m) high it is a monolith,

ranking as the tallest building in
Britain. Shops, restaurants, a
concert hall and a railway station
are incorporated into the plan.
But there is no viewing platform
at the top.

Mudchute

ISLE OF DOGS, E14
⊖ TOWER HILL, THEN
DOCKLANDS LIGHT RAILWAY:
MUDCHUTE
ATLAS REF 180 B2
Visitors seeking a 'master view' of
the Isle of Dogs will find a good
one from this curious mound. When
Millwall Docks were excavated in
the 1880s the mud was piled here
and has solidified to create a
plateau of allotments, a farm and
fields. **Beckton Alps**, a ski slope
much further away in the Royal
Docks, is another artificial mound
resulting from dock excavation.

Tobacco Dock

WAPPING HIGHWAY, E1
⊖ TOWER HILL, THEN
DOCKLANDS LIGHT RAILWAY:
SHADWELL
ATLAS REF 178 C3
This is Docklands' best example
of a fine old listed building
converted to a new use. Built in
1814 and covering about 4 acres
(1.6ha), this is where bonded
goods were stored. Now Virginia
tobacco, French brandy and
Jamaican rum have gone,
replaced by elegant shops and

restaurants, whose designers
have taken advantage of the
vaulted chambers of mellow
brick. Two 'pirate ships' are a
reminder that the warehouse was
once part of London Docks.

London City Airport

KING GEORGE V DOCKS, E16
⊖ PLAISTOW, THEN TAXI
⇌ SILVERTOWN AND CITY
AIRPORT
ATLAS REF 186
The airport is interesting to visit
even if you are not using the
turbo-jet planes taking off for
Paris, Brussels and other parts of
Europe. The runway lies between
two long, deep waterbasins,
which once berthed liners the
size of the *Mauritania*.
Watersports can be watched
from the airy restaurant.

Billingsgate Fish Market

ISLE OF DOGS, E14
⊖ TOWER HILL, THEN
DOCKLANDS LIGHT RAILWAY:
WEST INDIA QUAY
ATLAS REF 180 B4
Early birds with a taste for fish will
find Billingsgate (which was moved
here from Lower Thames Street in
1982) a place for bargains. London's
fish has been supplied by
Billingsgate since the 9th century,
and by ancient charter it is open
to the public as well as traders.
Open Tue–Sat 5.30am–9.00am.

*The Docklands Light
Railway at Heron
Quays, in the old West
India Docks on the Isle
of Dogs. This automatic
railway, opened in
1987, connects the new
Docklands
developments with the
City and gives
fascinating views of
modernistic buildings.*

⊖ KEW GARDENS
🚌 7, 27, 65, 90
♣ WESTMINSTER

Royal Botanic Gardens

ATLAS REF 184

◆ KEW, TW9 3AB ◆

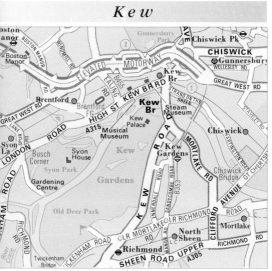

Kew

Before it was swallowed up by London's suburbs, Kew was an independent village. It still retains its delightful green, surrounded by Georgian houses, where cricket matches are played in summer. On the green is the charming Church of St Anne in red brick, consecrated in 1714 and standing on land given by Queen Anne. The great painter Thomas Gainsborough is buried in its churchyard.

Laid out by the Hanoverians in the early 18th century, Kew became the fashionably elegant neighbourhood it remains today. Handsome Georgian houses, many with Regency frills, surround Kew Green and St Anne's Church of 1714. King George II (1683–1760) lived in Richmond Lodge, and his son Frederick with his wife Augusta in Kew House, near the present Kew Palace. The widowed Augusta created a 9-acre (3.6ha) botanic garden in 1759 as part of landscaping which included an Orangery by Sir William Chambers, and a Japanese Pagoda.

Inheriting both estates, her son King George III and his wife Queen Charlotte occupied the Dutch House, now Kew Palace, and commissioned the landscaping of the grounds by Capability Brown. Plants were collected worldwide for the botanic garden which was given to the state by Queen Victoria in 1841. Under the direction of Sir William Hooker the Royal Botanic Gardens grew to 200 acres (81ha), and the superb hot houses designed by Decimus Burton were added.

Further royal bequests enlarged the gardens to 300 acres (121ha), while their scientific function expanded until they became, as they remain, the world's leading plant science institution.

A tour begins most logically at the **Main Gate** on **Kew Green**, though there is also access at Lion, Victoria and Cumberland Gates on Kew Road or by Brentford Gate on the Thames towpath. (An exit through the latter enables visitors taking the summertime ferry to go on a round tour before returning to Kew Green, or Kew Bridge and Kew Gardens stations.)

The first stop inside the Main Gate is likely to be the **Orangery**, now accommodating a shop and exhibitions. The **Fern House** is next door. Following the perimeter clockwise will lead you to Kew Gardens' busiest corner. The role of the **Wood Museum** within the walled **Cambridge Cottage Garden** is self-explanatory. Outside is the **Bulb Garden**, whose all-year-round displays are — like so much at Kew — a surprise to the non-expert gardener. Here plants flower not only in springtime, but at all seasons. Another all-year-round attraction is the **Alpine House** (opened in 1981), with its 3,000 mountain plants, including species from the Arctic to the Andes. The **Aquatic Garden** displays British species, while the **Grass Garden** exhibits some 600 members of this under-regarded family, with demonstrations of their fundamental usefulness in the human economy.

Continuing Kew's royal traditions, and in particular the patronage of Queens and Princesses of Wales, the modern **Princess of Wales Conservatory** (1987) replaces 26 greenhouses of tropical plants. Installed partially below ground to conserve heat, its 10 sections are computer-controlled to maintain temperature and humidity for specimens from the wet and dry tropics.

A stroll through the **Rock Garden** and the **Woodland Garden** brings you to the **Museum**,

Decimus Burton's spectacular Palm House is seen across the flowerbeds at Kew. Constructed of iron and glass, it was a forerunner of the Crystal Palace. Outside, the great conservatory is guarded by the figures of the Queen's Beasts, royal heraldic emblems.

which displays 'economic' or useful plants, such as those used for dyes, medicines, oils and waxes, rubber, and even poisoned arrows. Outside, **Palm House Pond** is overlooked by Kew's most spectacular building — the **Palm House**, a palace of glass designed by Decimus Burton in the 1840s. Recently renovated, the interior is like a tropical rainforest in miniature, exhibiting plants in their ecological context.

On its west side is the formal **Rose Garden** which, as well as demonstrating the provenance of today's popular hybrids, is the focus of Kew Gardens' three main vistas: Chestnut Vista towards the river and Syon House on the opposite bank; Pagoda Vista towards Britain's most splendid example of 18th-century *chinoiserie*; and Cedar Vista towards the tall cedar next to the beech clump. Northwards is the **Waterlily House** (1852), whose original centrepiece, the Giant Waterlily *Victoria amazonica*, now decorates the Princess of Wales Conservatory.

Through the Japanese cherry trees is one of Kew's other great buildings. The **Temperate House**, another Decimus Burton creation, houses a range of rare plants with the Chilean Wine Palm — probably the largest greenhouse plant anywhere — as its prize exhibit. A short distance away the **Australian House** contains plants indigenous to this subcontinent, notably eucalyptus and mimosas.

The south-west corner nearest to Richmond (and visitable through Lion Gate) includes, as well as the Refreshment Pavilion, the **Marianne North Gallery**. Inside are paintings of plants of various countries visited by Miss North during the 1870s and 1880s. Dominating the area is the **Pagoda**, 163ft (50m) tall, with 10 tapering stories.

Towards the river, **Queen Charlotte's Cottage** was built in the 1780s as a Marie Antoinette-style rustic refuge for the queen of George III and her family. The wildness survives in the 40-acre (16.2ha) cottage grounds, which are managed as a nature reserve. The masses of bluebells in spring are particularly beautiful.

The **Lake**, a Victorian feature, attracts a variety of wildfowl as well as pinioned ducks and geese. Running parallel to the riverbank, the **Rhododendron Dell** was originally planted with Himalayan species collected by Sir William Hooker's son Joseph, his successor as Director of Kew Gardens. Princesses' Walk continues past the **Azalea Garden**, which is especially fine in late May and June.

Kew Palace, built in 1631 by Samuel Fortrey, a City merchant of Dutch origin (hence its alternative name, the Dutch House) is a handsome early example of the red-brick style which became the model for comfortable country houses. It displays memorabilia of King George III and his era. The **Queen's Garden**, laid out in a 17th-century pattern with herbs of the time, was opened by Queen Elizabeth II in 1969.

Open daily, 9.30am to dusk. Admission fee.

The grounds at Kew were attractively embellished in the 18th century with follies and eye-catchers, strategically placed. Sir William Chambers, the architect of Somerset House, designed the Japanese pagoda which rises to the sky near the southern edge of the gardens

Nearby . . .

Kew Bridge Steam Museum

GREEN DRAGON LANE, BRENTFORD
⇌ KEW BRIDGE
ATLAS REF 184
The waterworks preserves steam-powered beam engines of impressive size and early vintage in working order. A Boulton and Watt pump of 1820 was installed when the pumping station was built in 1837. Exhibits include a working forge and traction engines.
Open daily, 11.00am–5.00pm. Admission fee.

Musical Museum

368 HIGH STREET, BRENTFORD
⇌ KEW BRIDGE
ATLAS REF 184
Inside this former church is an array of mechanical musical machines, ranging from pianolas to mighty fairground organs. Marvellous to look at, the instruments also produce an awe-inspiring volume of sound.
Open Apr–Oct, Sat and Sun 2.00pm–5.00pm; Jul and Aug, Wed–Fri 2.00pm–5.00pm. Admission fee.

The beautiful Temperate House is another of Decimus Burton's iron-and-glass creations and is home to some 3,000 species of plants. It is twice the size of the Palm House and took almost 40 years to build, being finally completed in 1899.

Hampstead and Highgate

ATLAS REF 182

◆ NW3, N6 ◆

Hampstead and Highgate

The grand Georgian façade of Kenwood House looks out over landscaped 18th-century grounds to Hampstead Heath. It was once the home of the Earls of Mansfield.

Hampstead and its twin village, Highgate, look down on London to the north. Once small villages, they were swallowed up in the 19th century by urban sprawl. Hampstead itself still follows street patterns of an earlier age.

Sitting on the northern heights 450ft (137m) above London, Hampstead preserves some of the isolation it enjoyed when access was steep for carriages and waggons. Narrow streets, alleys, courtyards and flights of steps have a charm which since the 18th century has attracted artists and writers and led prosperous City people to build here. To the north lie 800 acres (324ha) of woods and open spaces — Hampstead Heath — with two celebrated hostelries, Jack Straw's Castle and The Spaniards. The Vale of Health, a romantically named valley, Parliament Hill Fields and Highgate Ponds all contribute to Hampstead's aura of rural charm.

Hampstead's popularity began early in the 1700s when chalybeate (iron salt) spring water was discovered in Well Walk and drew the fashionable and wealthy to this hilltop village to take a cure. The water was also bottled and sold in flasks in what is now Flask Walk. Well-preserved houses, many open to the public, are Hampstead's greatest gift to the visitor today.

Also looking down on London from the north is Highgate, in many ways the twin village of Hampstead. Its height above London can best be appreciated by approaching it from Highgate Hill.

A delicate 18th-century figure in Meissen porcelain from Fenton House, the oldest house in Hampstead.

Kenwood House

HAMPSTEAD LANE, NW3
⊖ ARCHWAY
ATLAS REF 182
One of London's finest stately homes, and now a museum, Kenwood House is situated in a wooded estate with a lake (by which concerts are held in summer). The fine entrance portico, approached by a drive, is part of the transformation from an earlier Jacobean mansion which makes Kenwood unmistakably the creation of the 18th-century architect, Robert Adam. The ceiling of the Entrance Hall is by the Swiss painter Angelica Kauffmann, and the painting in the beautiful library is the work of her Venetian husband, Antonio Zucchi. On Lord Mansfield's

death in 1927, Kenwood was bequeathed to the nation. In rooms which retain the informal dimensions of a private house hang pictures by Rembrandt, Van Dyck, Vermeer and Gainsborough. Art exhibitions are held regularly.

Open Oct–Mar daily, 10.00am–4.00pm; Apr–Sep daily, 10.00am–6.00pm.

Keats' House

KEATS' GROVE, NE3
⊖ HAMPSTEAD
⊖ BELSIZE PARK
ATLAS REF 182
This small but distinctive house was the home of the poet John Keats from 1818 to 1820. It saw the writing of some of his most famous works until consumption made it essential for him to

convalesce in Italy. In John Keats' time the house was semi-detached and his fiancée, Fanny Browne, lived next door with her widowed mother. In this house *La Belle Dame sans Merci* and many of Keats' sonnets were written, while his famous *Ode to a Nightingale* was composed under a plane tree in the garden. This tree has gone, but other trees — saplings in 1820 — remain as a link with the poet. Keats died of tuberculosis in Rome in 1821 aged 25, and personal items such as his letters are displayed in the house.

Open Apr–Oct, Mon–Fri 2.00pm–6.00pm, Sat 10.00am– 1.00pm and 2.00pm–5.00pm, Sun 2.00pm–5.00pm; Nov–Mar, Mon–Fri 1.00pm– 5.00pm, Sat 10.00am–1.00pm and 2.00pm– 5.00pm, Sun 2.00pm–5.00pm.

Fenton House

HAMPSTEAD GROVE, NW3
⊖ HAMPSTEAD
ATLAS REF 182
To the north, in Hampstead Grove, is Fenton House, a nearly perfect example of a William-and-Mary building (1693). Here architecture and music blend melodically, for the house is now a museum of historic musical instruments. Among the exhibits is an early Stuart harpsichord, on which the great composer George Frederick Handel played when he was living in London.

Fenton House derives its name from its late-18th-century owner, Philip Fenton, a Continental merchant with Dutch interests. Now in the care of the National Trust, the house also displays porcelain and period furniture. Visitors are impressed by the beautiful wrought-iron gates at the Windmill Hill entrance. These are a source of an unresolved mystery; they are variously believed to have been brought from France by Fenton, to have come from Hampton Court Palace, or to be part of old St Paul's Cathedral.

Open Mar, Sat and Sun 2.00pm–6.00pm; Apr–Oct, Mon– Wed, Sat and Sun 11.00am–6.00pm. Admission fee payable by non-National Trust members.

Jack Straw's Castle and The Spaniards

HAMPSTEAD HEATH, NW3
⊖ HAMPSTEAD
⊖ GOLDER'S GREEN
ATLAS REF 182
On the west side of Hampstead Heath, these two famous inns are well-placed and historically interesting. Jack Straw's Castle is a famous coaching inn. It was also an important place during the Peasants' Revolt, when Straw and his supporters made the building a rallying point on their way to Highbury. More likely 'Jack Straw' is a generic name for a farm worker. But no-one questions that famous 19th-century novelists such as Thackeray, Dickens and Wilkie Collins were patrons, while the great Romantic poets such as Shelley, Keats and Lord Byron would visit The Spaniards in Hampstead Lane. In 1780 rioters on their way to destroy Kenwood House were decoyed by drinks here until soldiers arrived and disarmed them.

Freud Museum

20 MARESFIELD GARDENS, NW3
⊖ SWISS COTTAGE
ATLAS REF 182
The house is a memorial to Sigmund Freud. After the great psychoanalyst arrived as a refugee from Vienna in 1938, this was his home until his death a year later. For 40 years his daughter Anna — herself a psychoanalyst — continued to live here and kept the library and study as he knew it. Freud's letters and personal relics are on show, as is the prototype couch, which visitors may see but not lie on.

Open Mon–Sat 10.00am– 5.00pm. Admission fee.

Highgate Cemetery

SWAIN'S LANE, N6
⊖ HIGHGATE
⊖ ARCHWAY
ATLAS REF 182
Highgate has many charms and curiosities (among them a stone on Highgate Hill marking the spot where Dick Whittington traditionally turned again). But the outstanding attraction is sepulchral. Highgate Cemetery is one of the most famous in the world, not because of its size (17 acres or 6.8ha), but because of the whimsical charm of the monuments to be found in it. Nothing here, except perhaps the graves of children, induces melancholy: quite the contrary. So many of the internees appear to have gone to their graves with smiles on their faces.

At every turn there are tombs to arouse curiosity or a smile. A Victorian menagerie-keeper is remembered by a snoozing, cross-pawed lion. Splayed stumps on the headstone of a cricketer show that he has completed his innings. There is a stone accordion on the grave of a musician and his wife, and 'Alas, poor Yorick!' is inscribed on the tomb of a comedian.

Among the writers, artists and professional men to be found here are Charles Dickens, Michael Faraday, Sir Rowland Hill (inventor of the penny post) and Eric Blore, who took over the completion of Buckingham Palace from Nash. Here is the grave of Lizzie Siddal, the beautiful young wife of Dante Gabriel Rossetti, the Pre-Raphaelite artist and poet. Her grave was opened up at Rossetti's instigation, so that he could recover a book of manuscript poems which he had romantically buried with her, but later wanted to publish.

In recent years the cemetery, which had become a neglected wilderness, has been tended and carefully conserved by a dedicated local group, the Friends of Highgate Cemetery. Further burials cannot take place in the cemetery but opposite, on the east side of the hill, there is an extension, where the huge head of Karl Marx (buried in 1883) looks down on the vandals who find him an irresistible target.

Open for hourly guided tours (west side only), daily; summer 10.00am–4.00pm, winter 10.00am–3.00pm.

Highgate Cemetery is best known for its monument to Karl Marx (below).

Luxuriant trees and shrubs grow in Highgate Cemetery.

On the Perimeter: North-East

L ondon's north-eastern sector offers the inquiring explorer the mother church of the worldwide methodist movement and one of the world's largest collections of children's toys; a gallery devoted to the protean talents of William Morris, and the delights of Alexandra Palace.

Museum of the Order of St John

ST JOHN'S GATE, EC1
⊖ FARRINGDON
ATLAS REF 173 D3

The Order of the Hospital of St John of Jerusalem, or Knights Hospitallers, has left its mark on Clerkenwell, which was originally a country hamlet on the River Fleet, to the north of the City. From the 12th century onwards the order built a large priory here, and the site is now occupied by St John's Square, off Clerkenwell Road. St John's Church, an 18th-century building restored after the Second World War, stands on what was once the priory church. All that remains of the priory today is the 12th-century crypt and St John's Gate, across St John's Lane, dating from 1504. Housed on its ground floor is the Museum of the Order of St John, which tells the story of the knights and of the order's modern descendant, the St John Ambulance Brigade, which has a worldwide membership of more than 250,000.

Open Mon and Fri 10.00am–5.00pm, Sat 10.00am–4.00pm.

Wesley's House and Chapel

CITY ROAD, EC1
⊖ OLD STREET
ATLAS REF 173 F3

The chapel was opened by John Wesley, the founder of Methodism, in 1778 and stands on a site where 50,000 loads of rubble from old St Paul's were dumped in the 17th century before Sir Christopher Wren's rebuilding could start. The chapel was rebuilt in the 19th century and restored again in 1978. The original pulpit and font have survived. In front of the building there is a statue of Wesley, who is buried behind the chapel. More than 5,000 other Methodists are interred in and close to the building. (Across City Road lie **Bunhill Fields**, London's main burial ground for Nonconformists from 1658 until 1852. Here are the graves of John Bunyan, author of *The Pilgrim's Progress*, Isaac Watts the hymn-writer and the artist William Blake.)

Next to the chapel is the house where Wesley spent the last 12 years of his life, and where he

died in 1791. Still to be seen are furniture and books that he used, along with other personal items.

Chapel open Mon–Sat 8.00am–5.00pm, Sun service 11.00am. House and museum open Mon–Sat 10.00am–4.00pm. Admission fee.

Geffrye Museum

KINGSLAND ROAD, E2
⊖ OLD STREET
ATLAS REF 183

A pretty series of almshouses, erected early in the 18th century by the Ironmongers' Company around three sides of a little park, now houses this lively museum of period rooms, illustrating the history of interior design from Tudor times to the 1950s. There are Georgian shopfronts, as well, and a woodworker's workshop and kitchen of the same period. At the centre is the old chapel. The museum is a delightful, informal evocation of London life over many centuries.

Open Tue–Sat 10.00am–5.00pm, Sun 2.00pm–5.00pm.

Bethnal Green Museum of Childhood

CAMBRIDGE HEATH ROAD, E2
⊖ BETHNAL GREEN
ATLAS REF 183

The museum is in a Victorian structure of iron and glass, full of light and space, which was put up in Kensington in the 1850s. It was moved here in 1872 and given a brick exterior. For years the Bethnal Green Museum was a depository for duplicate or unfashionable objects from the V & A's collections. It has now cast aside this dusty and unloved image, and blossomed as the Museum of Childhood, making the most of its splendid assemblage of toys and dolls, dolls' houses, games and models, and children's playthings of all periods. There are rocking chairs, teddy bears, model trains, children's clothes and books, in

Simple elegance in the study of John Wesley's house. Over the fireplace is a modern portrait of the great man. His three-cornered hat, travelling cloak and shoes are in the display case.

one of the biggest collections of its kind in the world.

Among the dolls' houses is the **Tate Baby House**, a fully furnished Georgian mansion in miniature dating from about 1760. The galleries upstairs in the museum include educational toys and furniture.

Open Mon–Thu and Sat 10.00am–6.00pm, Sun 2.30pm–6.00pm.

Whitechapel Art Gallery

80 WHITECHAPEL HIGH STREET, E1
⊖ ALDGATE EAST
ATLAS REF 178 B4
Built by philanthropists in the 1890s to bring cultural life to the East End, the gallery has long enjoyed a reputation for staging excellent temporary exhibitions, usually of modern and highly avant-garde art. The building's dramatic Art Nouveau façade is by C Harrison Townsend, though it lacks the verve of his Horniman Museum building.

Open Tue–Sun 11.00am–5.00pm (till 8.00pm on Wed).

William Morris Gallery

WATER HOUSE,
FOREST ROAD, E17
⊖ WALTHAMSTOW CENTRAL
ATLAS REF 183
An unexpected find in suburban Walthamstow, the gallery celebrates the genius of William Morris as designer, artist-craftsman, writer, thinker and political reformer. Collected here are furniture, fabrics and other artefacts made by Morris's company, William Morris & Co., in the late-19th century. There are also fascinating photographs, and examples of work by Morris's associates, including Sir Edward Burne-Jones and Frank Brangwyn. Brangwyn is well represented as a painter, having given the gallery many of his own works.

Open Tue–Sat 10.00am–1.00pm and 2.00pm–5.00pm.

Vestry House Museum

VESTRY ROAD, E17
⊖ WALTHAMSTOW CENTRAL
ATLAS REF 183
This 18th-century workhouse now contains a local history collection.

Open Mon–Fri 10.00am–1.00pm and 2.00pm–5.30pm, Sat 10.00am–1.00pm and 2.00pm–5.00pm.

Alexandra Palace and Park

MUSWELL HILL, N22
⊖ WOOD GREEN, THEN BUS
ATLAS REF 182
Set high on a hill and surrounded by an extensive park, this grand exhibition hall was formally opened in 1873 and named after the then Princess of Wales, the future Queen Alexandra. It burned to the ground a couple of weeks later and was immediately rebuilt. During the First World War is was a camp for German prisoners, who were put to work in the grounds. It enjoys spectacular views across London as far as the North Downs, which are worth a visit by themselves. Following another disastrous fire, in 1980, the palace was restored. It is now a popular venue for exhibitions, concerts and meetings. Its other claim to fame is that it was used for Britain's earliest scheduled television transmissions in the 1930s, and continued to be used as a television studio until the 1950s.

*Right: **The Woodpecker**, designed by William Morris in the 1880s, hangs in the Walthamstow gallery.*

Hawksmoor Churches

Nicholas Hawksmoor's three churches in the East End are among London's greatest architectural treasures. Exotic, extravagant and complex, they are Baroque in a way that seems entirely un-English.

The first, **St Anne's**, in Commercial Road, Limehouse, was started in 1712 on what were then open fields north of the Thames. A theatrical composition of disparate parts, it shows that Hawksmoor was breaking away from the influence of his master, Sir Christopher Wren. The result was a tower that is still a vital ingredient of the riverside skyline.

Next came **St George's in the East** in Cannon Street Road, Shadwell. Begun in 1715, with a commanding tower, the church shows how Hawksmoor's increasing confidence brought all the elements of the building into harmony — a far cry from the comfortable Classicism of the late-18th century.

Christ Church in Commercial Street, Spitalfields, was started eight years later. It is a grand Venetian composition, huge in scale, and Venetian now in its glorious decay. These buildings represent the exciting but short-lived flowering of the Baroque in Britain. The style was soon

One of Nicholas Hawksmoor's most harmonious creations — the Church of St George's in the East.

to be driven out by Palladianism, and Hawksmoor's East End churches are a tantalising reminder of what might have been.

On the Perimeter: North-West

Attractions in London's north-western outskirts range from the canal boats of Little Venice to the commemoration of feats of flying and heroism at the RAF Museum, and from one of Britain's best-known boys' schools to two of the finest Robert Adam interiors in the country, at Syon House and Osterley Park.

Veteran First World War biplanes in the Royal Air Force Museum at Hendon, whose hangars also provide a resting-place for machines of more recent vintage.

Little Venice W2

⊖ WARWICK AVENUE
ATLAS REF 182
Given its name by the poet Robert Browning, who lived nearby (in a house since demolished), Little Venice is the part of Maida Vale where handsome stuccoed terraces flank the junction of the **Grand Union** and **Regent's Canals**, and their attendant basins. There are plenty of colourful canal boats to be seen. The first canal linking London with Birmingham and the Midlands opened early in the 19th century. An extension eastwards, linking it to the Thames at Wapping was opened in 1820 and called the Regent's Canal. John Nash included it in his newly created Regent's Park.

An excellent way to explore London's hidden waterways is to walk along the towpath from Little Venice through Regent's Park to Camden Town and Islington, and on to Hackney and the East End. A pleasant alternative is a trip on a waterbus or traditional narrowboat (starting from

Warwick Crescent or Blomfield Road).

St John's Wood NW8

⊖ ST JOHN'S WOOD
ATLAS REF 182
Lying to the north of Little Venice, this area takes its name from the Knights of St John of Jerusalem, who owned it in the Middle Ages when it was largely woodland. It was not developed until the turn of the 18th and 19th centuries and long retained a certain secluded charm which made it sought after by authors and artists, including George Eliot and Sir Edwin Landseer. St John's Wood was also notorious as an area where well-to-do gentlemen installed their mistresses in chic suburban houses, and was known as 'an Abode of Love and the Arts'. The principal attraction today is **Lord's Cricket Ground and Museum**. This is the best-known ground in the country and is the home of two clubs — Middlesex County Cricket Club and Marylebone Cricket Club (see page 162).

The Saatchi Collection

98A BOUNDARY ROAD, NW8
⊖ SWISS COTTAGE
ATLAS REF 182
This gallery, specialising in changing exhibitions of the very latest in modern art, is well worth visiting.
Open Fri and Sat 12.00noon–6.00pm.

Primrose Hill NW3

⊖ CHALK FARM
ATLAS REF 182
Rising just to the north of Regent's Park, Primrose Hill is the best place to enjoy a panoramic view of London's skyline. All the major structures can be clearly seen, from Tower Bridge in the east to the Millbank Tower in the west.

Royal Air Force Museum

GRAHAME PARK WAY, NW9
⊖ COLINDALE
ATLAS REF 182
When the Black Death struck London in the 14th century, the monks of Westminster Abbey had their cattle moved to Hendon to escape contagion. In modern times, however, the area is better known as the site of a pioneering aircraft factory. The first non-stop flight from London to Paris was made from here in 1911, and from 1920 to 1937 the Royal Air Force (RAF) put on an annual air display. Today, the old hangars house the Royal Air Force Museum, which was opened in 1972.

There are actually three parts to the museum, the first telling the story of the RAF from its formation in 1918, the second devoted to the Battle of Britain, and the third commemorating Bomber Command. Many famous planes can be seen, from the Sopwith Camel and Bristol fighter of the First World War to the Hurricane, Spitfire, Wellington, Mosquito and Lancaster of the

Second, along with a collection of German aircraft of the same period, and the Meteor, Lightning, Vulcan and Harrier of more recent history. There are also uniforms and memorabilia, and an interesting collection of paintings and sculpture.

Open daily, 10.00am–6.00pm. Admission fee.

Church Farm House Museum

GREYHOUND HILL, NW4
⊖ HENDON CENTRAL, THEN BUS
ATLAS REF 182
One of the oldest buildings in Hendon, dating from the 17th century, this is now a museum of local history, with period rooms and a fine 18th-century kitchen.

Open Mon and Wed–Sat 10.00am–1.00pm and 2.00pm –5.30pm, Sun 2.00pm–5.30pm, Tue 10.00am–1.00pm.

Harrow School and Village

HIGH STREET,
HARROW-ON-THE-HILL
⊖ HARROW-ON-THE-HILL
ATLAS REF 181
Set high on a hill, Harrow is an island village, surrounded by a sea of suburbia. The medieval church is its prominent feature, with terraces of 18th-century houses around it. The church was restored in the 19th century by Sir George Gilbert Scott, and there is a stone in the churchyard where the youthful Lord Byron liked to gaze dreamily upon the view. His daughter Allegra was buried beneath the church porch.

Harrow School, with its Victorian buildings, dominates the High Street. Founded in 1572, its famous pupils have included Lord Byron, Sir Robert Peel, Richard Brinsley Sheridan and Sir Winston Churchill, who used to return every year for the school songs. The school museum is in the Old Speech Room.

School museum open daily (except Wed). Times vary.

Pitshanger Manor

MATTOCK LANE, W5
⊖ EALING BROADWAY
ATLAS REF 181
This was the country house of Sir John Soane, the architect, in the early 19th century. It has been restored and is now a museum.

Open Tue–Sat 10.00am– 5.00pm.

Gunnersbury Park Museum

POPE'S LANE, W5
⊖ ACTON TOWN
ATLAS REF 184
Standing in the park is a Regency house once owned by the Rothschild family. It is now an interesting museum of the history of Ealing and Hounslow, with lively temporary exhibitions.

Open Mon–Fri 1.00pm– 5.00pm, Sat and Sun 2.00pm– 6.00pm (4.00pm in winter).

Osterley Park House

OSTERLEY LANE, MIDDLESEX
⊖ OSTERLEY
ATLAS REF 184
An oasis of calm sandwiched between suburbia and the M4 motorway, Osterley is an exciting blend of 18th-century architecture and landscape design. House and park were originally laid out in the 16th century, but from the 1750s both were extensively rebuilt. The exterior was remodelled by Sir William Chambers, the interior by Robert Adam, and the combined efforts of these two great rivals has created a splendid example of 18th-century Classical grandeur. Osterley is now owned by the National Trust and run by the V & A. Its interiors are a graceful monument to the Adam manner.

Open Tue–Sun 11.00am– 4.30pm. Admission fee for non-National Trust members.

Syon House

BRENTFORD, MIDDLESEX
⊖ GUNNERSBURY
ATLAS REF 184
The curiously grim exterior of Syon House, originally Tudor but altered in the 17th and early 19th centuries, conceals a magnificent suite of rooms designed by Robert Adam from 1761. The **Front Hall** is perhaps the most beautiful in Britain; wonderful plasterwork, rich marble, and painted walls and ceilings express both the delicacy and the extravagance of Adam's art. In the park there are botanical gardens and Charles Fowler's great conservatory of iron and glass, a graceful forerunner of the Crystal Palace. There is also a butterfly house.

House open Apr–Sep, Sun–Thu 12.00noon–5.00pm. Gardens open daily, 10.00am–dusk. Admission fee.

Chiswick House

BURLINGTON LANE, W4
⊖ TURNHAM GREEN, THEN BUS
ATLAS REF 185
The house, the launching pad for the Palladian Classical revival in Britain, was created from 1720 by Lord Burlington, the art connoisseur, and the architect William Kent to house the former's art collection and library. Everything is on a grand scale, and Kent was also the designer of the park. The property is now cared for by English Heritage.

Open daily, 10.00am–6.00pm (4.00pm in winter). Admission fee.

Hogarth's House

HOGARTH LANE, W4
⊖ TURNHAM GREEN
ATLAS REF 185
This is a humble house, where the 18th-century painter William Hogarth lived for 15 years. The secluded garden is overshadowed by a mulberry tree which Hogarth himself enjoyed.

Open Apr–Sep, Mon–Sat 11.00am–6.00pm, Sun 2.00pm– 6.00pm (4.00pm in winter). Admission fee.

The drawing-room at Osterley Park, which the connoisseur Horace Walpole praised as 'worthy of Eve before the Fall'.

On the Perimeter: South-East

S outh-east of central London visitors can enjoy shrunken heads in the Horniman Museum, admire Rembrandts and Poussins in the chaste confines of the Dulwich Picture Gallery, or gaze in astonishment at the figures of prehistoric monsters at Crystal Palace and the latest anti-flood technology of the Thames Barrier.

Camberwell   SE5

⊖ VICTORIA, THEN
⇌ DENMARK HILL
ATLAS REF 186
Little open space is left in an area that gave its name to the Camberwell Beauty butterfly — first spotted here in 1748 — but the district is not without interest. From the north the long and rather tatty Camberwell Road leads to Camberwell Green. Nearby is **Camberwell Grove**, a

Charming gardens provide a civilised counterpoint to the strange and fascinating assemblage of exotic objects in the Horniman Museum.

pleasant avenue of late Georgian houses. Joseph Chamberlain was born at 188 Camberwell Grove and Robert Browning at 179 Southampton Way. **Camberwell Green** itself inspired Mendelssohn's *Spring Song* in 1842.

Good Victorian churches in the area include the parish church of **St Giles**, in Camberwell Church Street, designed by Sir George Gilbert Scott and completed in 1844. More extravagant are the 1890s buildings of the **Camberwell School of Arts and Crafts** in Peckham Road, with the **South London Art Gallery** next door — late Victorian verging on Art Nouveau. In Denmark Hill, to the south, are the buildings of King's College Hospital.

Horniman Museum

LONDON ROAD, SE23
⊖ CHARING CROSS, THEN
⇌ FOREST HILL
ATLAS REF 186
One of London's hidden treasures, this museum near Dulwich is worth a visit for two reasons. The first is to enjoy the building itself, with its tall clock tower. Designed by C Harrison Townsend, it was completed in 1901 and is one of London's few Art Nouveau structures of quality. The second is to inspect the contents, an eccentric and delightfully old-fashioned blending of ethnographical objects with natural history, plus a large collection of musical instruments. There are masks, shrunken heads, a stuffed walrus and stuffed birds. Some of the more exotic items were acquired by the museum's founder, the tea magnate Frederick Horniman MP, in the course of his travels. He originally opened his collection to the public in his own home in 1890. The gardens of the museum command a fine view of London.
Open Mon–Sat 10.30am– 6.00pm, Sun 2.00pm–6.00pm.

Dulwich Picture Gallery

COLLEGE ROAD, SE21
⊖ VICTORIA, THEN
⇌ WEST DULWICH
ATLAS REF 186
Another hidden treasure, this was Britain's first public art gallery, opened in 1814. The collection of paintings is truly remarkable and includes important works by Rembrandt, Canaletto, Tiepolo, Claude and Poussin, Van Dyck, Teniers, Watteau, Hogarth, Reynolds, Gainsborough and many others. The nucleus of the collection was assembled by the 17th-century actor Edward Alleyn, who founded Dulwich College nearby. Much later, in 1811, the college acquired pictures that had been assembled for a national gallery for Poland at the bequest of Sir Francis Bourgeois.

The paintings are housed in a curious building designed by the architect Sir John Soane. It is an exercise in Neoclassicism at its most formal, and least human. From the outside it looks like a giant tomb, covered in Soanian perspectival tricks. It is a tomb, indeed, since it contains the mausoleum of Sir Francis Bourgeois and his friends, Mr and Mrs Noel Desenfans. The interior, however, is also an excellent place for hanging pictures.
Open Tue–Fri 10.00am– 1.00pm and 2.00pm–5.00pm, Sat 11.00am–5.00pm, Sun 2.00pm–5.00pm.

Crystal Palace Park   SE19

⊖ VICTORIA, THEN
⇌ CRYSTAL PALACE
ATLAS REF 186
Sir Joseph Paxton's palace of iron and glass was moved to Sydenham after the Great Exhibition of 1851, and re-erected there to serve as an exhibition and concert hall. It filled this role until 1936, when it was totally destroyed by a catastrophic fire. What remains

today of this wonderful Victorian dream are some terraces of the formal grounds in which the Crystal Palace stood, some sculpture (including a giant head of Paxton himself), and a large public park with lakes and a children's zoo. The most exciting inhabitants of this suburban playground are the life-size models of prehistoric animals, installed here for educational purposes in 1854. Giant scaly heads rise from the waters and horned creatures peer engagingly out of bushes, while rising over them all is a giant iguanodon, in whose enormous belly 21 Victorian gentlemen once sat down to dinner. The **National Sports Centre** houses Britain's leading athletics stadium (see page 162).

Eltham Palace

COURT YARD, SE9
CHARING CROSS, THEN
ELTHAM
ATLAS REF 186
One of the earliest of London's royal palaces, Eltham was at the height of its career and magnificence during the 14th and 15th centuries. The last monarch to live in it was Henry VIII, but he later preferred Greenwich and Hampton Court. By the 17th century much of the palace was in ruins and it had become primarily a source of building materials. The **Great Hall**, completed in a typically grandoise regal style in 1480 with a massive hammerbeam roof and oriel windows, was fully restored in the 1930s. The Great Hall and the Lord Chancellor's Lodgings in the Outer Court are all that is left of the palace today.

The Thames Barrier

UNITY WAY, SE18
CHARING CROSS, THEN
WOOLWICH DOCKYARD
ATLAS REF 186
Designed to overcome the serious risk of flooding in the London area, the barrier on the Thames at Woolwich was completed in 1983. Looking rather like the Sydney Opera House in Australia, it has 10 moveable gates, four of which are wide enough to allow the passage of shipping. In normal conditions the gates lie on the bed of the river, but when flood threatens they can be raised hydraulically to stop the flow of the water until the danger has passed. The barrier has only been used a few times as yet, but its line of piers

straddling the river and the complexity of its engineering have made it a major tourist attraction. There is a visitor centre and exhibition hall, and tourists can make boat trips around the barrier.
Open Mon–Fri 10.30am–5.00pm, Sat and Sun 10.30am–5.30pm.

Royal Artillery Regimental Museum

RED LION LANE, SE18
CHARING CROSS, THEN
WOOLWICH ARSENAL
ATLAS REF 186
Woolwich has a distinguished naval and military history. It was a village on the Thames early in the 16th century when Henry VIII founded a dockyard here to build the *Great Harry*, the pride of his navy. The yard launched many a famous ship until it was closed in 1869. Meanwhile, the Royal Arsenal had been established at the eastern end of the town in the 18th century. The earliest regiments of artillery were organised at the arsenal, (which was closed in the 1960s), and the massive, late 18th-century blocks of the **Royal Artillery Barracks** can still be seen on Woolwich Common.

The Royal Military Academy also began here and its handsome building is now home to the **Royal Artillery Regimental Museum**. Guns are housed in the **Rotunda**, designed by the 18th-century architect John Nash, in Repository Lane.
Regimental Museum open Mon–Fri 12.30pm–4.30pm, Sat and Sun 2.00pm–4.00pm; Museum of Artillery, Repository Lane open Mon–Fri 12.00noon–5.00pm, Sat and Sun 1.00pm–5.00pm (4.30pm in winter).

North Woolwich Old Railway Station Museum

PIER ROAD, E16
LIVERPOOL STREET, THEN
NORTH WOOLWICH
ATLAS REF 186
On the north bank of the Thames, linked by the free ferry which has been running for over a century from Woolwich, is this collection of locomotives, artefacts and photographs, telling the story of the Great Eastern Railway. The emphasis is on the railway's role in the development of the East End.
Open Mon–Sat 10.00am–5.00pm.

The futuristic Thames Barrier is the largest object of its kind in the world. The stainless-steel hoods cover concrete piers, which contain the machinery that raises the giant submerged steel gates into position, to stem a threatened flood.

On the Perimeter: South-West

The Thames winds its way sweetly through the south-western sector of London's suburbs, whose pleasures range from the village green at Richmond and the open spaces of Richmond Park and Wimbledon Common, to the royal grandeur of Hampton Court.

Old Battersea House

VICARAGE CRESCENT, SW11
⊖ WATERLOO, THEN
⇌ CLAPHAM JUNCTION
ATLAS REF 185
Built in the 17th century in the formal Dutch style, the house is close to the river and to Battersea Old Church. Hemmed in by indifferent later buildings, it is rather like a lion surrounded by jackals. It was restored in the 1970s and now houses a remarkable collection of Victorian paintings and colourful, Islamic-inspired pottery by William de Morgan.
Open Wed, by appointment only.

Richmond Village and Park

⊖ RICHMOND
ATLAS REF 184
The spirit of the 18th century is strong in Richmond, which is one of the few areas of London that can still be called a village. At its heart is **Richmond Green**, the setting for summer cricket matches. Along one side is a terrace of early 18th-century cottages, known as **Maids of Honour Row**, and at the far western end are the remains of the medieval **royal palace**, built here in 1125 by Henry I and then known as the Palace of Sheen. Richmond's royal connections encouraged the town to flourish. In 1499 the Palace of Sheen was rebuilt by Henry VII after a fire, and renamed Richmond Palace. Henry died in the palace, as did Queen Elizabeth I in 1603. Charles I moved his court here to escape an outbreak of bubonic plague in 1634, but in the following years it fell into decay. Today only the Tudor gatehouse remains.

Richmond's streets, easily explored on foot, have a pleasantly cosmopolitan air. The town is at its most 18th-century by the river, where there are pleasant walks and boats for hire.

A short distance away, up Richmond Hill, is **Richmond Park**, 2,500 acres (1,012ha) of land enclosed by Charles I in the 17th century for hunting. Today it is the largest area of natural wood and heath near London. Lakes and ponds, Classical mansions and deer wandering freely may all be seen here.

Strawberry Hill

WALDEGRAVE ROAD, TWICKENHAM
⊖ WATERLOO, THEN
⇌ STRAWBERRY HILL
ATLAS REF 184
Strawberry Hill was built by Horace Walpole in 1749–76 as a 'Gothik' extravaganza, and the style Walpole developed has come to be known as 'Strawberry Hill Gothic'. The interior of the house was carved, moulded and painted in complex detail. Many of the fireplaces were modelled on medieval tombs in Westminster Abbey and Canterbury Cathedral. The building is now used as a teacher training college.
Open by appointment only, Jan–Jun, Oct–Dec, Wed and Sat pm.

Marble Hill House

RICHMOND ROAD, TWICKENHAM
⊖ RICHMOND, THEN BUS
ATLAS REF 184
This perfect example of the 18th-century country house in a natural setting was designed in 1728 by Roger Morris. Set in a park by the Thames, it was built for the Countess of Suffolk, a mistress of King George II. Here English Palladian architecture is at its most formal and delicate, an exercise in Classical harmony through Georgian eyes. The interior contains 18th-century paintings and furniture.
Open Eas–Sep daily, 10.00am–6.00pm; Oct–Eas 10.00am–4.00pm. Admission fee.

Deer enjoy the shade under the spreading trees of Richmond Park, which was originally a royal hunting ground. The deer have to be culled regularly, to keep their numbers within bounds, and the venison still finds its way to the tables of Very Important Persons.

Orleans House Gallery

RIVERSIDE, TWICKENHAM
⊖ RICHMOND, THEN BUS
ATLAS REF 184

All that remains of the house, sadly, is the **Octagon**, built by James Gibbs in 1720. (The house was demolished in 1926). The Octagon stands in pleasant woodland, and has a richly decorated interior. It is a rare example of Baroque exuberance, which did not greatly appeal to British taste. Attached to it is Orleans House Gallery, used for displaying paintings and watercolours of Twickenham and Richmond.

Open Tue–Sat 1.00pm–5.30pm, Sun 2.00pm–5.30pm (4.30pm in winter).

Ham House

HAM STREET, RICHMOND
⊖ RICHMOND
ATLAS REF 184

Originally a conventional Jacobean house of 1610, Ham House was extravagantly rebuilt in the 1670s by the Duke and Duchess of Lauderdale, who created a mansion and park of princely magnificence. The Lauderdales were great keepers of inventories and archives, and thanks to the information they preserved, the house has been restored to its splendour of 1678. It has a fine staircase, marble Dining Room with leather wall hangings, Mortlake tapestries and portraits by Sir Peter Lely. The formal gardens have also been reconstructed. The house is owned by the National Trust, and run by the V & A Museum.

Open Tue–Sun 11.00am–5.00pm. Admission fee for non-National Trust members.

Bushy Park

TEDDINGTON, MIDDLESEX
⊖ WATERLOO, THEN
≋ TEDDINGTON
ATLAS REF 184

Ten rows of chestnuts and limes, stretching across Bushy Park for over 1 mile (1.6km), are a magnificent memorial to Sir Christopher Wren, who laid out the Chestnut Avenue in the 17th century as part of his unfulfilled plan to give Hampton Court a new front. There are 274 chestnut trees, planted 42ft (67m) apart. The sight of the Chestnut Avenue in flower in May is one of the best in London, a perfect expression of the Classical ideal of nature and man in harmony.

Hampton Court Palace

EAST MOLESEY, SURREY
≋ HAMPTON COURT
ATLAS REF 184

Set by the Thames and reachable in summer by boat from Westminster Pier and from Kingston-upon-Thames, Hampton Court is the most sumptuous and the most varied of London's royal palaces. Cardinal Wolsey, its first owner, began building in 1514, and intended that it would surpass every house in the kingdom in splendour. Henry VIII confiscated it from him 15 years later and made it even bigger and grander. In the 17th century, part of it was rebuilt by Sir Christopher Wren for King William III.

The drive leads past an array of heraldic figures to the **Great Gateway** of mellow red brick. Beyond is a succession of courtyards. **Clock Court** is named after the remarkable astronomical clock built for Henry VIII in 1540. The **Great Hall**, built for the same monarch in the 1540s, has a stupendous hammerbeam roof. There are also cavernous Tudor kitchens. The **State Apartments** contain fine paintings by Brueghel, Holbein, Tintoretto and others, ceilings by Andrea Verrio, furniture and tapestries.

Outside is the noble park with the most famous **maze** in Britain, planted in William III's time, and beautiful gardens and walks. The old game of real tennis is still played in the royal court and the great vine which was planted by the landscape architect, Capability Brown, in 1768 still produces grapes. The **Orangery** has a notable collection of Mantegna paintings.

Open daily, 9.30am–5.30pm (4.30pm in winter).

Wimbledon Common and Windmill

WIMBLEDON, SW19
⊖ WIMBLEDON
ATLAS REF 185

After Richmond Park, this is the largest area of wild space in London accessible to the public. Acquired as a wasteland in 1871, the common was extensively planted with trees and it is now a natural environment whose diversity attracts many species of birds, butterflies, reptiles and fungi. All of them seem to survive happily alongside joggers, dog-walkers and exploring children. The old windmill is now a museum.

Windmill open Eas–Oct, Sat, Sun and Bank Holidays 2.00pm–5.00pm. Admission fee.

Formal flowerbeds and shapely urns grace the grounds of Hampton Court, with the warm red brick of the palace itself in the background. It was originally built by Cardinal Wolsey and was enlarged and made even more splendid by kings from Henry VIII onwards.

London's
River

To travel along the central stretch of
the River Thames, from
Battersea Reach downstream to
Tower Bridge, is to journey through
much of London's history,
as the boat ripples past palaces and
pubs, churches and power stations,
gardens and office blocks, under a
succession of brightly painted bridges.

London's River

The Houses of Parliament, seen from a riverboat on the Thames.

From Battersea Reach to Vauxhall Bridge

A view up Battersea Reach, to Chelsea Harbour tower and Lots Road power station.

Battersea Reach is the stretch of water leading to Battersea Bridge. On the right bank, Battersea was long noted for its market gardens and especially for delicious asparagus. **Battersea Old Church**, dedicated to St Mary, with its Classical portico and conical spire, dates from 1777, though there has been a church on this site since Saxon times. William Blake was married here in 1782. His bride, Catherine Boucher, was the daughter of one of Battersea's market gardeners. The 19th century artist J M W Turner liked to sketch the river from the church.

On the opposite side of the water, **Chelsea Harbour** is a 1980s development of flats and offices, with a yacht marina. Cremorne Road preserves the name of the Cremorne pleasure gardens, famous for dancing, concerts and daring balloon ascents. In 1861 a certain Madame Genevieve skipped lightly across the Thames here on a tightrope, but Victorian Puritanism disapproved of the pleasure grounds. They were seen as a nursery of immorality and were closed down in 1877.

Battersea Bridge was built in 1890, designed by the great Victorian engineer Sir Joseph Bazalgette. His bridge replaced an old wooden one of 1772, a slender construction strung with lamps, whose memory is romantically preserved in 19th-century paintings by Turner and Whistler. The wooden bridge had itself replaced a ferry across the river at this point.

There is a good view from the river of **Cheyne Walk**, on the left bank. This celebrated street was named after the family which owned the manor of Chelsea in the 17th and 18th centuries. Droves of famous people have lived here. Starting from the western end, No. 119 was the last home of Turner, who delighted to paint this stretch of water. He lived here under the name of Booth, in the hope of anonymity, and died here in 1851. Hilaire Belloc lived at No. 104 and Isambard Kingdom Brunel resided as a boy at No. 98. Whistler lived at No. 96 with his mother — the subject of his best-known painting. On Sunday mornings he used to walk with her along to **Chelsea Old Church** nearby, which was rebuilt after bomb damage in the Second World War (see page 77). The statue outside the church is of Sir Thomas More. His house and garden were here in the 16th century.

Further along Cheyne Walk, the **King's Head and Eight Bells** has stood on this site for 400 years and was rebuilt in the 18th century. At No. 16 the Pre-Raphaelite painter D G Rossetti and his friend, the poet Algernon Swinburne, lived a Bohemian life in the 19th century. They kept kangaroos, peacocks and a wombat in their garden. The statesman David Lloyd George lived at No. 10, and the Victorian novelist Mary Ann Evans (better known by her pseudonymn, George Eliot) died at No. 4.

The delightful pink-and-white **Albert Bridge** with its cat's cradle of iron girders is many people's favourite of all the London bridges. Dating from 1873, it has cars surging over it, but it is sufficiently fragile for troops to be ordered to break step before crossing it. Opposite the Chelsea end of the bridge is one of London's famous statues, David Wynne's spectacular *Boy with a Dolphin* (1975).

Royal Hospital Gardens

EMBANKMENT

Chelsea Physic Gdn

CHELSEA

King's Head and Eight Bells

Chelsea Old Church

Chelsea Reach

Peace Pagoda

PARK

ALBERT BRIDGE

BATTERSEA

WALK

BATTERSEA BRIDGE

CHEYNE

CREMORNE RD

Chelsea Harbour

Battersea Reach

Battersea Old Church

The next stretch of the river is Chelsea Reach. On the north bank the traffic roars along **Chelsea Embankment**, designed by Sir Joseph Bazalgette and opened in 1874. There are attractive iron lamps along the wall. It runs for about a mile (1.6km) to Chelsea Bridge, passing on the way the charming **Chelsea Physic Garden** (see page 77) and the extensive grounds of the **Royal Hospital** (see page 76). At low water the outfall of the Ranelagh Sewer can be seen in the embankment wall. This is where the Westbourne, one of London's 'lost' rivers, joins the Thames.

Stretching all along the opposite,

The Victorian fragility of Albert Bridge, a delicate cat's cradle of girders.

Almost immediately comes **Grosvenor Bridge**, with trains clattering overhead into Victoria station. The Grosvenor family, the Dukes of Westminster, own a substantial part of Pimlico. The bridge was first constructed in the 1850s and 1860s to bring steam trains of the London, Dover and Chatham Railway and the London, Brighton and South Coast Railway puffing into Victoria.

The southern bank is now

William IV pub is followed by another monument of the 1930s, **Dolphin Square**. Covering 7½ acres (3ha), with 1,250 flats and its own shops, garden and restaurant, it was the biggest block of flats erected in Europe in its time.

Opened in 1906 to replace an earlier structure, **Vauxhall Bridge** is engagingly adorned with allegorical statues of substantial proportions and austere demeanour. On the upstream side the figures represent Agriculture, equipped with a scythe; Architecture, holding a model of St Paul's Cathedral; Engineering and Pottery. On the other side are ranged Science, Fine Art, Local Government and Education.

Until 1859 Vauxhall Gardens were on the south bank here. They were the leafy scene of many 18th-century parties and sportive revels. The Battle of Waterloo was re-enacted here by 1,000 soldiers in 1827.

Westminster Pumping Station

Dolphin Square

King William IV

GROSVENOR ROAD

GROSVENOR ROAD

CHELSEA BRIDGE

Grosvenor Bridge

Battersea Power Station

NINE ELMS LANE

Covent Garden Flower Market

VAUXHALL BRIDGE

ALBERT EMBANKMENT

ROAD

southern bank are the trees and greenery of **Battersea Park** (see page 37), which was opened in 1853. The prominent pagoda was built by Buddhist monks in 1985.

Chelsea Bridge was built in 1934 to replace a bridge of 1858. On the north bank the eye is taken by the tall, Italianate tower of **Westminster Pumping Station**, constructed in 1875 as part of Sir Joseph Bazalgette's drainage schemes. On the other side of the river the striking **Marco Polo Building** of 1988 can be seen, with its broken pediment.

dominated by the vast bulk of **Battersea Power Station**, designed by Sir Giles Gilbert Scott and opened in 1937. The massive industrial temple with its four towering chimneys is one of the finest buildings of its period. Along the river beyond it is the **Nine Elms** district, with Battersea Dogs' Home — London's rescue centre for unwanted dogs — new Covent Garden Market and the grim, blank-faced Nine Elms Cold Store.

On the northern bank the **King**

A message of peace in Battersea Park.

From Millbank to Waterloo Bridge

The 'Mother of Parliaments' seen by night from the river, with Victoria Tower to the left and Big Ben at the opposite end.

Millbank was still a quiet riverside lane between Chelsea and Westminster in the 18th century. It developed from the 1820s on, when a singularly grim, silent and labyrinthine prison called Millbank Penitentiary was built here. It closed in 1890 and its site is now occupied by the dignified Classical portico of the **Tate Gallery**, with James Stirling's modern wing beside it, where only works of art are confined (see page 50). The hulking 387ft (118m) **Millbank Tower** of 1963 is totally out of proportion with its surroundings.

Opposite, on the right bank, is **Albert Embankment**, another creation of Sir Joseph Bazalgette, completed in 1870. The fire boats moored here belong to the London Fire Brigade headquarters.

Lambeth Bridge, with a pair of obelisks rising at each end, dates from 1932. The first bridge at this point was constructed in 1861. Earlier, a ferry carrying horses and carriages had operated here, sometimes hazardously. The boat carrying Oliver Cromwell's coach and horses sank in 1656, and previously in the century the weight of Archbishop Laud's belongings as they were moved across river to Lambeth Palace had proved too much for the ferry.

Beyond Lambeth Bridge are Church and State. Next to the bridge on the right bank rise the mellow walls of **Lambeth Palace**, the London home of the Archbishop of Canterbury (see page 121). Dominating the scene on the other bank is the splendid Victorian Gothic bulk of the **Houses of Parliament**, seen at its best from the river and designed by Sir Charles Barry to replace the previous building, which was destroyed by fire in 1834 (see page 46). The House of Commons was reduced to rubble by a bomb in 1941, but by 1945 it had been rebuilt under the supervision of Sir Giles Gilbert Scott. If a flag is flying on the great Victoria Tower, it means that Parliament is in session, and in fine weather Members of Parliament (MPs) may be seen taking tea on the riverside terrace. At the far end, nearest Westminster Bridge, is one of London's best-loved landmarks, **Big Ben**.

Opposite Big Ben, on the Lambeth bank, is the 19th-century front of **St Thomas's Hospital**, associated with Florence Nightingale and now home to a museum named in her honour (see page 121).

The seven-arched **Westminster Bridge** was designed by Thomas Page, with Sir Charles Barry as consultant, and opened in 1862. It replaced one of 1750, which was

only the second bridge built across the Thames in London (after London Bridge itself). City aldermen and the Thames watermen, who made their living rowing passengers across the river, always fiercely objected to the construction of new bridges. It was on the old Westminster Bridge that the author James Boswell made love enjoyably to a girl in 1763, with the Thames rolling mightily below, and here 40 years later Wordsworth saw the view which inspired his famous sonnet.

At the northern end of the bridge, on the downsteam side, is the well-loved 1850s statue of Queen Boudicca (Boadicea) and her daughters by Thomas Thornycroft. The sculptor was encouraged by the Prince Consort, who would have liked to have seen the group erected over the main entrance to Hyde Park. The two rearing horses were modelled on animals specially lent by the prince. The bridge's southern end is guarded by a splendid lion, made in Coade stone in Lambeth in 1837. Next to the lion, spreading along the right bank, is the imposing façade of **County Hall**, formerly the home of the Greater London Council.

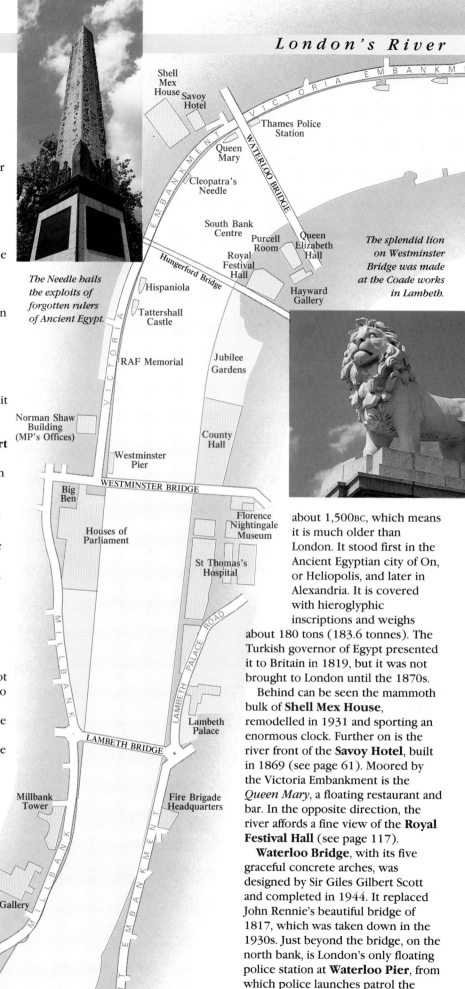

On the northern bank, **Westminster Pier** is the starting point of many river boat trips and excursions. Behind it, **Victoria Embankment** starts on its way to Blackfriars. A companion piece to Albert Embankment, it is yet another creation of Sir Joseph Bazalgette, completed in 1870. Here there are handsome iron lamps with coiled dolphins at the base. Beneath the embankment run a tube line and a huge sewer pipe. Its creation was the most ambitious engineering project carried out in London to that date.

Rising above the trees, close to Westminster Bridge, is the R Norman Shaw Building (formerly **New Scotland Yard**), built by the architect of that name in the 1880s, in Sherlock Holmes Baronial. It was famous as the headquarters of the Metropolitan Police until 1967, but it is now used by MPs. Further along are two more 1880s blocks, the exuberantly ornate **Whitehall Court** and the **National Liberal Club**, by Alfred Waterhouse. The great golden eagle atop the cenotaph on the Victoria Embankment crowns the **RAF Memorial** of 1923. Moored by the wall here are two ships, the *Tattershall Castle*, which started life on the River Clyde, and the *Hispaniola*, respectively a bar and a restaurant. Over on the southern bank, meanwhile, the **Jubilee Gardens** were laid out in 1977 as part of the celebrations of the Queen's 25th year on the throne.

Hungerford Bridge is central London's only combined rail and foot bridge, carrying trains from Waterloo East over the river to Charing Cross station. Completed in 1864, the same year that the station was opened, it replaced an earlier suspension bridge by Isambard Kingdom Brunel. In those days, before Sir Joseph Bazalgette's great schemes were completed, the stench from the sewage-filled river was so frightful that few people, it was said, ventured to use the footbridge. Nowadays it is crossed by many commuters in rush hours. On the north bank it leads to a striking new building, **Embankment Place**, designed by Terry Farrell and completed in 1990, with a soaring double arch above Charing Cross station.

The obelisk called **Cleopatra's Needle** on the left bank dates from

The Needle hails the exploits of forgotten rulers of Ancient Egypt.

The splendid lion on Westminster Bridge was made at the Coade works in Lambeth.

about 1,500BC, which means it is much older than London. It stood first in the Ancient Egyptian city of On, or Heliopolis, and later in Alexandria. It is covered with hieroglyphic inscriptions and weighs about 180 tons (183.6 tonnes). The Turkish governor of Egypt presented it to Britain in 1819, but it was not brought to London until the 1870s.

Behind can be seen the mammoth bulk of **Shell Mex House**, remodelled in 1931 and sporting an enormous clock. Further on is the river front of the **Savoy Hotel**, built in 1869 (see page 61). Moored by the Victoria Embankment is the *Queen Mary*, a floating restaurant and bar. In the opposite direction, the river affords a fine view of the **Royal Festival Hall** (see page 117).

Waterloo Bridge, with its five graceful concrete arches, was designed by Sir Giles Gilbert Scott and completed in 1944. It replaced John Rennie's beautiful bridge of 1817, which was taken down in the 1930s. Just beyond the bridge, on the north bank, is London's only floating police station at **Waterloo Pier**, from which police launches patrol the river. At this point the Thames makes a right-angled bend and turns more or less due east.

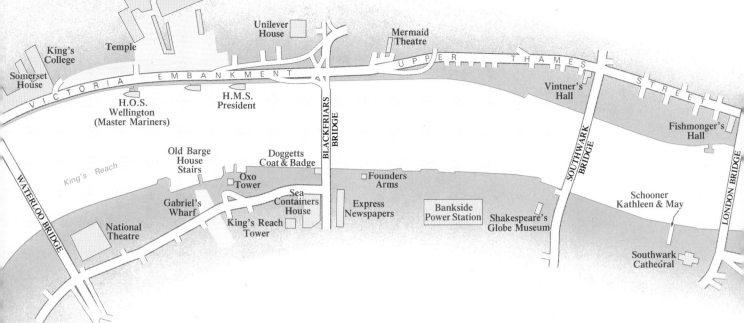

From Somerset House to Tower Bridge

Beyond Waterloo Bridge the dome of St Paul's and City office blocks greet the morning.

Beyond Waterloo Bridge, on the north bank of the river, is one of London's most impressive waterfront façades, the 800ft (244m) stately and beautiful 18th-century frontage of **Somerset House** (see page 100). It rose from the river bank originally on a line of huge arches with a terrace above. Looking across the other way, there is a stark contrast with the post-war concrete of the **Royal National Theatre** (see page 118) on the right bank.

This stretch of the river is known as **King's Reach**, in memory of King George V (1865–1936). The east wing of Somerset House is occupied by King's College, part of the University of London. Beside it, the **Temple** (see page 103) comes into view. The stairs and arch on the Victoria Embankment are at the point where the City of Westminster ends and the City of London begins. On the way towards Blackfriars there are

views of **St Paul's Cathedral** (see page 104) up on the northern side, with its great dome breasting the sky. Moored along here is the sloop HOS *Wellington*, the unique floating livery hall of the Honourable Company of Master Mariners. Further on, HMS *President* is the headquarters of the charity Inter-Action.

On the opposite bank are the **Old Barge House Stairs**, where Thames watermen once used to collect and land passengers. The playful 1920s **Oxo Tower** behind **Gabriel's Wharf** makes a sharp contrast to the post-war and attractively decorated **Sea Containers House**, with 380ft (115.9m) **King's Reach Tower** looming up behind it.

Just this side of Blackfriars Bridge, on the left bank, one of London's 'lost' rivers, the Fleet, joins the Thames on its underground journey from Hampstead Heath. At the northern end of Blackfriars Bridge is

Unilever House, an imposing edifice of 1931, with statues by Sir William Reid Dick and others. On the opposite bank, the modern pub is the **Doggetts Coat and Badge**, named in honour of the annual river race by Thames watermen.

Blackfriars Bridge itself is a handsome 1860s creation, savagely vilified in its own time as a piece of 'desperate imbecility', though it is impossible now to see what all the fuss was about. Immediately beyond the bridge, on the south side, is the modernistic **Express Newspapers Building**.

On the right bank is the solitary and ominous chimney of the disused **Bankside Power Station** of 1963, by Sir Giles Gilbert Scott. The Bankside area was once London's most raffish entertainment and red-light district. Today, Shakespeare's **Globe Theatre** is being reconstructed here (see page 125). The modern **Founders Arms** pub stands on the site of a foundry where the bells of St Paul's were cast.

On the left bank is the **Mermaid Theatre**, at Puddle Dock. Hiding behind a new development next to Southwark Bridge stands **Vintners' Hall**, the 17th-century livery hall of the Vintners' Company, which owns some of the Thames swans.

The unobtrusive **Southwark Bridge**, by Sir Ernest George, opened in 1921 and has never attracted much attention. Beyond it, another railway bridge crosses the river to the turreted entrance to Cannon Street station. This stretch of the Thames is the scene of the haunting opening of Dickens's *Our Mutual Friend*, where two figures in a boat are described searching for floating

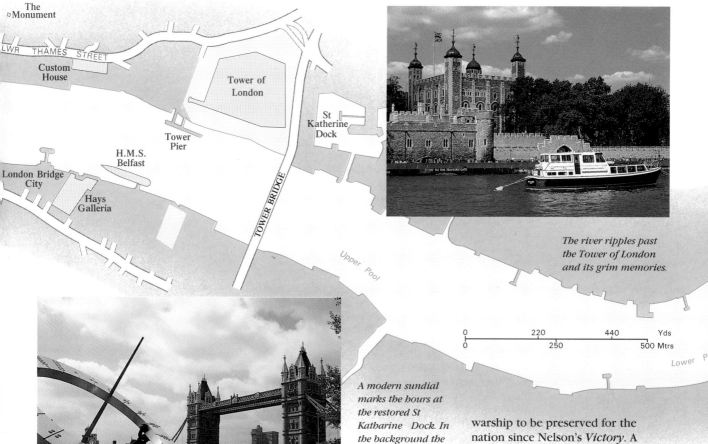

The Monument

LWR THAMES STREET

Custom House

Tower of London

Tower Pier

St Katharine Dock

H.M.S. Belfast

TOWER BRIDGE

London Bridge City

Hays Galleria

Upper Pool

Lower Pool

0   220   440   Yds
0   250   500 Mtrs

The river ripples past the Tower of London and its grim memories.

A modern sundial marks the hours at the restored St Katharine Dock. In the background the bastions of Tower Bridge deliberately echo the architecture of the Tower of London.

corpses to rob. The Classical building nestling against London Bridge on the left bank is **Fishmongers' Hall**, the headquarters of one of the major City livery companies. Built in the 1830s, it was restored after severe bomb damage in the Second World War. On the opposite bank are **St Mary Overie Dock**, with the *Kathleen & May* schooner (see page 125) and **Southwark Cathedral** (see page 124).

London Bridge opened in 1973 and is generally judged a disappointment. Its venerable predecessors stood a little way further down river. The last of them, built by John Rennie, was sold for £1 million in 1970 and taken, slab by slab, to Lake Havasu City in Arizona, USA. The Rennie bridge dated from the 1820s and replaced the most famous London Bridge of all, the one completed in 1209. This was the bridge which had houses and shops perched crazily along the road across it and a fortified gate at each end, on

top of which were displayed the grisly heads of traitors. This bridge had 19 narrow arches, which were difficult to pass.

Beyond London Bridge the **Pool of London** starts, the furthest stretch of the Thames inland to which ships of any size can navigate. Along the right bank rise the modern blocks of **London Bridge City** and the redeveloped **Hays Galleria** (see page 123). Close to the bridge, on the other side, is the tall pillar of the **Monument** (see page 109), topped by a flaming urn and commemorating the Great Fire of 1666. Further along is the façade of the **Custom House**, designed by Sir Robert Smirke in Classical style in the 1820s. Then comes **Tower Pier**, which is just before the **Tower of London** (see page 112), a great fortress which has stood on guard here for nine centuries. In the background loom modern City office blocks.

Moored at the south bank is **HMS Belfast** (see page 123), the first

warship to be preserved for the nation since Nelson's *Victory*. A powerful 11,500-ton (11,730-tonne) cruiser, launched in 1938, she saw service on Arctic convoys, in the sinking of the German *Scharnhorst* and in the Normandy landings, and later in the Korean War. She is kept in fighting trim.

Since it was formally opened in 1894 by the Prince of Wales (the future King Edward VII), **Tower Bridge** (see page 114) has become a symbol of London for many visitors. The architect was Sir Horace Jones and the engineer was Sir John Wolfe Barry. The bridge neatly reconciled two conflicting demands, for ships to move unhindered up and down river and for road traffic to get across it. The huge 1,000-ton (1,020-tonne) leaves of the drawbridge no longer rise ponderously to let ships through as often as of yore, but the vastly impressive hydraulic machinery is still there.

Beyond Tower Bridge on the left bank, **St Katharine Dock** has been attractively redeveloped (see page 115). By the waterside is another spectacular statue by David Wynne, *Girl with a Dolphin* (1973). Downstream lies the **Lower Pool of London**, where once the masts and rigging of ships were thickly clustered. Limehouse Reach leads to **Docklands** (see page 129) and **Greenwich** (see page 126). Beyond is the Thames Estuary and the tang of the open sea.

A London

Directory

*Whether your interests are
in the arts and entertainment,
eating out, shopping, sport,
or simply sightseeing, you will find
plenty in London to fill hours,
days or weeks. This directory lists
some of the best of London's
experiences to help you make the
most of your time in the capital.*

Directory

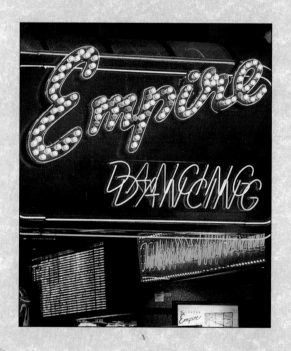

*London offers its visitors entertainment of
unrivalled variety and quality*

Out and About in London

London has an efficient, if sometimes overcrowded, transport system and is not a difficult place to get about in. The simplest and slowest, but also the most enlightening way to see the town is on foot. There is no real substitute for walking along London's streets and through its squares and alleys to see the city properly. Faster methods range from the underground (or 'tube') to buses, cars, taxis and boats. If you are brave enough or rich enough, you can even hire a bicycle or a helicopter.

London's famous red buses are used for sightseeing.

BUSES AND TUBES

To savour the taste of London life as experienced by Londoners themselves, it is essential to take at least one or two journeys by bus and tube; however, unless you enjoy discomfort, it is best to avoid morning and evening rush hours (from about 8.00am to 9.30am and from 4.30pm to 6.00pm), when Londoners are on their way to and from work. Buses and tubes run from about 6.00am to midnight. There are also some all-night bus services.

Excellent and inexpensive views of London's streets, buildings and people can be obtained from the red double-decker buses which are one of the city's trademarks. You are not likely to travel very quickly, but buses can help you to understand the city's layout. The bus network is ingenious and you can get from and to almost anywhere in London on a bus.

Travel by tube is usually quicker than by bus. Deep down underground, you will not see London, but you will see Londoners, in all their variety. You will also hear music of every kind, from jazz to classical, played by buskers in the echoing passages. Smoking is not allowed.

The London tube is one of the world's biggest electric underground railways, serving 273 stations. It is efficiently signposted and there are maps at all stations and platforms. The different lines are colour-coded for ease of identification.

TRAVELCARDS

It is worth enquiring at any tube station about these special tickets, which give you one or more days' unlimited travel by bus, tube and rail in any combination, for a reduced price. They are good value and save time and trouble paying for every separate stage of a journey.

SIGHTSEEING TOURS

London Transport runs good sightseeing tours of London in red double-decker buses with live commentaries. Open-topped buses are used on fine days. The tours include Piccadilly Circus, Trafalgar Square and Nelson's Column, Big Ben and Westminster Abbey, St Paul's, the Bank of England and the Tower of London. Trips take about 1½ hours and run daily at half-hourly intervals from 10.00am until dusk (from 9.00am between July and mid-September). Pick-up-points are at the Haymarket, the top of Park Lane, Baker Street tube and Victoria Street. There is also a special one-hour 'London by Night' bus tour, running every night from April through to mid-October, leaving Lancaster Gate at 9.00pm and Piccadilly Circus at 9.30pm.

London Transport also runs guided coach tours of London and others from London to historic places in the south of England. The starting point is Wilton Road coach station, near Victoria.

Numerous other bus and coach tours of London are run by private companies. Consult Tourist Information Centres for full details.

TAXIS

The old-fashioned London taxicabs or 'Hackney carriages' (originally from a French word for a horse) were once as characteristic of London as red buses. They have now been largely phased out and replaced by an uglier breed. Taxi drivers have to pass a formidable examination to prove they have 'the knowledge' — a profound and detailed grasp of the city's streets. You can hail a taxi in the street when its 'For Hire' sign is lit up, or from taxi ranks at mainline British Rail stations. It is customary to tip 10 to 15 per cent of the fare. There may be an extra charge for luggage, or if you are travelling after midnight.

GUIDED WALKS

Tourist Information Centres can provide a map of the 10 mile (16km) Silver Jubilee Walkway. This waymarked route starts in Leicester Square and passes many points of interest on its course through the City, the South Bank and Westminster, before finishing back in Leicester Square again. There are shorter heritage walks and a London Wall walk in the City; details are available from the City of London Tourist Infromation Centre outside St Paul's. There are pleasant walks too, along the towpaths of the Grand Union and Regent Canals.

Numerous guided walks set off every day to explore different areas and aspects of London. Themes include royal and aristocratic London, London's archaeology, and Dickensian London. There are pub walks and ghost walks, a walk in the shadow of Jack the Ripper, a walk in the footsteps of Sherlock Holmes, and many more. These are often very good value. Details are available from Tourist Information Centres.

CARS

Travelling in London by car is not really an option, unless you enjoy traffic jams. If you decide to use your car, you should find somewhere to park in one of the outer London suburbs without too much difficulty. From there, it is easy to travel by tube into the centre. Street parking in central London is extremely scarce. Multi-storey car parks are usually full by 9.00am on weekdays and can be very expensive.

BOATS

Boats travel all year round from Westminster Pier and Charing Cross Pier to the Tower, Greenwich and the Thames Barrier. In summer there are also boats to Kew, Richmond and Hampton Court from Westminster Pier. Circular sightseeing trips are available from Westminster Pier, where you can also go on evening disco and dinner-dance cruises. A high-speed catamaran service operates between Charing Cross Pier, the City and Greenwich. For information on times and services, contact the London Tourist Board (tel. 071-730 4812).

There are enjoyable canal trips available between Camden Lock, Regent's Park and Little Venice. They run from Easter to October, and there are also lunch and dinner cruises. Information is available from Regent's Canal Information Centre, 289 Camden High Street, NW1 (tel. 071-482 0523).

THE DOCKLANDS LIGHT RAILWAY

Opened in 1987, the Docklands Light Railway runs between the City and Docklands. The trains run above ground and there are striking views.

The Docklands Light Railway can be picked up from Stratford, Bow Road, Shadwell, Bank and Tower Hill underground stations. At Bow Road and Tower Hill the Docklands Light Railway stations (called 'Bow Church' and 'Tower Gateway') are a short walk away from the tube stations.

TOURIST INFORMATION CENTRES

Publications and advice are available from the following information centres:
Victoria Station Forecourt, SW1 (≋ ⊖ Victoria). Open daily, 8.00am–8.30pm (until 7.00pm on Mon–Fri and 5.00pm on Sun in winter).
Harrods, 87–135 Brompton Road, SW1 (⊖ Knightsbridge). Open during shop hours.
Selfridges, 400 Oxford Street, W1 (⊖ Bond Street). Open during shop hours.
Tower of London, West Gate, EC3 (⊖ Tower Hill). Open Eas–Nov, Mon–Sat 9.30am– 6.00pm, Sun

10.00am–6.00pm.
Liverpool Street Station, EC2 (≋ ⊖ Liverpool Street). Open Mon–Fri 9.30am–6.30pm, Sat 8.30am–6.30pm, Sun 8.30am–3.30pm
Heathrow Airport Underground Station Concourse (Terminals 1, 2 and 3, ⊖ Heathrow Central). Open daily, 8.00am–6.30pm.

For information from **London Tourist Information Centres,** tel. 071–730 3488 (Mon–Fri 9.00am–6.00pm only; a queuing system is in operation).

Publications and further information are available from **The British Travel Centre,** 12 Regent Street, SW1 (⊖ Piccadilly Circus). Open Mon–Fri 9.00am–6.30pm, Sat and Sun 10.00am–4.00pm (tel. 071·730 3400).

LONDON TRANSPORT CENTRES

Tickets, guidebooks, free maps and details of what's on are available from: Piccadilly Circus, Victoria, Oxford Circus, Euston, King's Cross, Liverpool Street and St James's Park stations.

Three specialist weekly magazines — *Time Out, What's On* and *City Limits* — provide detailed listings of shows, films, events, walks and amusements of all kinds. For general

information about London transport, tel. 071·222 1234 day or night.

HEATHROW, GATWICK AND LONDON CITY AIRPORT

There are frequent and rapid connections from Heathrow Airport to central London by A1 airbus (to Victoria) and A2 airbus (to Euston and Russell Square); and by underground (Piccadilly Line). From Gatwick Airport the 'Gatwick Express' service runs every 15 minutes to Victoria station.

From London City Airport in Silvertown a bus shuttle operates to London City Airport Pier. From here there is a regular high-speed Riverbus service on weekdays, calling direct at either Chelsea Harbour, Charing Cross Pier, Festival Pier, Swan Lane Pier, London Bridge City Pier, West India/Canary Wharf Pier and Greenwich Pier. Alternatively, take the Docklands Light Railway from Silvertown and City Airport station to connect with Central London tube services at Stratford or West Ham.

MAINLINE STATIONS

London is the hub of Britain's railway system and the

principal passenger stations connect the city with the rest of the country. Take trains from the following British Rail mainline stations to the following destinations:
West Country: Paddington, Waterloo
Southern England: Paddington, Victoria, Waterloo
South-east England: Charing Cross, London Bridge, Waterloo, Waterloo East and Victoria
South Wales: Paddington
West Midlands, North-west England and western Scotland: Euston
North Wales: Euston
North-east England and eastern Scotland: King's Cross
East Midlands: St Pancras
Norfolk, Suffolk and Essex: Liverpool Street

BRITISH RAIL INFORMATION

For departures from Charing Cross, Waterloo, Waterloo East, Liverpool Street, London Bridge and Victoria tel. 071–928 5100.
For departures from Euston and St Pancras tel. 071–387 7070.
For departures from Paddington tel. 071–262 6767.
For departures from King's Cross tel. 071–278 2477.

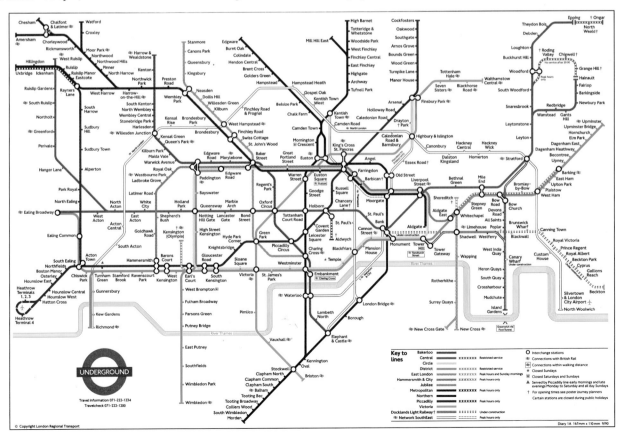

London's Markets

· · · · · · · · · · · · · · · · · · · ·

Adding colour, humour, enterprise and lively cut-and-thrust to the London scene, street markets and street vendors are vigorous survivors of the London's long tradition of open-air trading, which in the old days reached its peak in August every year at Bartholomew Fair. This great three-day cloth fair, held in Smithfield outside St Bartholomew's Priory, attracted stalls and entertainers of every description — from jugglers and acrobats to wrestlers and tightrope performers. The fair was suppressed in 1855, but its spiritual descendants still flourish in the form of markets here and there, selling everything from fresh fruit and vegetables to clothes, antiques, novelties and junk. The following are some of the most enjoyable.

STREET MARKETS

BERWICK STREET, W1
⊖ OXFORD CIRCUS
Nowadays this cramped, lively Soho market deals mainly in fresh produce. The market started 200 years ago or more, when local tradesmen and craftsmen began putting their goods out on the street, but it was not given official status until 1892. Berwick Street Market occupies the single block between Broadwick Street, where William Blake was born in 1758, and Peter Street, where saltpetre was once made for gunpowder. There has been a pub on the site of the Blue Posts since at least the 1730s.
Open Mon–Sat 9.00am–5.00pm.

BRICK LANE, E1
⊖ LIVERPOOL STREET
A market in the Spitalfields area for produce, clothes, jewellery, hardware and oddments. The street gets its name from the fact that bricks and tiles were made here in the 16th century.
Open Sun 8.00am–1.00pm.

BRIXTON MARKET,
ELECTRIC AVENUE, SW9
⊖ BRIXTON
One of London's most colourful street markets, Brixton caters to the local West Indian population among others, and you can buy ackee and goat fish, as well as clothes, costume jewellery and domestic items to the beat of Caribbean music. Electric Avenue, dating from 1888, was one of the first electrically lit shopping streets in London.
Open Thu–Tue 9.00am–5.30pm, Wed 9.00am–1.00pm.

CAMDEN LOCK, CAMDEN
LOCK PLACE, NW1
⊖ CAMDEN TOWN
Books, records and antiques, as well as snacks and bric-à-brac are available from this entertaining market which is popular with young people. It stretches for a mile (1.6km), but the main market area is by Regent's Canal.
Open Sat and Sun 9.00am–6.00pm.

CAMDEN PASSAGE,
OFF UPPER STREET, N1
⊖ ANGEL
Antique shops have occupied this picturesque alley since the 1960s and on market days stalls are set up here.
Open Wed 6.45am–4.00pm and Sat 8.00am–5.00pm (antiques); Thu 7.00am–4.00pm (books, prints and drawings).

COLUMBIA ROAD, E2
⊖ OLD STREET
A major flower and plant market, with an excellent choice of houseplants. The original market here was founded by Baroness Burdett-Coutts, the Victorian social reformer.
Open Sun 7.00am–2.00pm.

All the way from treasures to tat in Portobello Road.

EAST STREET, SE17
⊖ ELEPHANT & CASTLE
In the Old Kent Road area, this is one of the biggest street markets in London and some stalls have been handed down in the same family for 100 years or more. Produce, clothes, shoes and toys, household goods, plants, oddments and just about everything can be bought here.
Open Tue–Fri 7.00am–5.00pm, Sat 7.00am–6.30pm, Sun 8.00am–2.00pm.

GABRIEL'S WHARF,
56 UPPER GROUND, SE1
⊖ WATERLOO
⊖ TEMPLE
A recently established open-air market with craft workshops and street entertainers, Gabriel's Wharf is on the South Bank near the Royal National Theatre. It is part of the Coin Street redevelopment project, which began in the late 1980s.
Open Fri–Sun 10.30am–4.00pm.

JUBILEE MARKET HALL,
THE PIAZZA, COVENT GARDEN, WC2
⊖ COVENT GARDEN
⊖ LEICESTER SQUARE
Established when the main market moved away across the river, the Jubilee Market Hall's stalls sell crafted goods, clothes, jewellery, records, and assorted antiques. (See also page 62).
Open Mon 6.00am–5.00pm (antiques), Tue–Fri 9.00am–5.00pm (general goods), Sat and Sun 9.00am–5.00pm (crafts).

LEADENHALL MARKET,
GRACECHURCH STREET, EC3
⊖ BANK
⊖ MONUMENT
In a handsome building of 1881 by Sir Horace Jones, Leadenhall Market is close to the heart of what was once Roman London. A market has thrived on this site since the Middle Ages. Today it deals principally in meat, game, fish, vegetables and plants. Samuel Pepys recorded in his diary that he bought a leg of beef for 6d (about 2½p) here in 1663. The market has a pleasant atmosphere. Its pubs and cafés are thronged with City workers.
Open Mon–Fri 9.00am–5.00pm.

LEATHER LANE,
OFF HOLBORN, EC1
✪ CHANCERY LANE
Always crowded with office
workers at lunchtime and
alive with repartee, this
market is of crockery and
household goods, hardware,
clothes, groceries, fruit and
vegetables. In the 19th
century Leather Lane was a
slum area, described as being
infested with thieves, beggars
and organ-grinders.
*Open Mon–Fri 10.00am–
2.30pm.*

**NEW CALEDONIAN
MARKET,** BERMONDSEY
SQUARE, SE1
✪ LONDON BRIDGE
An enormous selection of
antiques is on view at this
market, which begins very
early between 5.00am and
7.00am on Fridays. Although
primarily for dealers, casual
browsers are also welcome.
There are curios of all
descriptions on the stalls, and
plenty of colourful local
characters.
Open Fri 5.00am–2.00pm.

NORTH END ROAD, SW6
✪ FULHAM BROADWAY
This lively market for
produce, plants, domestic
items, clothes and other goods
runs all the way from Lillie
Road down towards Fulham
Broadway.
*Open Mon–Sat 8.00am–
6.00pm.*

PETTICOAT LANE,
MIDDLESEX STREET, E1
✪ ALDGATE
The best-known of all
London's street markets,
Petticoat Lane is famed for its
Cockney atmosphere and is a
magnet to tourists. It takes its
name from its long history of
selling second-hand clothes,
which it has been famed for
since the mid-18th century.
Today, stalls sell all sorts of
domestic items as well. There
is also a daily fruit and
vegetable market in
Wentworth Street nearby.
*Open Sun only, 7.00am–
2.00pm.*

PICCADILLY MARKET,
ST JAMES'S CHURCH,
PICCADILLY, W1
✪ PICCADILLY CIRCUS
In the forecourt of the church
and popular with tourists, the
market sells antiques, craft
objects and bric-à-brac.
*Open Fri and Sat 9.30am–
6.00pm.*

PORTOBELLO ROAD, W11
✪ NOTTING HILL GATE
✪ LADBROKE GROVE
Though not officially
designated for street trading
until the 1920s, Portobello
Road's street market was
flourishing for 50 years before
that. In the 1950s the stalls
here on Saturdays became the
best-known antiques market
in London with everything
from antiques to tat.
*Open Sat 7.00am–5.00pm
(antiques), Mon–Wed and Fri
8.00am–6.00pm (general),
Thu 8.00am–1.00pm (general).*

SHEPHERD'S BUSH, W12
✪ SHEPHERD'S BUSH
Off Goldhawk Road are lively
stalls offering fruit and
vegetables, household items
and oddments, with a strong
West Indian flavour. This area
was still a country village in
the 1830s and there were
farms nearby until late in the
19th century. The triangular
common was once called
Gabblegoose Green.
*Open Mon–Sat 9.00am–
5.00pm.*

STRUTTON GROUND, SW1
✪ ST JAMES'S PARK
✪ VICTORIA
Off Victoria Street, this is the
only produce market in the
area, catering mainly to office
workers at lunchtime.
*Open Mon–Fri 11.30am–
3.00pm.*

WHOLESALE
MARKETS

These markets deal in bulk
and do not cater primarily for
the ordinary visitor. They are
also tending to move away
from the centre of London.
The most famous of them, the
Covent Garden fruit,
vegetable and flower market
with its *My Fair Lady*
associations, departed south of
the Thames to Nine Elms in
1974. The historic
Billingsgate fish market, once
in Lower Thames Street not
far from the Tower of London,
has been on the Isle of Dogs in
Docklands since 1982 (see
page 129). The future of
Smithfield meat market, West
Smithfield, EC1 is uncertain.
The old **Borough** fruit and
vegetable market in Stoney
Street, SE1 is still noisily alive
early on weekday mornings
under the railway arches
leading into London Bridge
station.

'STRAWBERRY RIPE' — STREET SELLERS AND STREET CRIES

food that was on offer, but
everything from pets to
clothes, from firewood and
rat poison to matches and
flowers. All had their own
cries: 'buy a fine singing
bird', 'oh rare shoes', 'small
coal', 'knives and scissors to
grind'. The muffin man
walked the streets with a
tray of muffins on his head,
ringing a handbell. Ballad
singers sang their wares at
the tops of their voices.

Until the 1850s street
vendors supplied London's
shopping requirements more
than markets or shops.
There were about 30,000
costermongers selling fruit,
vegetables and fish from
donkey carts and barrows in
the London of 1851. Right
down to the end of the
century, street criers
covering 10 miles (16km)
or so a day were a familiar
sight in the capital. The
costermongers were the
aristocracy of the street.
They chose 'kings' to keep
order and settle disputes in
different areas — the fore-
runners of today's Pearly
Kings and Queens, who
raise money for charity in
their colourful costumes
sewn with cascades of pearl
buttons.

Street traders announced
their presence and adver-
tised their wares with noisy
cries which, along with the
shouts of beggars and street
entertainers, set up a
hubbub of sound which
astonished and sometimes
alarmed country visitors. A
monk who went to London
in the 15th century wrote of
street sellers bawling
'strawberry ripe', 'hot
sheep's feet', 'mackerel' and
'ribs of beef'. It was not only

Some cries became so
formalised that they were
incomprehensible except to
those in the know.

The Industrial Revolution
swept most of this away
with a tide of factory
products, but in London
today you can still find the
chestnut-seller with his
glowing brazier, hear the
strangled cry of the rag-and-
bone man and the patter of
the salesman on street
corners, with his trays of
toys or ties.

Shopping in London

London boasts one of the world's richest and most varied collections of shops, selling goods of every type, quality and price. The smartest, best-known shops are concentrated in the West End. Major shopping streets and areas are Bond Street, St James's Street, Piccadilly, Jermyn Street, Regent Street, Oxford Street, Covent Garden, Brompton Road and Kensington High Street. Some streets have attracted shops of the same sort: Charing Cross Road is known for bookshops, Bond Street for picture dealers, jewellers and high fashion shops, Tottenham Court Road for electrical goods and furniture stores and Kensington High Street for its starry cluster of antique shops.

The following is a browsing selection of well-known and particularly intriguing shops. Normal opening hours are between 9.00am and 5.30pm, Monday to Saturday.

At Burlington Arcade.

FAMOUS NAMES

ASPREY, 165 NEW BOND STREET, W1
⊖ BOND STREET
⊖ GREEN PARK
The tops in goldsmiths' and silversmiths' work, with fabulous objects at fabulous prices. The Asprey family, of Huguenot descent, moved to Bond Street in the 1830s and have been royal jewellers since Queen Victoria's time.

BERRY BROS & RUDD,
3 ST JAMES'S STREET, SW1
⊖ GREEN PARK
London's grandest wine merchant, in premises little changed since 1699. The shop has an atmosphere of immemorial dignity.

BURBERRYS,
18 HAYMARKET, W1
⊖ PICCADILLY CIRCUS
The honoured name in raincoats was founded in 1901 by Thomas Burberry, who prospered on the demand for weatherproof clothing in the early days of motoring. (There is another branch at 165 Regent Street.)

BURLINGTON ARCADE,
OFF PICCADILLY, W1
⊖ GREEN PARK
⊖ PICCADILLY CIRCUS
Running, singing, whistling and opening an umbrella are against the rules of this august arcade. It consists of a row of small, smart shops next door to the Royal Academy. First constructed in 1819, the arcade has been rebuilt several times. (See page 67.)

FORTNUM & MASON,
181 PICCADILLY, W1
⊖ PICCADILLY CIRCUS
On the hour, Mr Fortnum and Mr Mason bow to each other on the clock above the main entrance of London's top grocer's. The shop was founded in 1707 by Hugh Mason, a grocer, and William Fortnum, a footman to Queen Anne. The shop specialised in exotic foods and the two partners began by importing saffron and gable worm seed from the Orient. The shop later sent provisions to officers of the Duke of Wellington's army in the Peninsular War and in the palmy days of Empire it established a reputation for supplying exiles in the remotest corners of the globe with rations of Oxford marmalade and gentleman's relish. Its hampers are still famous. (See page 68.)

GARRARD & CO.,
112 REGENT STREET, W1
⊖ OXFORD CIRCUS
⊖ PICCADILLY CIRCUS
Makers of crowns to the world's monarchs, Garrard & Co. are suppliers of jewellery, porcelain and other exquisite items to the rest of us. The firm's history goes back to 1735. Garrard's made the Imperial State Crown for the coronation of George V in 1911.

GIEVES & HAWKES,
1 SAVILE ROW, W1
⊖ PICCADILLY CIRCUS
Renowned for quality in the street which is the holy of holies of men's tailoring, Gieves & Hawkes was founded by two 18th-century naval and military outfitters: one dressed Nelson, and the other Wellington. They joined forces to clothe civilians as well.

HAMLEY'S, 188 REGENT STREET, W1
⊖ OXFORD CIRCUS
A five-storey paradise for children, Hamley's claims to be the world's biggest toyshop, with dolls, games and other playthings for all ages. William Hamley opened the first shop, called Noah's Ark Toy Emporium, in High Holborn in 1760.

HATCHARDS,
187 PICCADILLY, W1
⊖ GREEN PARK
⊖ PICCADILLY CIRCUS
This fashionable Regency bookseller is still one of the most engaging shops in London. John Hatchard founded the business in 1797; distinguished past customers have included Lord Byron,

For the shooting set at the Mayfair gunmakers, Purdey's.

Thomas Macaulay and William Makepeace Thackeray, Oscar Wilde and G K Chesterton.

JOHN LOBB, 9 ST JAMES'S STREET, SW1
⊖ GREEN PARK
Royal bootmakers, who have traded here for 150 years.

JOHN LOCK & CO,
6 ST JAMES'S STREET, SW1
⊖ GREEN PARK
These are the hatters who first developed the bowler hat, originally designed for wear by gamekeepers contending with poachers. James Lock succeeded his father-in-law in the business in 1759. Lock's made the plumed hat worn by the Duke of Wellington at the Battle of Waterloo in 1815.

MARKS & SPENCER,
458 OXFORD STREET, W1
⊖ MARBLE ARCH
Extremely popular with tourists, 'M & S' has many other London branches, but this is the biggest, opened in 1930. Michael Marks, an immigrant from Poland, started a penny arcade in Leeds in 1884 and it all grew from there.

PAXTON & WHITFIELD,
93 JERMYN STREET, SW1
⊖ GREEN PARK
⊖ PICCADILLY CIRCUS
London's classiest cheese shop has been in business since the 18th century. It sells more than 250 varieties today.

JAMES PURDEY & SONS,
57 SOUTH AUDLEY STREET, W1
⊖ MARBLE ARCH
Specialists in sporting guns, founded by James Purdey in 1814.

SPINK & SON, 5 KING STREET, ST JAMES'S, SW1
⊖ PICCADILLY CIRCUS
The doyen of London's coin dealers. Founded in the 1660s by John Spink and his cousin, Elwes Spink, today it deals in medals and rare banknotes as well as silver, jewellery and art.

TRUEFITT AND HILL, 23 OLD BOND STREET, W1
⊖ GREEN PARK
These awesomely prestigious barbers were wigmakers to King George IV in the 1820s. Francis Truefitt first set up in business in Bond Street in 1805.

TURNBULL & ASSER, 71-2 JERMYN STREET, SW1
⊖ PICCADILLY CIRCUS
The smartest of smart shirtmakers, founded in 1885.

ART DEALERS AND AUCTION HOUSES

BOND STREET, W1
⊖ BOND STREET
The Bond Street area bristles with classy art dealers. Both Old and New Bond Street are a delight to explore, even if you can't afford the merchandise. **Arthur Ackermann & Son**, at 33 New Bond Street, have been London's leading dealers in sporting art for more than two centuries, while **Agnew's** at 43 Old Bond Street are old-established, prestigious picture dealers. Other famous names are **P & D Colnaghi & Co.**, at 14 Old Bond Street, established in 1760, the **Fine Art Society** at 148 New Bond Street, established in 1876, and **Wildenstein** at 147 New Bond Street (the house in which Lord Nelson lived).

CHRISTIE'S, 8 KING STREET, ST JAMES'S, SW1
⊖ PICCADILLY CIRCUS
An internationally famous auction house, holding sales on most days of the week. Thousands of pounds change hands on the nod here. Christie's was established in 1766 by James Christie, who auctioned everything from chamber pots up; he became a close friend of Sir Joshua Reynolds and other members of the art establishment of the day. The Christie family remained active in the firm until 1889.

SOTHEBY'S, 34 NEW BOND STREET, W1
⊖ BOND STREET
London's other heavyweight international auction house

was founded in 1744, originally as a book auctioneer. The Sotheby family were connected with the firm from 1776 to 1861.

SPECIALITIES . . .

R ALLEN & CO., 117 MOUNT STREET, W1
⊖ MARBLE ARCH
These old-fashioned Mayfair butchers have been here for 200 years.

THE BACK SHOP, 24 NEW CAVENDISH STREET, W1
⊖ BOND STREET
Everything for martyrs to back pain.

BETJEMAN & BARTON, 43 ELIZABETH STREET, SW1
⊖ SLOANE SQUARE
⊖ VICTORIA
Specialists in fine teas.

BILL LEWINGTON, 144 SHAFTESBURY AVENUE, W1
⊖ LEICESTER SQUARE
Brass and wind instruments, even bagpipes.

BUTTON QUEEN, 19 MARYLEBONE LANE, W1
⊖ BOND STREET
Buttons of all kinds, ancient and modern.

CHARBONNEL ET WALKER, 28 OLD BOND STREET, W1
⊖ GREEN PARK
Mme Charbonnel set up here in the 1870s, at the request of the Prince of Wales (later King Edward VII). It has been the most aristocratic place to buy chocolates in London ever since.

ELLS AND FARRIER, 20 PRINCES STREET, W1
⊖ OXFORD CIRCUS
Beads and sequins.

J FLORIS, 89 JERMYN STREET, SW1
⊖ PICCADILLY CIRCUS
Perfumes and scented products.

STANLEY GIBBONS, 399 STRAND, WC2
⊖ CHARING CROSS
The world's largest stamp dealers.

THOMAS GOODE, 19 SOUTH AUDLEY STREET, W1
⊖ BOND STREET
Glass and crystal.

HOPE AND GLORY, 131A KENSINGTON CHURCH STREET, W8
⊖ NOTTING HILL GATE
Commemorative china.

INDERWICK & CO., 45 CARNABY STREET, W1
⊖ OXFORD CIRCUS
Vendors of pipes since 1797.

BY ROYAL APPOINTMENT

Some shops are entitled to display a royal coat-of-arms because they hold a warrant of appointment as suppliers to the Queen or certain other members of the royal family. The system goes far back into the Middle Ages. William Caxton, who established the first printing press in England, was appointed printer to the King in 1476. A list of tradesmen who supplied the Palace in 1684 included a hatter, a locksmith and a maker of golf clubs. Purveyors of bacon, beer, poultry, fish, butcher's meat and oysters to William III and Queen Mary were listed in 1700. Lists from the 18th century include a royal mole-taker and a rat-catcher, and in 1775 there was a furious row over who should be acknowledged as the royal bedbug operative.

Things were getting out of hand and in 1782 the whole matter was put in charge of the Lord Chamberlain of the Household, in whose department it remains.

The number of warrants increased substantially in Queen Victoria's day. Among other household names, she patronised Fry's for chocolate, Twinings for tea and Wall's for pork. The list changes from time to time, but it includes many of the shops listed in this section. Among them are: Asprey; Berry Bros & Rudd; Burberrys; Garrard & Co.; Gieves & Hawkes; Hamley's; Hatchards; John Lobb; John Lock & Co.; Paxton & Whitfield; James Purdey & Sons; Spink & Son; Turnbull & Asser; Charbonnel et Walker; J Floris; Stanley Gibbons; and Ede & Ravenscroft.

KEITH JOHNSON & PELLING, 11 GREAT MARLBOROUGH STREET, W1
⊖ OXFORD CIRCUS
Cameras and photographic equipment.

LILLYWHITES, 24-36 LOWER REGENT STREET, SW1
⊖ PICCADILLY CIRCUS
Sports gear.

JANET REGER, 2 BEAUCHAMP PLACE, SW3
⊖ KNIGHTSBRIDGE
Lingerie.

JAMES SMITH & SONS, 53 NEW OXFORD STREET, WC1
⊖ TOTTENHAM COURT ROAD
Umbrellas, walking sticks and swordsticks.

THROUGH THE LOOKING-GLASS, 563 KING'S ROAD, SW6
⊖ FULHAM BROADWAY
Antique mirrors.

TRADITION, 2 SHEPHERD STREET, W1
⊖ GREEN PARK
⊖ HYDE PARK CORNER
Model soldiers.

THE WHITE HOUSE, 51 NEW BOND STREET, W1
⊖ GREEN PARK
Fine linen.

CHRISTOPHER WRAY LIGHTING EMPORIUM, 591 AND 600 KING'S ROAD, SW6
⊖ FULHAM BROADWAY
Lights and lamps.

. . . AND CURIOSITIES

ALAN ALAN'S MAGIC SHOP, 88 SOUTHAMPTON ROW, WC1
⊖ HOLBORN
Jokes and horrors.

AND SO TO BED, 638 KING'S ROAD, SW6
⊖ FULHAM BROADWAY
Antique and brass beds.

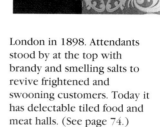

ANYTHING LEFT-HANDED,
65 BEAK STREET, W1
⊖ OXFORD CIRCUS
⊖ PICCADILLY CIRCUS
Just what it says, this shop
sells everything for
left-handed people.

BERMANS & NATHANS,
18 IRVING STREET, WC2
⊖ LEICESTER SQUARE
Fancy dress and theatre
costumes are available here
for hire.

**CAMDEN LOCK BALLOON
CO.,** 31 CAMDEN LOCK, NW1
⊖ CAMDEN TOWN
Balloons and balloon
sculptures.

THE CANDLE SHOP,
30 THE MARKET,
COVENT GARDEN, WC2
⊖ COVENT GARDEN
Novelty candles.

**DAVENPORTS MAGIC
SHOP,** UNDERGROUND
CONCOURSE, CHARING
CROSS, WC2
⊖ CHARING CROSS
The place in London for
conjurer's equipment.

BARRY DEW,
20 CHAPEL MARKET, N1
⊖ ANGEL
London's only specialist banjo
shop.

EATON SHELL SHOP,
30 NEAL STREET, WC2
⊖ COVENT GARDEN
Not at the seashore, but they
sell seashells.

EDE & RAVENSCROFT,
93 CHANCERY LANE, WC2
⊖ CHANCERY LANE
Robes and wigs for judges,
barristers and academics.

GET STUFFED,
105 ESSEX ROAD, N1
⊖ HIGHBURY & ISLINGTON
Stuffed animals are sold at this,
one of Britain's few taxidermy
shops.

KNUTZ, 1 RUSSELL STREET,
WC2
⊖ COVENT GARDEN
Crudities and ruderies to suit
all tastes.

PETAPHERNALIA,
31A HIGHGATE HIGH
STREET, N6
⊖ HIGHGATE
Specialists in cages and pet
equipment.

THEATRE ZOO,
21 EARLHAM STREET, WC2
⊖ COVENT GARDEN
Animal masks and costumes.

DEPARTMENT STORES

ARMY AND NAVY STORES,
105 VICTORIA STREET, SW1
⊖ ST JAMES'S PARK
⊖ VICTORIA
Completely rebuilt in 1977,
the Army and Navy started
100 years before as a
co-operative supplying
provisions at a discount to
members of the armed forces.
It soon developed its own
factories, and today it boasts a
good food and wine hall.

BARKERS, 63 KENSINGTON
HIGH STREET, W8
⊖ HIGH STREET
KENSINGTON
Barkers occupies a striking
1930s building by Bernard
George, with Art Deco
ornament. The same architect
was responsible for the
attractive building next door,
formerly occupied by Derry &
Toms, which has an unusual
roof garden.

DEBENHAMS,
334 OXFORD STREET, W1
⊖ OXFORD CIRCUS
Earlier Debenham and
Freebody, of Wigmore Street,
Debenhams began in the 18th
century as a small draper's
shop in Marylebone. William
Debenham became a partner
and his daughter married
Clement Freebody. The
business gradually grew and
acquired others. At one time it
rejoiced in the telephone
number 'Mayfair One'. Today
it is best known for smart
women's clothes.

DICKINS AND JONES, 224
REGENT STREET, W1
⊖ OXFORD CIRCUS
Now in a 1920s building,
Dickins and Jones originally
opened at 54 Oxford Street, at
the sign of the Golden Lion, in
1790. John Pritchard Jones
joined the Dickins family as a
partner 100 years later. When
Queen Victoria died in 1901,
the store dyed all its
impending white sale stock
black overnight and made a
killing selling mourning.

HARRODS,
87-135 BROMPTON ROAD,
SW1
⊖ KNIGHTSBRIDGE
The shop of shops, which will
sell you anything from an
aardvark to a zither.
Characteristically, Harrods
installed the first 'moving
staircase' (or escalator) in

London in 1898. Attendants
stood by at the top with
brandy and smelling salts to
revive frightened and
swooning customers. Today it
has delectable tiled food and
meat halls. (See page 74.)

HARVEY NICHOLS,
109 KNIGHTSBRIDGE, SW1
⊖ KNIGHTSBRIDGE
Smart, expensive designer
clothes are sold in this shop,
which is celebrated for its
window-dressing. It started
life in 1813 as Benjamin
Harvey's diminutive draper's
shop.

JOHN LEWIS,
278 OXFORD STREET, W1
⊖ OXFORD CIRCUS
The original John Lewis was a
dress material buyer who set
up on his own account in
Oxford Street in 1864. The
shop prospered, the business
expanded and a rival store,
Peter Jones, was acquired. The
Lewis family were pioneers of
profit-sharing and the business
is now owned by its staff. The
Oxford Street store was
rebuilt in the 1950s. There is a
Barbara Hepworth sculpture
on the east wall.

LIBERTY, 210-20 REGENT
STREET, W1
⊖ OXFORD CIRCUS
A department store with
character and a byword for
good taste. Founded by Arthur
Lasenby Liberty, a
Buckinghamshire draper's son,
in 1875, the store had a strong
influence on Art Nouveau
fashion and design and was
rebuilt in 1924. The
remarkable mock-Tudor
exterior on Great Marlborough
Street was constructed using
timbers from two old 'wooden
wall' battleships. St George
and the dragon do battle on
the store's clock every hour.
(See page 65.)

PETER JONES,
SLOANE SQUARE, SW1
⊖ SLOANE SQUARE
This pleasantly conventional

*Stylishness and fun: a carousel
graces a store which originally
sold oriental silks.*

store is in one of London's
most fascinating 1930s
buildings. It was designed by
William Crabtree, who was
only 25 when he began work
on it. The original Peter Jones
was a Welsh draper who came
to London in the 1860s. He
was bought out by John Lewis
in 1906.

SELFRIDGES,
400 OXFORD STREET, W1
⊖ MARBLE ARCH
Secondly only to Harrods in
size, this is the proud creation
of an American tycoon,
Gordon Selfridge, who as a
young man worked for the
Chicago department store
colossus, Marshall Field.
Selfridge opened the store in
1909. Today it has a
reputation for reasonable
prices. Its food halls were
recently refurbished and it has
the largest perfume
department in Europe.

WHITELEYS,
QUEENSWAY, W2
⊖ BAYSWATER
⊖ QUEENSWAY
Restored to its Edwardian
splendour, this former
department store now houses
an assortment of shops,
cinemas and restaurants. It is
worth visiting just to enjoy
the décor. The founder was a
Yorkshireman named William
Whiteley, who called himself
'the Universal Provider', ready
to sell 'anything from a pin to
an elephant at short notice'.
He opened the store in
Bayswater in 1863, to take
advantage of the opening of
the new Metropolitan Railway,
the first underground line in
London. He was murdered in
his office in 1907. In the
Second World War it was
rumoured that Hitler meant to
use the opulent building as his
headquarters after capturing
London.

London's Pubs

· ·

London's pubs come in all shapes and sizes and styles of décor, from venerable taverns where strong ale has poured down thirsty throats for three centuries or more, to foursquare Georgian inns and glittering Victorian gin palaces. Some have connections with famous people, some are haunted (see page 31), some have strange names. Among the most attractive are the riverside pubs.

What follows is a selection of pubs of character. Opening times vary. Although pubs can stay open from 11.00am to 11.00pm on weekdays (Sundays from 12.00noon to 3.00pm and again from 7.00pm to 10.30pm), but not all stay open all day. City pubs often close at weekends.

CLAIMS TO FAME

Many London pubs have links with famous people. There is a **Samuel Pepys** in Clarges Street, Mayfair, and a **Charlie Chaplin** at the Elephant and Castle. The discoverer of penicillin is honoured at the **Sir Alexander Fleming** in Bouverie Place, Bayswater, while **Nelson's Head** is suitably placed in Horatio Street, in the East End. On the fictitious side, **Eliza Doolittle** is immortalised in Ossulston Street, St Pancras, and **The Artful Dodger** in Royal Mint Street, near the Tower.

THE ADMIRAL CODRINGTON,
17 MOSSOP STREET, SW1
⊖ SOUTH KENSINGTON
This is a handsome Victorian-style pub — mirrored, panelled and gas-lit — with an attractive conservatory. It is named after Sir Edward Codrington, who commanded HMS *Orion* at Trafalgar in 1805 and defeated the Turks at the Battle of Navarino in 1827.

THE ALBERT,
52 VICTORIA STREET, SW1
⊖ ST JAMES'S PARK
A plush Victorian pub, named after the Prince Consort, whose portrait is displayed on the sign.

THE ANCHOR,
BANKSIDE, SE1
⊖ LONDON BRIDGE
Close to the Cannon Street railway bridge, and rebuilt in the 1770s, the Anchor once knew all the roughs and toughs of the Southwark waterside, among them smugglers, press gangs and criminals on the run. (It has

hideyholes for the latter.) Probably the place from which the diarist Samuel Pepys watched the Great Fire in 1666, it also has 18th-century associations with Dr Johnson and his biographer, James Boswell. The interior has been refurbished in what has been unkindly described as 'all-purpose brewer's Dickensian'.

THE ANGEL, 101
BERMONDSEY WALL EAST, SE16
⊖ ROTHERHITHE
Originally the Salutation, this pub has been called the Angel since Tudor times. It is built on piles over the Thames, with trapdoors said to have been used by smugglers. Famous customers, such as Samuel Pepys, Captain Cook and Laurel and Hardy, have enjoyed its superb river views.

THE BULL AND BUSH,
NORTH END WAY, NW3
⊖ GOLDERS GREEN
⊖ HAMPSTEAD
This is the 'old Bull and Bush' of the music hall song, with a history going back to about 1645. William Hogarth lived here at one time in the 18th century and the pub later numbered Sir Joshua Reynolds, David Garrick, Lawrence Sterne, Percy Bysshe Shelley and Charles Dickens among its famous patrons.

THE FLASK, 77 HIGHGATE
WEST HILL, N6
⊖ HIGHGATE
⊖ ARCHWAY
Dating from 1663, but later rebuilt, this pub was a favourite haunt of William Hogarth and Karl Marx. It has a pleasant forecourt for outdoor drinking.

THE FRENCH HOUSE,
49 DEAN STREET, W1
⊖ TOTTENHAM COURT ROAD
General de Gaulle sank a glass or two during the Second World War in this little Soho pub, which was a rendezvous for the Free French. Later Dylan Thomas and Brendan Behan were disorderly regulars. Formerly called the York Minster, the pub became known as 'the French' after the Berlemont family took it over in 1914.

THE GEORGE INN,
77 BOROUGH HIGH STREET, SE1
⊖ BOROUGH
A magnificent galleried coaching inn of medieval origin, the George was rebuilt in the 1670s and is now owned by the National Trust. Shakespeare himself may well have enjoyed a drink or two on this site (see page 123).

THE JOHN SNOW,
39 BROADWICK STREET, W1
⊖ PICCADILLY CIRCUS
⊖ OXFORD CIRCUS
Formerly the Newcastle on Tyne, this Soho pub changed its name when the original John Snow in the same street was demolished. Snow was a local doctor in the 19th century who traced an epidemic of cholera to a contaminated well and persuaded the authorities to close the pump, thereby saving many lives. It is said that the pump is sometimes seen in spectral form outside the pub.

The Angel has heavenly views of the Thames.

THE MAYFLOWER, 117
ROTHERHITHE STREET, SE16
⊖ ROTHERHITHE
This pub changed its name from the Ship in honour of the Pilgrim Fathers' vessel, which sailed from hereabouts in 1620. Today it is the only pub in the country licensed to sell American and English postage stamps.

THE MUSEUM TAVERN,
49 GREAT RUSSELL STREET, WC1
⊖ TOTTENHAM COURT ROAD
The pub claims Karl Marx, Dylan Thomas and luminaries of the Bloomsbury Group among its past customers — refreshing themselves after their dusty labours in the Reading Room of the British Museum across the way. It has a nice Victorian interior.

NELL OF OLD DRURY,
29 CATHERINE STREET, WC2
⊖ COVENT GARDEN
This delightful old Covent Garden pub is one of the oldest in the area. It is named after Charles II's mistress, Nell Gwyn, who was an actress at the Theatre Royal opposite. Today it is decorated with playbills. Customers can hear the theatre's bell signalling the end of the interval.

THE PROSPECT OF WHITBY,
57 WAPPING WALL, E1
⊖ WAPPING
One of London's most famous hostelries, much visited by tourists, the Prospect of Whitby dates from 1520. It was long frequented by smugglers and river thieves, and was once known as the Devil's Tavern. Samuel Pepys,

Judge Jeffreys, Charles Dickens, and J M W Turner all drank here in their time. Needless to say, the pub has no view of Whitby. It is named after a ship which used to moor here.

THE RED LION,
23 CROWN PASSAGE, PALL MALL, SW1
⊖ GREEN PARK
Dating from 1902, this is a popular, crowded pub. A tavern has been on the site for much longer. It is said that a secret passage once linked the building with St James's Palace, and that King Charles II kept many secret assignations with his mistress, Nell Gwyn, here.

THE RED LION,
217 WHITECHAPEL ROAD, E1
⊖ ALDGATE EAST
The highwayman Dick Turpin unintentionally shot and mortally wounded his friend Tom King in this pub's yard during a mêlée with Bow Street Runners in 1739. Turpin was hanged at York a few months later.

SHAKESPEARE'S HEAD,
29 GREAT MARLBOROUGH STREET, W1
⊖ OXFORD CIRCUS
Built in 1735, the pub was originally owned by Thomas and John Shakespeare, brothers who claimed descent from the Bard. His bust outside has one hand missing, blown off by a bomb in the Blitz.

THE SHERLOCK HOLMES,
10 NORTHUMBERLAND STREET, WC2
⊖ EMBANKMENT
Formerly the Northumberland Hotel, which is mentioned in Conan Doyle's *Hound of the Baskervilles*, it changed its name in the 1950s and became a shrine to the great fictional detective. It is full of Holmes mementos and curios.

YE OLDE CHESHIRE CHEESE, WINE OFFICE
COURT, 145 FLEET STREET, EC4
⊖ TEMPLE
⊖ BLACKFRIARS
This atmospheric pub and chop house surviving from 1667 is one of the most famous, and least altered, in London. Low-ceilinged, oak-beamed, sawdust-floored, it has medieval cellars underneath. Its star-studded roll of literary customers includes Dr Johnson, Pope, Voltaire, Dickens (who mentions it in *A Tale of Two Cities*), Tennyson and Mark Twain, as well as Conan Doyle, G K Chesterton and W B Yeats. The pub once had a parrot, celebrated for its frightful language, whose death in 1926 elicited obituaries in dozens of newspapers, and even a report by the BBC.

YE OLDE MITRE TAVERN,
ELY COURT, EC1
⊖ FARRINGDON
⊖ CHANCERY LANE
Built in 1546 by the bishops of Ely as a lodging for the servants at their town house, Ye Olde Mitre Tavern was rebuilt in the 18th century. Sir Christopher Hatton, one of Queen Elizabeth I's favourites, had a garden here. It is said that Good Queen Bess once danced round the cherry tree whose trunk is preserved in the bar.

The mitre of the bishops of Ely crowns the entrance to the pub.

OTHERS OF INTEREST

THE BLACKFRIAR, 174 QUEEN VICTORIA STREET, EC4
⊖ BLACKFRIARS
On the site of the Blackfriars monastery, this weird triangular hostelry with the figure of a black friar above its door was built in 1875. It has a marvellous Art Nouveau interior in bronze and marble, unique in London, with bas-reliefs of jolly monks.

THE CITTIE OF YORK,
22 HIGH HOLBORN, WC1
⊖ HOLBORN
An imposing pub frequented by lawyers, the Cittie of York was rebuilt in the 19th century, but has a history going back to 1430. It boasts the longest bar counter in Britain and a row of huge, 1,000-gallon (4,550-litre) wine barrels beneath its wooden beams, as well as a fireplace with no apparent chimney — the smoke is carried away under the floor.

THE CITY BARGE,
27 STRAND-ON-THE-GREEN, W4
⊖ GUNNERSBURY
On the river front at Chiswick, the pub is named after the Lord Mayor's barges, which

THE NAME'S THE THING

London has its fair share of pubs with odd and evocative names, from the **Salmon and Compasses** in Penton Street, near King's Cross to the **Ship Aground** not far from the river in Wolseley Street, Bermondsey. The **Three Swedish Crowns** lord it over Wapping Lane in the East End, and the **Pillars of Hercules** are appropriately located in Greek Street, Soho. Another well-known Soho drinking spot is the **Intrepid Fox** in Wardour Street, while Chelsea offers a choice between the **Magpie and Stump** and the **World's End,** both in the King's Road. The weird **Frog and Nightgown** inhabits the Old Kent Road, and the **Vulture's Perch** roosts in Kentish Town Road. There is a **Friend in Need** in Herbrand Street near Russell Square, and a **Blue-Eyed Maid** in the Borough High Street.

An atmospheric 17th-century tavern is the **Old Dr**

London's longest pub name.

Butler's Head in Mason's Avenue, off Coleman Street, Moorgate. It preserves the name and fame of the eccentric Dr William Butler, who recommended that King James I should drink ale for sciatica, and was promptly appointed royal physician. An unconventional practitioner, he would try to cure epilepsy by firing a gun beside the sufferer's ear, and threw patients with the ague into the Thames.

Another pub with an interesting name is the **Jamaica Wine House,** in St Michael's Alley, Cornhill. Originally a coffee house in the heart of the City, it was rebuilt after the Great Fire of 1666. In the 18th century it had a reputation for fine rum. It also attracted old seadogs, and was the place to pick up information about sailings to Jamaica.

The **Printer's Devil** at 98 Fetter Lane was once called the Vintner. Renamed in 1957 it doubles as a museum of printing, with presses and samples of printers' work. The 'devil' was a boy who did odd jobs.

Another pub named after an occupation is the **Running Footman** at 5 Charles Street. Its full name, 'I Am the Only Running Footman', is the longest pub name in London. The particular type of footman in question was employed to run ahead of a carriage and blow a horn to clear the way.

used to be moored here. It has a history going back to Elizabethan times at least.

THE DOVE,
19 UPPER MALL, W6
☖ RAVENSCOURT PARK
A charming little 18th-century Hammersmith hostelry, overlooking the river and claiming to have the smallest sung in London. *Rule Britannia* is said to have been written here.

THE LAMB AND FLAG,
33 ROSE STREET, WC2
☖ COVENT GARDEN
This celebrated Covent Garden pub has a Georgian front added to its 17th-century building. It was once known as the Bucket of Blood because bare-knuckled prizefights were staged upstairs.

THE LONDON APPRENTICE, 62 CHURCH STREET, ISLEWORTH
☖ RICHMOND
This famous hostelry near Syon House is named after the young men from the London docks who would row here for a pint on a day off. Rebuilt in the 18th century, it goes back to the 15th. There is a delightful terrace by the river.

THE RED LION, 2 DUKE OF YORK STREET, SW1
☖ PICCADILLY CIRCUS
A nice little Victorian gin palace with a well-preserved 1840s interior of rich mahogany panelling and mirrors, elaborately engraved with British flowers.

THE SALISBURY, 90 ST MARTIN'S LANE, WC2
☖ LEICESTER SQUARE
Richly opulent, this Edwardian bar lies at the heart of London's theatre district. Its interior is a symphony of red plush, brass and mirrors.

THE SUN, 63 LAMB'S CONDUIT STREET, WC1
☖ HOLBORN
More different types of draught beer can be bought here than in any other London pub. They are stored in cellars spreading under the street.

THE TABARD INN,
BATH ROAD, W4
☖ TURNHAM GREEN
A comforting 'Old English' inn of red brick, designed by the Victorian architect R Norman Shaw, who also built St Michael's church opposite. In

Conviviality at the former 'Bucket of Blood' hostelry in the Covent Garden area.

Bedford Park there is a delightful suburb of Queen Anne-style houses, begun in 1875 as one of the earliest garden suburbs in England.

THE TWO CHAIRMEN,
39 DARTMOUTH STREET, SW1
☖ ST JAMES'S PARK
Named after the sedan chairmen who brought customers to a famous cockpit next door, this is a snug 18th-century tavern with many regulars.

POP GOES THE WEASEL!

The **Eagle Tavern** in Shepherdess Walk, just off City Road, is immortalised in a well-known nursery rhyme:

*Up and down the City Road,
In and out the Eagle,
That's the way the money goes,
Pop goes the weasel!*

This may not be as meaningless as it seems. It is said that the verse refers to a local saddler who was devoted to his beer. A weasel is a tool used in leatherworking and he used to 'pop', or pawn, his weasel when necessary to pay for a drink. Whether this is true is anybody's guess. The Eagle has another claim to fame; Marie Lloyd, the great music hall comedienne, made her first appearance in the theatre on the tavern's first floor.

Many veteran London pubs famed in song and story have not survived the

Florrie Forde, the music-hall queen, at the sign of the Old Bull and Bush.

passing years. Among them is the **Tabard** in Southwark, the hostelry from which Chaucer's pilgrims set out in *The Canterbury Tales*. Later called the Talbot, it stood where Talbot Yard is now. The last vestiges of it were demolished in 1880.

Also departed are the **Mermaid** in Bread Street, a favourite tavern of the 17th-century dramatist Ben Jonson, and the **Star and**

Garter in Pall Mall, where Jonathan Swift, the satirist and novelist, liked to hold forth. The playwright Richard Brinsley Sheridan and his friends enjoyed many a glass at the **Queen of Bohemia** in Covent Garden and at the **Adam and Eve** in Kensington (which has left its name to Adam and Eve Mews, off Kensington High Street).

Men of letters such as Samuel Taylor Coleridge and Charles Lamb preferred the strangely named **Salutation and Cat** inn in Newgate Street. 'Salutation' refers to the Annunciation, when the Angel Gabriel brought the Virgin Mary the news that she was to be the mother of Christ. 'Cat' is an abbreviation of the Catherine Wheel on which St Catherine of Alexandria was tortured and martyred. This pub was once simply known as 'the Cat', but it added 'the Salutation' when it merged with a nearby tavern of that name.

Sport in London

From strawberries and cream at Wimbledon to *Abide With Me* at Wembley, or from the thrills and spills of the Royal Tournament at Earl's Court to the ritual of a Lord's test match, sporting events and annual spectacles are an important aspect of London life.

THE BOAT RACE
Rowed over a distance of about 4¼ miles (7.2km) on the Thames, from Putney to Mortlake, this annual contest between the universities of Oxford and Cambridge attracts lively interest and passionate partisanship as crowds of spectators gather along the river bank. The race has been rowed on the Thames since 1845 and is held around Easter time.

CRYSTAL PALACE NATIONAL SPORTS CENTRE,
LEDRINGTON ROAD, SE19
⊖ VICTORIA, THEN ⇌ CRYSTAL PALACE
Opened in 1964, in the grounds where the Crystal Palace stood until it was destroyed by fire in 1936, the centre is Britain's leading athletics stadium. Internationals and other important meetings are held here.

EARL'S COURT EXHIBITION CENTRE, WARWICK ROAD, SW5
⊖ EARL'S COURT
Designed by C Howard Crane and built in 1937, this was then the largest reinforced concrete building in Europe. It has been used for spectacular opera productions, but is mainly occupied by large-scale exhibitions, such as the annual International Boat Show. In July every year it is the scene of the Royal Tournament, a spectacular display of the armed services' skill and rivalry in field-gun races, tug-of-war and other contests.

HACKNEY WICK STADIUM,
WATERDEN ROAD, E15
⊖ LEYTON
Speedway and greyhound racing take place here. Speedway has grown into one of the most popular spectator sports since its introduction to Britain in the 1920s. Greyhound racing, or 'going to the dogs', has always been popular with East End Londoners.

HURLINGHAM CLUB,
RANELAGH GARDENS, SW6
⊖ PUTNEY BRIDGE
This is the august scene of major croquet matches, and it is also the headquarters of the game in Britain.

THE LONDON MARATHON
Held every year in April over a course of 26 miles 385 yards, (42km 352m) the marathon starts from Blackheath and Greenwich Park, finishing at Westminster Bridge. First run in 1981, it attracts thousands of entrants and spectators.

LORD'S CRICKET GROUND,
ST JOHN'S WOOD ROAD, NW8
⊖ ST JOHN'S WOOD
This famous ground is the headquarters of the game. It takes its name from Thomas Lord, a Yorkshireman connected with the founding of the Marylebone Cricket Club (MCC) in 1787. The present ground opened in 1814 and is also the home of the Middlesex County Cricket Club (MCCC). All the great names of cricket history, from W G Grace and Jack Hobbs, to Don Bradman, Len Hutton, Gary Sobers and Viv Richards have graced the venerable turf.

The first of many test matches was played here in 1884, when MCC defeated Australia. The playing area covers about 5 acres (2ha). The main entrance gates were designed in 1923 by Sir Herbert Baker as a tribute to W G Grace. The Father Time weathervane dates from 1926, and the striking Mound Stand, designed by Michael Hopkins, was built in 1987.

The Cricket Memorial Gallery was opened in 1953 as a museum in honour of cricketers killed in the First and Second World Wars. Covering the history of the game, it houses portraits of great players, bats and equipment, a stuffed sparrow killed by a cricket ball on the ground in 1936 and the urn containing the Ashes (of a bail burned by Australians lamenting defeat in 1883).
Open on match days, Mon–Sat 10.30am–5.00pm.

OLYMPIA, HAMMERSMITH ROAD, W14
⊖ OLYMPIA
This is a massive exhibition building, with 500,000 sq ft (46,500 sq m) of space. It opened in 1884 as the National Agricultural Hall, but the name was changed to Olympia two years later, when it was intended to use the building to stage circuses. The Bertram Mills Circus appeared here for many years. The first Motor Show was held at Olympia in 1905, and more buildings were added in the 1920s. Olympia is now the scene of the International Showjumping Championships every year, and until 1991 Cruft's Dog Show was always held here.

THE OVAL,
KENNINGTON OVAL, SE11
⊖ OVAL
London's other famous test cricket ground, the Oval, is the headquarters of the Surrey County Cricket Club. The club was founded in 1845 at a nearby pub, The Horns, and the first test match in England was played here in 1880, when England beat Australia. The Hobbs Gates at the ground's main entrance were erected in 1934 in honour of Jack Hobbs, Surrey's great batsman. It was on this ground in 1938 that the young Len Hutton took 364 runs off the Australian attack, then the highest score ever made in test cricket.

RUGBY FOOTBALL UNION MUSEUM, WHITTON ROAD, TWICKENHAM, MIDDLESEX
⊖ WATERLOO, THEN ⇌ TWICKENHAM
At the ground which is to Rugby Union what Lord's is to cricket, the museum traces the history of the game since William Webb Ellis picked up the ball and ran with it at Rugby School in 1823.
Open all year, Mon–Fri 9.30am–1.00pm and 2.15pm–5.00pm.

WEMBLEY STADIUM,
EMPIRE WAY, WEMBLEY
⊖ WEMBLEY PARK
The giant, concrete, 100,000-seater stadium with its twin domed towers was originally built for the British Empire Exhibition of 1924. Next to it is the Wembley Arena of 1934, originally built as the Empire Pool, then the largest swimming pool in the world.

In the old and new traditions: competitors in the London Marathon, passing the Tower.

The Wembley Stadium is used today for indoor tennis, horse shows and other sports, and even pop concerts. The sporting highlight of the stadium's year is the Football Association (FA) Cup soccer game in May. It is also used for football internationals, the annual Rugby League Cup Final, hockey and greyhound racing. It was the principal stadium used for the Olympic Games in London in 1948, when the Dutch athlete, Fanny Blankers-Koen, won four gold medals and Emil Zatopek of Czechoslovakia won the 10,000 metres by almost an entire lap. In 1966 England won the final of the soccer World Cup against West Germany at Wembley.

WIMBLEDON TENNIS,
ALL ENGLAND LAWN TENNIS CLUB, CHURCH ROAD, WIMBLEDON, SW19
⊖ SOUTHFIELDS
The club was founded as the All England Croquet Club in 1869, but by the 1880s tennis had pushed croquet into the back seat. The club moved to its present ground in 1922. The annual championships held here are the world's most celebrated tennis event, and the hallowed Centre Court at Wimbledon has seen great moments in the lives of all the world's great players, from Jean Borotra and Suzanne Lenglen to Bjorn Borg, John McEnroe and Martina Navratilova.

In 1977, to mark the centenary of the Wimbledon Championships, the Lawn Tennis Museum was opened at the ground, with displays covering the history of the game, tennis clothes and equipment, trophies, famous players and tennis bric-à-brac.
Museum open all year, Tue–Sat 11.00am–5.00pm, Sun 2.00pm–5.00pm.

FOOTBALL CLUBS

ARSENAL, ARSENAL
STADIUM, HIGHBURY, N5
⊖ ARSENAL
One of the most famous clubs in the country, Arsenal was originally founded in Woolwich in 1886 as Royal Arsenal. In 1913 it was moved to Highbury in North London. Arsenal have been FA Cup winners and League champions many times.
Colours: red and white.

Men's singles trophy, Wimbledon.

BRENTFORD, GRIFFIN PARK,
BRAEMAR ROAD, BRENTFORD, MIDDLESEX
⊖ WATERLOO, THEN ⇄ BRENTFORD CENTRAL
Founded in the 1880s and nicknamed 'the Bees', Brentford has been in the lower divisions for most of its history.
Colours: red, white and black.

CHARLTON ATHLETIC, THE
VALLEY, FLOYD ROAD, SE7
⊖ CHARING CROSS, THEN ⇄ CHARLTON
Charlton Athletic enjoyed its best days in the 1940s, when it played in the first post-war Cup Final in 1946.
Colours: red and white.

CHELSEA, STAMFORD
BRIDGE, FULHAM ROAD, SW6
⊖ FULHAM BROADWAY
Founded in 1905, Chelsea won the FA Cup in 1970 after the first Wembley final to go to a replay.
Colours: blue and white.

CRYSTAL PALACE,
SELHURST PARK, SE25
⊖ VICTORIA, THEN ⇄ SELHURST
Founded in 1905, the club gained the First Division in 1979.
Colours: white, scarlet and blue.

FULHAM, CRAVEN COTTAGE,
STEVENAGE ROAD, SW6
⊖ PARSON'S GREEN
⊖ PUTNEY BRIDGE
A veteran club, which began as a Sunday school side in West Kensington in 1879.
Colours: white and black.

LEYTON ORIENT, LEYTON
STADIUM, BRISBANE ROAD, E10
⊖ LEYTON
Originally Clapton Orient, this is an East End team, never in the limelight.
Colours: red and white.

MILLWALL, THE DEN, COLD
BLOW LANE, SE14
⊖ NEW CROSS
Known as the Lions, Millwall are the team of the old South London docks. They were founded in 1855 as amateurs Millwall Rovers.
Colours: royal blue and white.

QUEEN'S PARK RANGERS,
LOFTUS ROAD, SOUTH AFRICA ROAD, W12
⊖ WHITE CITY
This club began as St Jude's Institute's amateur team, in the Queen's Park area of Kensal Town.
Colours: blue and white.

TOTTENHAM HOTSPUR,
WHITE HART LANE, 748 HIGH ROAD, N17
⊖ SEVEN SISTERS
An exceptionally distinguished club with numerous trophies

to its credit, Tottenham Hotspur started life as the Hotspur Cricket Club's football team in 1882 and played on Tottenham Marshes.
Colours: blue and white.

WEST HAM UNITED, UPTON
PARK, GREEN STREET, E13
⊖ UPTON PARK
West Ham United grew out of the Thames Ironworks side. It has been a professional team since 1900, and has won the FA Cup several times.
Colours: claret and blue.

WIMBLEDON, SELHURST
PARK, SE25
⊖ VICTORIA, THEN ⇄ SELHURST
Wimbledon was not a fully professional side until the 1960s, when the club moved up from the Southern League.
Colours: blue and yellow.

The FA Cup Final at Wembley, the culmination of the football season.

ASSOCIATION FOOTBALL

The origins of Association Football are lost in the mists of history. In medieval times games might involve dozens of players on either side and be contested over open country and across streams and ditches in a giant, heaving scrimmage. The ball was tugged or smuggled to a mark that counted as a goal. It was a vigorous sport with few rules; injuries were common and deaths not unknown. In the 17th century rival teams of London apprentices enjoyed similar sessions of street football, but it was not until well into the Victorian age that the

game as we know it today developed from the older variety, and was first played with the feet.

The game was first properly organised by amateur clubs composed of ex-public schoolboys. One such was Old Harrovians, founded in 1859. In 1863 a meeting took place in London to form the Football Association (FA), and the first code of rules was published. Within the next 20 years or so professional clubs had been organised. Today's leading London clubs mostly date from the 1880s and 1890s. In many cases they started as amateur sides.

Theatres, Cinemas, Opera Houses and Concert Halls

. . . .

London is one of the cultural and entertainment capitals of the world. There are upwards of 40 theatres open in the West End and two resident opera companies, as well as several highly regarded symphony orchestras and ballet companies. There is also a lively sphere of fringe theatre and music in arts centres and pubs. *Time Out, What's On* and *City Limits* are weekly magazines which specialise in supplying full entertainment listings. The Society of West End Theatres runs a ticket booth in Leicester Square, with last-minute seats at half-price.

Her Majesty's Theatre, Haymarket, in 1890s splendour.

GENERAL

THE BARBICAN CENTRE,
SILK STREET, EC2
⊖ BARBICAN
⊖ MOORGATE
Opened in 1982, and grim in concrete, besides being huge and labyrinthinely confusing, the Barbican is home to high-quality concerts, theatre, cinema and art exhibitions (see page 107).

INSTITUTE OF CONTEMPORARY ARTS,
THE MALL, SW1
⊖ CHARING CROSS
In the elegant Regency setting of Carlton House Terrace, the ICA has a theatre, a cinema, and two art galleries.

SOUTH BANK CENTRE,
SOUTH BANK, SE1
⊖ WATERLOO
⊖ EMBANKMENT
The Royal Festival Hall, two other concert halls, the Royal National Theatre, the National Film Theatre, the Museum of the Moving Image and the Hayward Gallery comprise this complex (see page 116).

THEATRES

London is rich in Victorian and Edwardian theatres, including opulent masterpieces by the great theatre architect Frank Matcham. The following is a selection of particularly fine theatre buildings.

ALBERY, ST MARTIN'S LANE, WC2
⊖ LEICESTER SQUARE
Opened in 1903, the Albery has a lovely Edwardian interior by W G R Sprague, a pupil of Frank Matcham.

APOLLO VICTORIA,
WILTON ROAD, SW1
⊖ VICTORIA
Originally a striking Art Deco cinema; few of the decorative features are left.

CRITERION, PICCADILLY CIRCUS, W1
⊖ PICCADILLY CIRCUS
Underground, the Criterion has a delightful 1870s interior.

DUKE OF YORK'S,
ST MARTIN'S LANE, WC2
⊖ LEICESTER SQUARE
Opened in 1892, this theatre saw the first performance of Sir J M Barrie's *Peter Pan* in 1904.

GARRICK, CHARING CROSS ROAD, WC2
⊖ LEICESTER SQUARE
The Garrick, with its attractive Italianate façade, opened in 1889.

GLOBE, SHAFTESBURY AVENUE, W1
⊖ PICCADILLY CIRCUS
Opened in 1906, the Globe has a handsome, Regency-style interior.

HACKNEY EMPIRE,
291 MARE STREET, E8
⊖ BETHNAL GREEN
Opened in 1900 and designed by Frank Matcham for circuses and spectaculars, the Hackney Empire is tremendously ornate in brick and terracotta.

HAYMARKET, HAYMARKET, SW1
⊖ PICCADILLY CIRCUS
Built in 1821, to replace a theatre of 1720, the Haymarket has a grand Classical portico by John Nash. Lilly Langtry, the mistress of Edward VII, made her stage début here in the 19th century.

HER MAJESTY'S,
HAYMARKET, SW1
⊖ PICCADILLY CIRCUS
Founded by Sir Herbert Beerbohm Tree in 1897, the year of Queen Victoria's Diamond Jubilee, this pavilioned theatre is crowned by a Baroque copper dome.

HIPPODROME,
CRANBOURN STREET, WC2
⊖ LEICESTER SQUARE
Now a nightclub, the Hippodrome was designed by Frank Matcham in 1900 in grandiose style for spectacular stage shows.

LONDON PALLADIUM,
ARGYLL STREET, W1
⊖ OXFORD CIRCUS
Designed by Frank Matcham to seat an audience of 2,300, the Palladium opened in 1910. It had a sumptuous interior of marble columns, arches and staircases, mosaic floors, a barber's for gentlemen, and a spacious ladies' boudoir with hairdressing rooms. The Argyll Street front is Matcham's re-modelling of an 1860s original. Famous for variety shows, the Palladium is home to the annual Royal Command Performance.

MERMAID, PUDDLE DOCK, EC4
⊖ BLACKFRIARS
A converted Victorian warehouse, now imprisoned in an enormous 1981 office block by Richard Seifert and Partners, the Mermaid has retained its river views.

'MATCHLESS MATCHAM'

Frank Matcham was born in 1854 at Newton Abbot in Devon, the son of a brewery manager. He joined an architectural practice in Torquay at the age of 14, later moving to London and forming his own firm.

Matcham specialised in theatres. He had plenty of commissions, for in the 1890s and early 1900s theatre owners were busy transforming the old music halls, with their spit-and-sawdust image, into smart places of entertainment for middle-class and family audiences. Matcham's predilection for red-plush opulence and gilded grandeur made him ideally suited to the task. His major London theatres were the Coliseum, the Palladium and the Hippodrome.

Matcham also built many theatres in the provinces, and travelled all over Britain, chain-smoking cigars in the back of his Daimler-Benz. He died at his home in Southend in 1920, aged 66. After years of neglect, his lavish style is once again being appreciated.

OLD VIC, WATERLOO ROAD, SE1

⊖ WATERLOO

The 'Old Vic', as it is commonly known, was restored to its 19th-century splendour in 1982 (see page 119).

RICHMOND THEATRE, LITTLE GREEN, RICHMOND

⊖ RICHMOND

Built in 1899 by Frank Matcham, the Richmond Theatre has a charming interior, beautifully preserved.

ROYAL COURT, SLOANE SQUARE, SW1

⊖ SLOANE SQUARE

Opened in 1888, the Royal Court has a reputation for new and avant-garde drama. Many of George Bernard Shaw's plays were first performed here.

THEATRE ROYAL, DRURY LANE, WC2

⊖ COVENT GARDEN

Dating from 1812, this is the fourth theatre on this site. It has associations with Garrick and Sheridan. King Charles II's mistress, Nell Gwyn, appeared in this building, in which Sir Henry Irving also played (see page 63).

VICTORIA PALACE, VICTORIA STREET, SW1

⊖ VICTORIA

Designed by Frank Matcham as a music hall, Victoria Palace opened in 1911. It became the home of the Crazy Gang, and, later, of the Black-and-White Minstrels.

WYNDHAM'S, CHARING CROSS ROAD, WC2

⊖ LEICESTER SQUARE

⊖ CHARING CROSS

A handsome Victorian theatre of 1899 with a Classical façade, Wyndham's saw 2,084 performances of *The Boy Friend*.

CINEMAS

Most of London's impressive 1920s and 1930s cinemas have been demolished or turned into bingo halls. There is no shortage of films in London, but few cinemas of character are left.

EVERYMAN, HOLLYBUSH VALE, NW3

⊖ HAMPSTEAD

A distinguished repertory cinema in what was originally an 1880s drill hall, showing a mixture of English and foreign films.

MINEMA, 45 KNIGHTSBRIDGE, SW1

⊖ HYDE PARK CORNER

Small and luxuriously comfortable.

ODEON, LEICESTER SQUARE, WC2

⊖ LEICESTER SQUARE

A great black brute of a building. Dating from 1937, it was the flagship of the Odeon chain.

WARNER WEST END, LEICESTER SQUARE, WC2

⊖ LEICESTER SQUARE

A 1930s modernistic building, with sub-Epstein statuary.

OPERA HOUSES AND CONCERT HALLS

LONDON COLISEUM, ST MARTIN'S LANE, WC2

⊖ LEICESTER SQUARE

The Coliseum is a splendid Baroque building with a tower supporting a giant illuminated globe, which originally revolved. The view of it down St Martin's Lane, with the spire of St Martin-in-the-Fields beyond, is one of London's great vistas. Designed by Frank Matcham it opened in 1904, and boasted the first revolving stage in Britain. It is now the home of the English National Opera.

ROYAL ALBERT HALL, KENSINGTON GORE, SW7

⊖ KNIGHTSBRIDGE

⊖ HIGH STREET KENSINGTON

This much-loved Victorian concert hall in mellow red brick is scene of the famous annual promenade concerts (see page 82).

ROYAL OPERA HOUSE, BOW STREET, COVENT GARDEN, WC2

⊖ COVENT GARDEN

⊖ LEICESTER SQUARE

Home of the Royal Opera and the Royal Ballet, the Royal Opera House was designed by Edward Barry, and built in 1858. Its magnificent auditorium seats 2,110 people (see page 63).

ST JOHN'S CHURCH, SMITH SQUARE, SW1

⊖ WESTMINSTER

This 18th-century church is now used for concerts and is also an arts centre

WIGMORE HALL, 36 WIGMORE STREET, W1

⊖ BOND STREET

A small concert hall, with Art Nouveau decorations, used for chamber music and recitals.

THE PROMS

The basic idea of a promenade concert is that people can saunter about while listening to music. To this day part of the Proms audience listens standing up, though there may not be much room for strolling. The Proms began in 1895, but they had predecessors in the popular concerts of classical music held earlier in the 19th century. The French conductor and impresario Louis Jullien staged promenade concerts in London in the 1840s and 1850s on a heroic scale, with hundreds of musicians, massed choirs and military bands. A German conductor, August Manns, also held Saturday concerts at the Crystal Palace from the 1850s until the end of the century.

The first concert of the series of Proms as we know them today was staged on 10 August 1895 at the newly built Queen's Hall in Langham Place. The conductor was 26-year-old Henry Wood. The early concerts were extremely successful and in 1911 Wood was knighted. By 1927, however, the Proms were suffering from chronic box-office difficulties. At that point they were saved by the newly founded BBC, which has run and broadcast them live ever since. Wood's first concert under the new regime opened joyfully with a performance of Elgar's *Cockaigne* overture. When Queen's Hall was destroyed in the Blitz in 1941, the Proms moved to the Royal Albert Hall.

Wood went on planning and conducting the concerts until almost the end of his life. He gave his last performance in July 1944, at the age of 76, and died the following month. The job of planning the programmes and the task of conducting them were now separated.

After some uncertainty, Sir Malcolm Sargent became principal conductor of the Proms in 1948 and he continued as such until 1966, the year before his death. Since then Sir Colin Davis, Pierre Boulez and other distinguished conductors have officiated. Simon Rattle, aged 21, became the youngest Proms conductor ever in 1976.

During the 1960s Sir William Glock, the BBC's music controller, became a major influence on the Proms, which now saw the introduction of more works by 20th-century composers, and more early music as well. Glock's last season of the Proms was in 1974. Every summer since the concerts have continued to bring a wide range of serious music to London audiences, as well as internationally acclaimed soloists and musicians.

Flags and fervour at the last night of the Proms.

Eating out in London

· · · · · · · · · · · · · · · ·

You could eat out every day in a different London restaurant, hotel, pub, wine bar, café, department store, fast-food joint, pizza parlour or fish-and-chip emporium for several years without having to repeat yourself. On the way you would sample practically every known cuisine, from African to Indian, Chinese, Thai, American and Vietnamese. Soho has the heaviest concentration of restaurants in a single area in London, and there is a cluster of Chinese eating places in and around Gerrard Street in Chinatown. The Covent Garden area rejoices in trendy eateries, while Mayfair and the Kensington/Notting Hill Gate areas boast many lavish establishments.

The selection below picks out a small number of famous and intriguing places to try in central London, with prices climbing from the inexpensive (by London standards) to figures which might make a millionaire wince. Opening hours vary, but lunchtime generally runs from around 12.00noon to 2.00pm. Evening meals start from 6.30pm.

Tea at the Ritz has almost become a British institution.

GRAND HOTELS

CONNAUGHT HOTEL, CARLOS PLACE, W1
✠ BOND STREET
Originally the Coburg Hotel, built in 1901, the Connaught was rechristened because of anti-German feeling during the First World War. Today it has a very highly regarded, beautiful and stratospherically expensive restaurant.

DORCHESTER HOTEL, PARK LANE, W1
✠ HYDE PARK CORNER
Opened in 1931, the Dorchester was General Eisenhower's headquarters in the Second World War. It contains a remarkable 1950s

penthouse suite with décor by Oliver Messel. Reopened in 1990 after a complete revamp, it has a terrace restaurant and grill.

RITZ HOTEL, PICCADILLY, W1
✠ GREEN PARK
A London landmark since 1906, when it was completed as the city's first important steel-framed building. The *Louis XVI* interior by Waring and Gillow is a byword for Edwardian luxury. Afternoon tea in the Palm Court is a special treat. Famous past guests are depicted in a mural in the foyer.

SAVOY HOTEL, STRAND, WC2
✠ CHARING CROSS
Opened in 1869, and set back from the Strand, the Savoy has an eye-catching Art Deco fascia in stainless steel. The Savoy's first chef was the great Auguste Escoffier, who invented Peach Melba here, and the Grill Room and the Savoy restaurant have been famous ever since. The Savoy is a favourite place for expensive breakfasts and afternoon teas (see also page 61).

WALDORF HOTEL, ALDWYCH, WC2
✠ TEMPLE
✠ COVENT GARDEN
This is a handsome Edwardian hotel of 1908, with an attractive palm court. The tea dance was revived here in the 1980s.

TRADITIONAL BRITISH

COOKE'S, 41 KINGSLAND HIGH STREET, E8
✠ DALSTON JUNCTION
For your authentic jellied eels, stewed eels and a selection of East End delicacies.

GEALE'S, 2 FARMER STREET, W8
✠ NOTTING HILL GATE
This fish restaurant is strongly recommended for fish and chips.

THE GEORGE AND VULTURE, 3 CASTLE COURT, EC3
✠ BANK
A strangely named, venerable and atmospheric chop house in the heart of the City (not open evenings and at weekends).

RULES, 35 MAIDEN LANE, WC2
✠ COVENT GARDEN
This is where Dickens, Thackeray and King Edward VII liked to eat. Opened as an oyster bar in 1786, it gives substantial helpings of old school-tie food.

SIMPSONS-IN-THE-STRAND, 100 STRAND, WC2
✠ CHARING CROSS
✠ EMBANKMENT
Founded in 1828, this is another fine old traditional establishment, serving roast beef, saddle of lamb, Lancashire hot-pot and Stilton with a glass of port.

SHOPPING AND CULTURAL

FORTNUM & MASON, 181 PICCADILLY, W1
✠ PICCADILLY CIRCUS
Fortnum's has two restaurants and a buttery, which are well thought of for breakfast, lunch, and afternoon tea (see also pages 68 and 156).

HEAL'S, 196 TOTTENHAM COURT ROAD, W1
✠ TOTTENHAM COURT ROAD
The restaurant in this well-known furniture store serves highly rated afternoon teas.

SIMPSON'S WINE BAR, 203 PICCADILLY, W1
✠ PICCADILLY CIRCUS
A soothing wine bar, quietly tucked away upstairs in a fashionable clothes shop.

TATE GALLERY RESTAURANT, MILLBANK, SW1
✠ PIMLICO
In the bowels of the Tate Gallery, the restaurant has wonderful murals by Rex Whistler, which make a pleasant backdrop to English-style meals which are served at lunchtime (see also page 50).

VICTORIA & ALBERT MUSEUM, CROMWELL ROAD, SW7
✠ SOUTH KENSINGTON
This simple self-service café tucked away down a corridor serves a selection of lunches, light meals, tea and coffee (see also page 78).

ORIENTAL PLEASURES

BOMBAY BRASSERIE, 140 GLOUCESTER ROAD, SW7
✠ GLOUCESTER ROAD
Very grand, very large, highly regarded Indian restaurant with Raj-style décor, next to Bailey's Hotel.

LEY ONS, 56 WARDOUR STREET, W1
✠ PICCADILLY CIRCUS
A celebrated Cantonese restaurant in the heart of Soho's film district, with more than 200 varieties of *dim sum*.

SINGAPURA, 839 FULHAM ROAD, SW6
✠ FULHAM BROADWAY
Singapore and Indonesian cuisine is served here. There is an excellent *rijstaffel*.

SUNTORY, 72 ST JAMES'S STREET, SW1
✠ GREEN PARK
This prestigious Japanese restaurant sets high standards of food and service, with matching prices.

THE VEERASWAMY, 99 REGENT STREET, W1
✠ PICCADILLY CIRCUS
The oldest Indian restaurant in London, founded in 1927 by a daughter of the Nizam of Hyderabad, the Veeraswany has colonial décor and smartly turbanned waiters.

MIXED TREATS

THE ARCHDUKE, CONCERT HALL APPROACH, SE1
✠ WATERLOO
A wine bar, close to the Royal Festival Hall.

All ready to carve the joint at Simpson's-in-the-Strand.

ATHENAEUM BAR,
ATHENAEUM HOTEL,
116 PICCADILLY, W1
⊖ HYDE PARK CORNER
The bar is famous for the
biggest range of malt whiskies
in London. It has a Windsor
Lounge restaurant.

BIBENDUM, MICHELIN
HOUSE, 81 FULHAM ROAD,
SW3
⊖ SOUTH KENSINGTON
French food is served here,
in a delightful building of
1910, constructed as an
advertisement for Michelin
products. The building has
cupolas like piles of tyres, and
tiled murals of cars and
bicycles.

BLOOM'S, 90 WHITECHAPEL
HIGH STREET, E1
⊖ ALDGATE EAST
This famous Jewish resort for
kosher food gives generous
portions and lively backchat.

**CRANK'S HEALTH FOOD
RESTAURANT,** 8 MARSHALL
STREET, W1
⊖ PICCADILLY CIRCUS
London's best-known
vegetarian restaurant serves
salads, soups, pasta, sweets
and cakes. It is highly spoken
of. There are several branches
in central London.

THE GAY HUSSAR, 2 GREEK
STREET, W1
⊖ TOTTENHAM COURT
ROAD
A renowned Hungarian
restaurant, long popular with
leftish politicos and
intellectuals. Delectable
goulash and smoked goose.

GRAHAM'S, 38 POLAND
STREET, W1
⊖ OXFORD CIRCUS
This friendly kosher fish
restaurant caters to the local
rag trade.

INIGO JONES, 14 GARRICK
STREET, WC2
⊖ LEICESTER SQUARE
Smart and highly regarded, in
a converted Victorian stained-
glass factory, the Inigo Jones
serves French cuisine, with
excellent pre-theatre set
dinners.

LE CAPRICE, ARLINGTON
HOUSE, ARLINGTON STREET,
SW1
⊖ PICCADILLY CIRCUS
Very fashionable, this French
restaurant is near the Ritz. The
bar is said to serve the best
Bloody Mary in London.

LE GAVROCHE, 43 UPPER
BROOK STREET, W1
⊖ BOND STREET
⊖ MARBLE ARCH
A celebrated and luxurious
French restaurant, owned and
run by the Roux Brothers of
television fame.

LUIGI'S, 15 TAVISTOCK
STREET, WC2
⊖ COVENT GARDEN
Italian restaurant of character,
near the renowned Royal
Opera House.

MAISON BERTAUD,
28 GREEK STREET, W1
⊖ TOTTENHAM COURT
ROAD
Mouth-watering treats at this
long-established Soho
patisserie include tea,
croissants, éclairs and
chocolate truffles.

PATISSERIE VALERIE, 44
OLD COMPTON STREET, W1
⊖ LEICESTER SQUARE
Another favourite Soho haunt
for pastries, cakes and
afternoon tea. It has been
catering to public tastes for 40
years and more.

PIZZA ON THE PARK, 11
KNIGHTSBRIDGE, SW1
⊖ HYDE PARK CORNER
London's most stylish pizza
parlour.

SAN FREDIANO, 62 FULHAM
ROAD, SW3
⊖ SOUTH KENSINGTON
Friendly, bustling and Italian,
San Frediano is greatly loved
by its regulars. It has the most
delicious display of *hors
d'oeuvres* in London and an
animated atmosphere.

OUT OF THE ORDINARY

The credit for creating the
first modern restaurant is
assigned to a Frenchman
named Boulanger. In 1765
he opened an establishment
in Paris whose patrons
could consume a choice
of nourishing soups and
broths. These he described
on the sign above his
premises as *restaurants*,
meaning 'restoratives'. The
name has stuck.

Ever since Boulanger's
initiative the French have
led the development of
the civilised and civilising
restaurant, which has
carried the glories of the
French table across the
world. In 19th-century
England, inns and chop-
houses provided food for
their guests and patrons. A
common feature was the
'ordinary', a forerunner of
today's *table d'hôte*. The
customers sat together at a
common table and ate as
much as they liked from a
limited selection of main
dishes, for a single price.

In 18th-century London,
for instance, a 'three-and-

a-half penny ordinary'
would provide boiled beef,
shin of beef, cow-heel and
tripe. A chairman might sit
at the head of the table to
preside over the feast and
stimulate a bluffly genial
atmosphere. As late as 1926
a restaurant in Cheapside
called Simpson's still had a
daily ordinary at 1.00pm,
complete with a chairman
and a prize for guessing the
weight of a cheese.

The writing had been on
the wall for the ordinary,
however, since the spread
of the French restaurant to
London in the 19th century,
which put old-fashioned
chop-houses out of business.
The Soho area took a leading
part in this process and has
remained London's principal
restaurant quarter ever since.
A landmark was the founding
of Kettner's at 29 Romilly
Street. It was opened in
1867 by Auguste Kettner,
chef to no less a personage
than the Emperor Napoleon
III of France. Immensely
fashionable, renowned for
its gourmet cooking and its

discretion, it was Oscar
Wilde's favourite restaurant.

At about the same time
the Café Royal opened in
Regent Street. Its plush
Domino Room became a
smart meeting place in the
late 19th century, where
Wilde held court with
literary friends and the
young artist Aubrey
Beardsley rubbed shoulders
with the great painter
Whistler. The rococo décor
of the Grill Room at 68
Regent Street still preserves
something of the atmos-
phere today.

Smart society and its
emulators brought enough
money to Soho to support
numerous restaurants with a
wide variety of cuisines.
Around 1900 it was common
practice for waiters in
Italian restaurants to pay the
owner for their jobs. One
Italian establishment in
Soho even made them
provide their own note-
books and pencils for
writing down orders. The
tips were enough to make it
worthwhile.

London
Atlas

*From Knightsbridge in the
west to the Isle of Dogs in
the east, the central London street
atlas charts the capital at
approximately six inches to one mile.
The conurbation mapping at one inch
to one mile extends out into the
suburbs, and there is a useful
theatreland map.*

Atlas

North, south, east and west: a compass atop the Tower

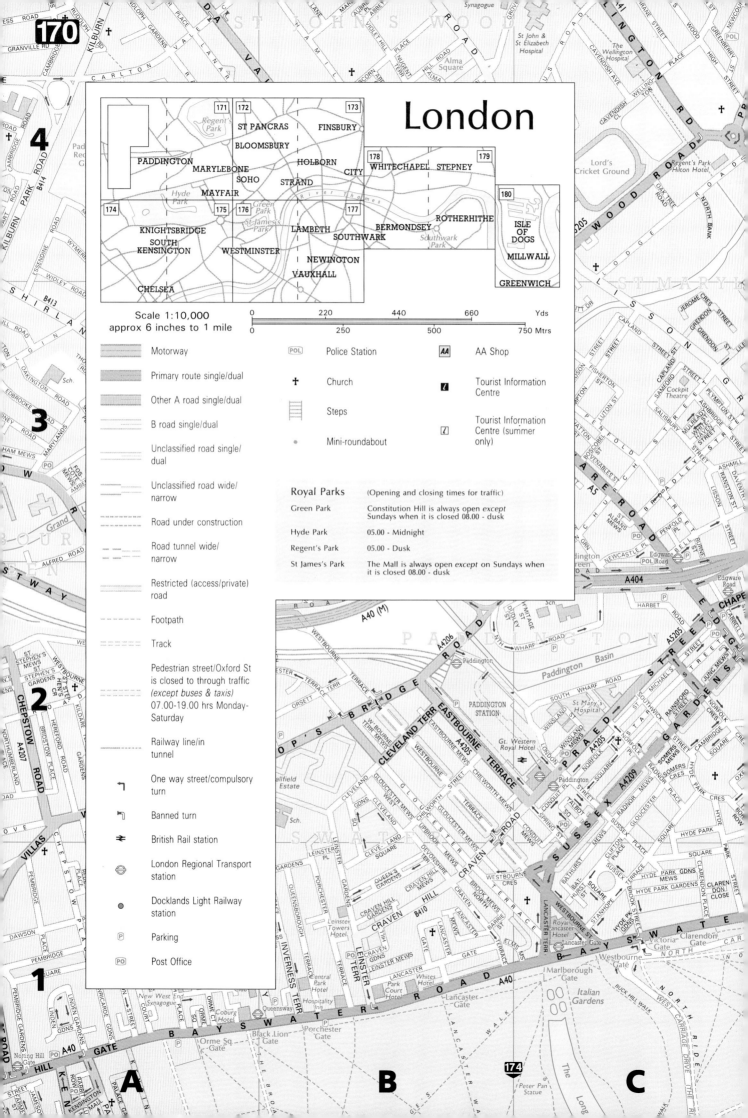

London

170

| 171 | 172 | | 173 |

St Pancras   Finsbury

Bloomsbury

Paddington   Marylebone   Holborn

Soho   City

Strand

Hyde Park   Mayfair

| 178 | | 179 |

Whitechapel   Stepney

| 174 | 175 | 176 | 177 |

| 180 |

Rotherhithe

Knightsbridge   Lambeth

South Kensington   Southwark   Bermondsey

Westminster

Newington

Vauxhall

Isle of Dogs

Millwall

Chelsea

Greenwich

Scale 1:10,000
approx 6 inches to 1 mile

0   220   440   660   Yds

0   250   500   750 Mtrs

Symbol	Description
	Motorway
	Primary route single/dual
	Other A road single/dual
	B road single/dual
	Unclassified road single/dual
	Unclassified road wide/narrow
	Road under construction
	Road tunnel wide/narrow
	Restricted (access/private) road
	Footpath
	Track
	Pedestrian street/Oxford St is closed to through traffic (except buses & taxis) 07.00-19.00 hrs Monday-Saturday
	Railway line/in tunnel
	One way street/compulsory turn
	Banned turn
⇌	British Rail station
	London Regional Transport station
	Docklands Light Railway station
(P)	Parking
PO	Post Office

Symbol	Description
POL	Police Station
†	Church
	Steps
•	Mini-roundabout
AA	AA Shop
	Tourist Information Centre
	Tourist Information Centre (summer only)

Royal Parks   (Opening and closing times for traffic)

Green Park   Constitution Hill is always open *except* Sundays when it is closed 08.00 - dusk

Hyde Park   05.00 - Midnight

Regent's Park   05.00 - Dusk

St James's Park   The Mall is always open *except* on Sundays when it is closed 08.00 - dusk

4

3

2

1

A   B   174   C

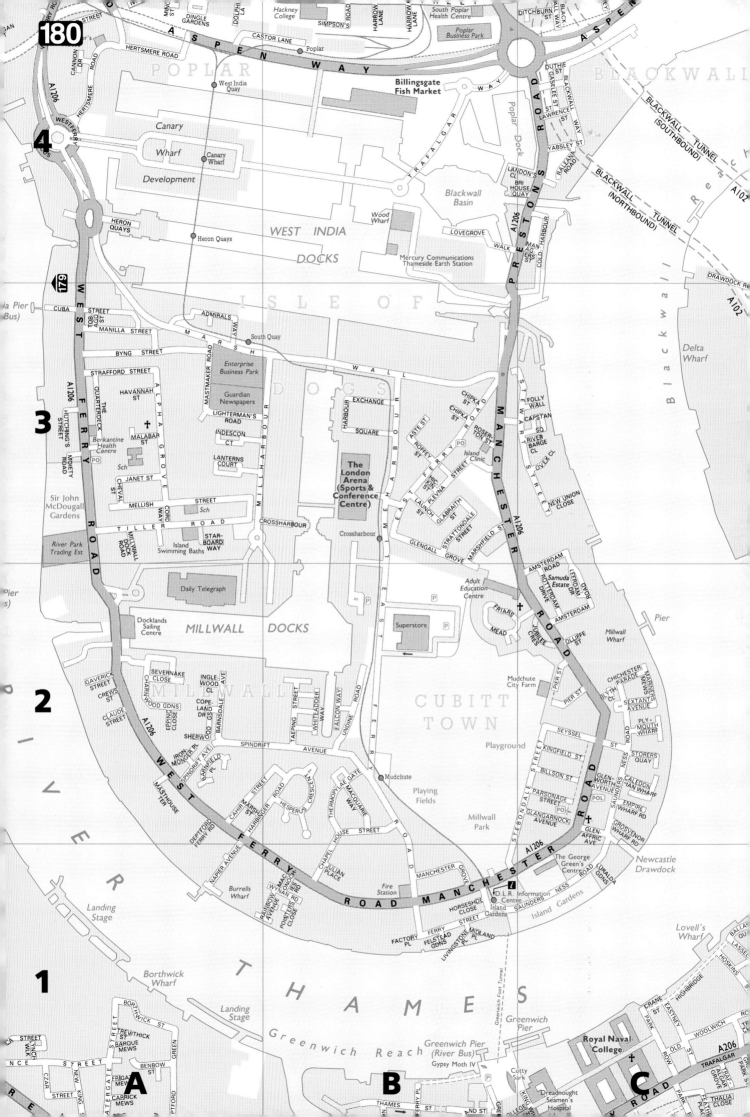

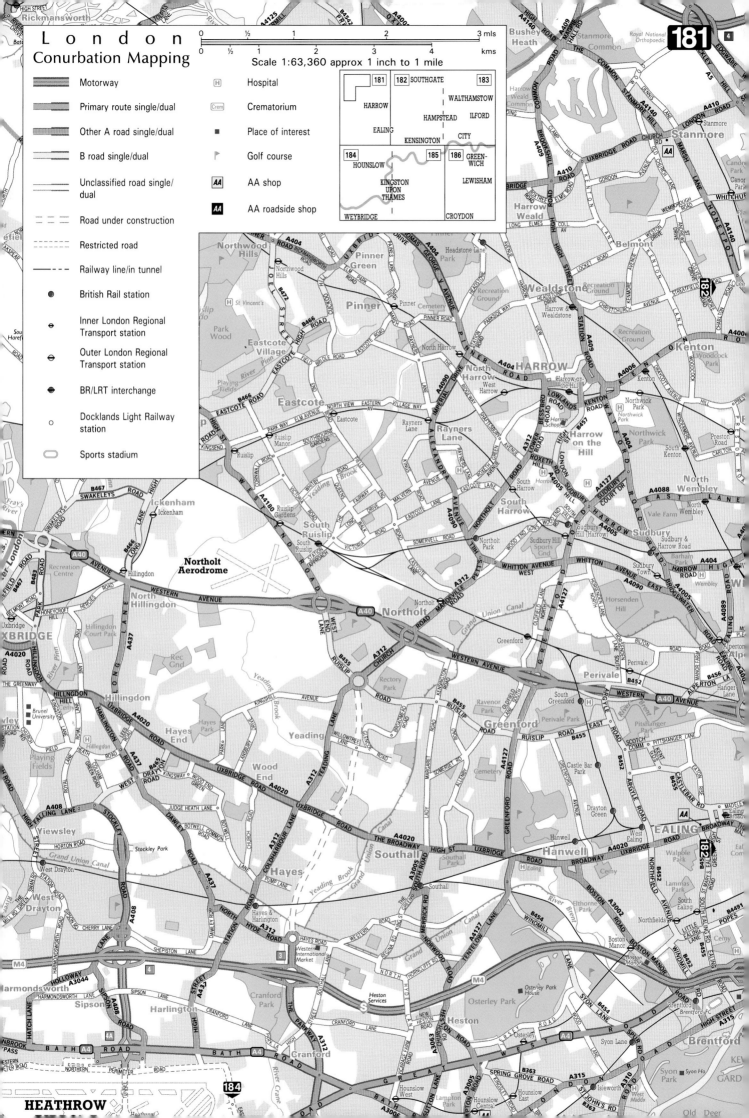

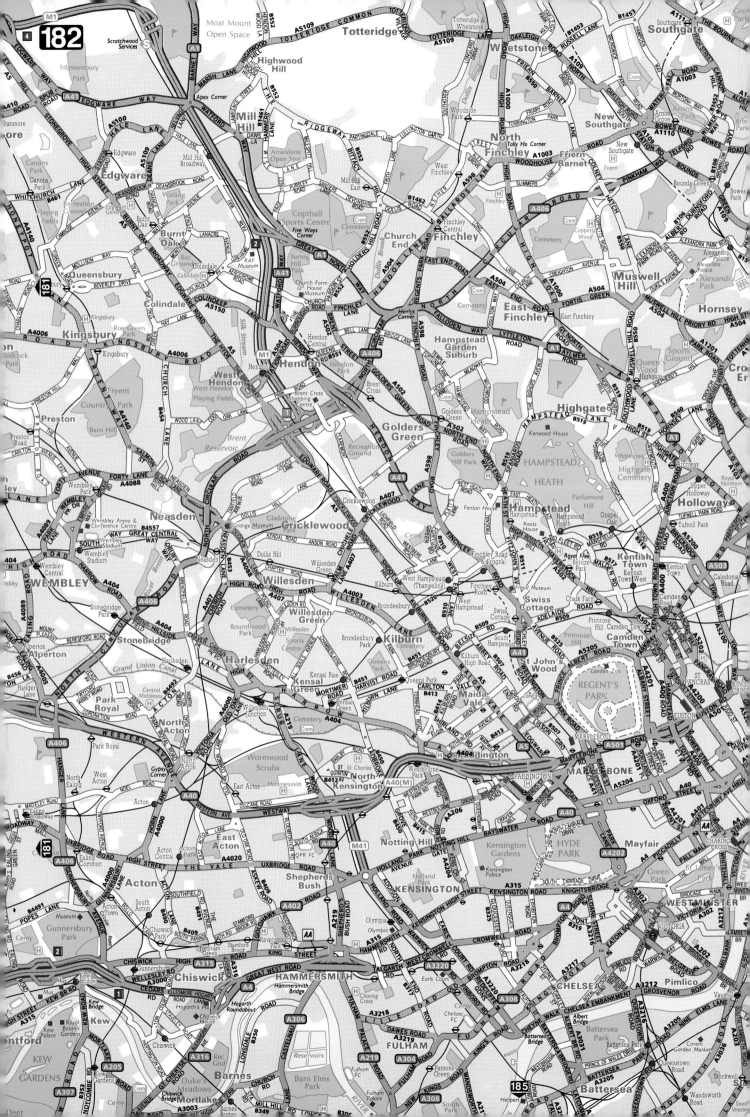

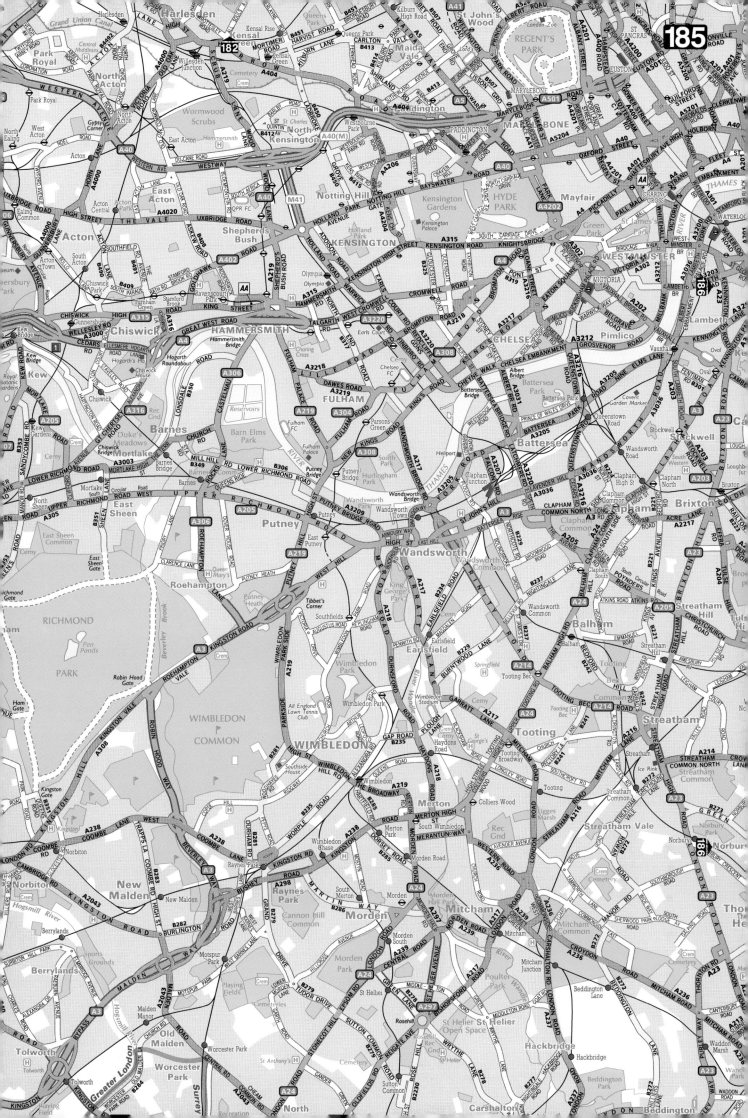

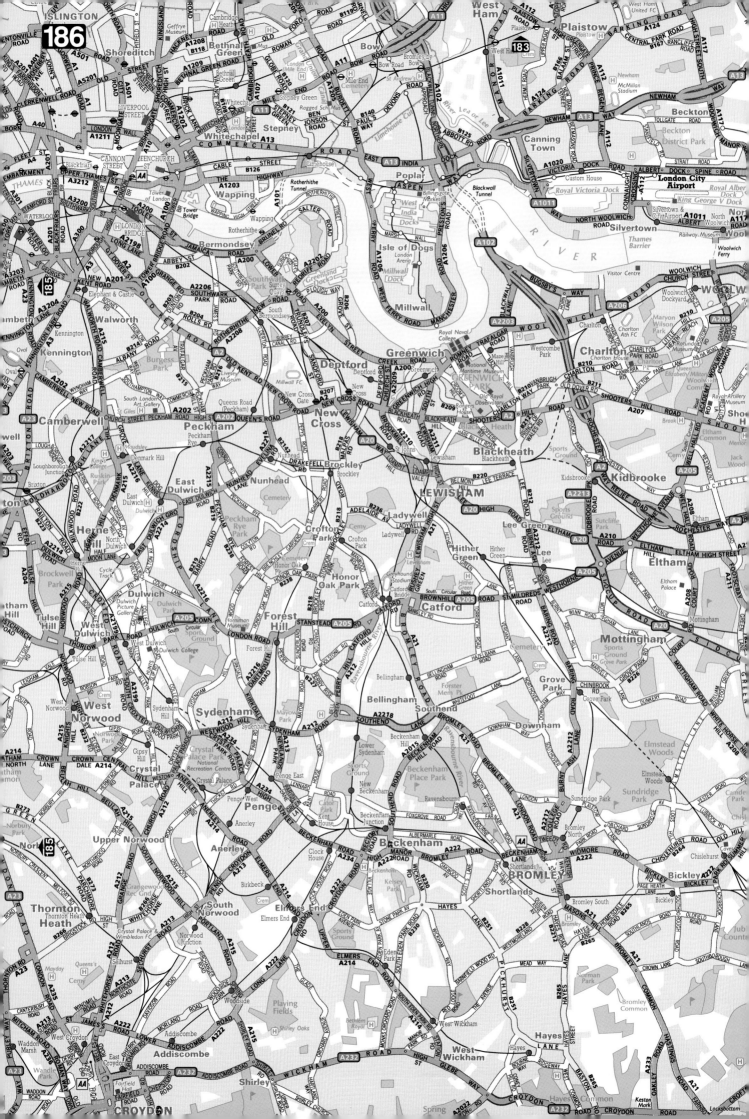

London Theatres, Cinemas and Concert Halls

THEATRES AND CONCERT HALLS

1 **Adelphi,** The Strand, WC2. Tel: 071-836 7611
2 **Albery,** St Martin's Lane, WC2. Tel: 071-867 1115
3 **Aldwych,** Aldwych, WC2. Tel: 071-836 6404
4 **Ambassadors,** West Street, WC2. Tel: 071-836 6111
5 **Apollo,** Shaftesbury Avenue, W1. Tel: 071-437 2663
6 **Apollo,** (Victoria), Wilton Road, SW1. Tel: 071-828 8665 (Not on plan)
7 **Arts** (Club)/Unicorn, Gt Newport Street WC2. Tel: 071-836 2132
8 **Barbican Centre,** Silk Street, EC2. Tel: 071-638 8891 (Not on plan)
9 **Bloomsbury,** Gordon Street, WC1. Tel: 071-387 9629 (Not on plan)
10 **Cambridge** Earlham Street, WC2. Tel: 071-379 5299
11 **Coliseum,** St Martin's Lane, WC2. Tel: 071-836 3161
12 **Comedy,** Panton Street, SW1. Tel: 071-867 1045
   Dominion see cinemas
13 **Drill Hall,** Chenies Street, WC1. Tel: 071-631 1353 (on plan)
14 **Duchess,** Catherine Street, WC2. Tel: 071-836 8243
15 **Duke of York's,** St Martin's Lane, WC2. Tel: 071-836 5122
16 **Fortune,** Russell Street, WC2. Tel: 071-836 2238
17 **Garrick,** Charing Cross Rd, WC2. Tel: 071-379 6107
18 **Globe,** Shaftesbury Avenue, W1. Tel: 071-437 3667
19 **Her Majesty's,** Haymarket, SW1. Tel: 071-839 2244
   Institute of Contemporary Arts – see cinemas
20 **Jeanette Cochrane,** Theobalds Road, WC1. Tel: 071-242 7040

21 **Lyric,** Shaftesbury Avenue, W1. Tel: 071-437 3686
22 **Mermaid,** Puddle Dock, EC4. Tel: 071-410 0000 (Not on plan)
23 **Royal National Theatre** South Bank, SE1. Tel: 071-928 2252
24 **New London,** Parker Street, WC2. Tel: 071-405 0072
25 **Old Vic,** Waterloo Road, SE1. Tel: 071-928 7616
26 **Palace,** Shaftesbury Avenue, W1. Tel: 071-434 0909
27 **Palladium,** Argyll Street, W1. Tel: 071-494 5038
28 **Phoenix,** Charing Cross Road, WC2. Tel: 071-867 1044
29 **Piccadilly,** Denman Street, W1. Tel: 071-867 1118
30 **Playhouse,** Northumberland Avenue, WC2. Tel: 071-839 4401
31 **Players,** Villiers Street, WC2. Tel: 071-839 1134
32 **Prince Edward,** Old Compton Street, W1. Tel: 071-734 8951
33 **Prince of Wales,** Coventry Street, W1. Tel: 071-839 5972
34 **Queen Elizabeth Hall,** South Bank, SE1. Tel: 071-928 8800
35 **Queen's,** Shaftesbury Avenue, W1. Tel: 071-494 5040
36 **Royal Albert Hall,** Kensington Gore, SW7. Tel: 071-589 8212 (Not on plan)
37 **Royal Court,** Sloane Square, SW1. Tel: 071-730 1745 (Not on plan)
38 **Royal Festival Hall,** South Bank, SE1. Tel: 071-928 8800
39 **Royal Opera House,** Covent Garden, WC2. Tel: 071-240 1066
40 **Royalty,** Portugal Street, WC2. Tel: 071-831 0660
41 **St John's,** Smith Square, SW1. Tel: 071-222 1061 (Not on plan)
42 **St Martin's,** West Street, WC2. Tel: 071-836 1443
43 **Sadler's Wells,** Roseberry Avenue, EC1. Tel: 071-278 8916 (Not on plan)
44 **Savoy,** Strand, WC2. Tel: 071-836 8888

45 **Shaftesbury,** Shaftesbury Avenue, WC2. Tel: 071-379 5399
46 **Strand,** Aldwych, WC2. Tel: 071-240 0300
47 **Theatre Royal,** (Drury Lane) Catherine Street, WC2. Tel: 071-836 8108
48 **Theatre Royal,** Haymarket, SW1. Tel: 071-930 8800
49 **Vanburgh (RADA),** Malet Street, WC1. Tel: 071-580 7982 (Not on plan)
50 **Vaudeville,** Strand, WC2. Tel: 071-836 9987
51 **Victoria Palace,** Victoria Street, SW1. Tel: 071-834 1317 (Not on plan)
52 **Westminster,** Palace Street, SW1. Tel: 071-834 0283 (Not on plan)
53 **Whitehall,** Whitehall, SW1. Tel: 071-867 1119
54 **Wigmore Hall,** Wigmore Street, W1. Tel: 071-935 2141
55 **Wyndhams,** Charing Cross Rd, WC2. Tel: 071-867 1116
56 **Young Vic,** The Cut, SE1. Tel: 071-928 6363

CINEMAS

   Barbican Centre – see theatres
1 **Cannon (Baker Street),** Marylebone Road, NW1. Tel: 071-935 9772
2 **Cannon,** Haymarket, SW1. Tel: 071-839 1527
3 **Cannon,** Oxford Street, SW1 Tel: 071-636 0310
4 **Cannon,** Panton Street, SW1. Tel: 071-930 0631
5 **Cannon,** Piccadilly, W1. Tel: 071-437 3561
6 **Cannon Premiere,** Swiss Centre, Wardour Street, W1. Tel: 071-439 4470
7 **Cannon,** Shaftesbury Avenue, WC2. Tel: 071-836 6279
8 **Cannon,** Tottenham Court Road, W1. Tel: 071-636 6148
9 **Curzon (Mayfair),** Curzon Street, W1. Tel: 071-465 8865
10 **Curzon Phoenix,** Charing Cross Road, WC2. Tel: 071-240 9661

11 **Curzon, (West End),** Shaftesbury Avenue, WC2. Tel: 071-439 4805
12 **Dominion,** Tottenham Court Road, W1. Tel: 071-580 9562
13 **Empire,** Leicester Square, WC2. Tel: 071-437 1234
14 **Institute of Contemporary Arts,** Carlton House, Terrace, SW1. Tel: 071-930 3647
15 **Lumiere,** St Martin's Lane, WC2. Tel: 071-836 0691
16 **Metro,** Rupert Street, W1. Tel: 071-437 0757
17 **Minema,** Knightsbridge, SW7. Tel: 071-235 4225 (Not on plan)
18 **National Film Theatre,** South Bank, SE1. Tel: 071-928 3232
19 **Odeon,** Haymarket, SW1. Tel: 071-839 7697.
20 **Odeon,** Leicester Square, WC2. (Including **Odeon Mezzanine)** Tel: 071-930 6111
21 **Odeon,** Marble Arch, W2. Tel: 071-723 2011 (Not on plan)
22 **Odeon, West End,** Leicester Square, WC2. Tel: 071-930 5252
23 **Plaza,** Regent Street, W1. Tel: 071-200 0200
24 **Prince Charles,** Leicester Place, WC2. Tel: 071-437 8181
25 **Renoir,** Brunswick Square, WC1. Tel: 071-837 8402 (Not on plan)
26 **Screen on Baker Street,** Baker Street, W1. Tel: 071-935 2772
27 **Warner West End,** Cranbourne Street, WC2. Tel: 071-439 0791

NOTE: the telephone number against each entry is for the Box Office, although a recorded information service may be obtained in some instances. Venues are subject to temporary closure due to change of programme or refurbishment.

Key

Parking	
Cinema	
Theatre	
Underground	

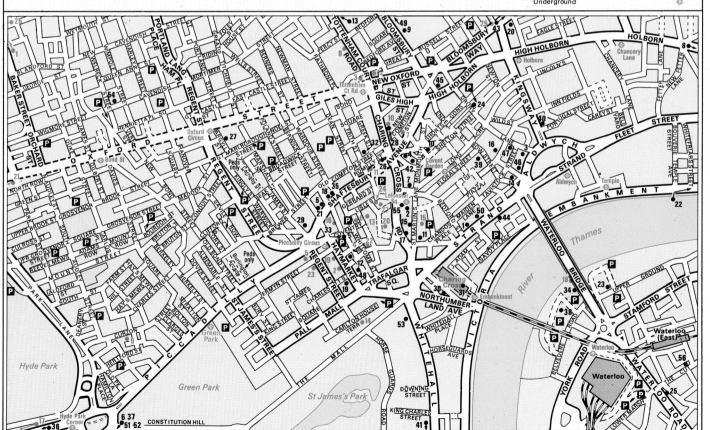

Index

◆ ◆ ◆

Acknowledgements

◆ ◆ ◆

The Automobile Association would like to thank the following photographers, libraries and associations for their assistance in the preparation of this book.

Allsport UK Ltd *162 London Marathon,* **163** *Wimbledon Men's Trophy (D Canron), FA Cup Final (S Bruty).*

Clive Barda Photography **165** *Last Night of the Proms.*

F Bolton and J Quinn **100** *Rubens'* Descent from the Cross.

British Dental Association **89** *Cartoon – Dentist.*

British Museum **94** *British Museum.*

Christie's Colour Library **12** *King's Cross Station.*

By courtesy of the Dean & Chapter of Westminster **44** *Rose Window & Poets' Corner,* **45** *Procession of Knights.*

Michael Holford **35** *Jeremy Bentham.*

Imperial War Museum **13** *Heinkel III.*

London Dungeon **122** *London Dungeon.*

Mary Evans Picture Library **27** *Earl of Burlington, Thomas Cubitt,* **33** *Rotherhithe Tunnel,* **111** *St Mary-le-Bow.*

William Morris Gallery **135** *The Woodpecker.*

Museum of London **8** *Silver Penny of King Alfred,* **9** *Rings,* **10** *London Plate,* **11** *Great Fire of London.*

National Gallery **59** *Seurat's* Bathers at Asnières.

Natural History Museum **79** *Natural History Museum.*

Postal Museum **106** *Stamps.*

Rex Features Ltd **19** *Royal Family.*

Ritz Hotel **166** *Tea at the Ritz.*

Doc Rowe **21** *Clowns,* **23** *Swan Upping, Pearly Kings & Queens,* **114** *Beating the Bounds.*

Simpsons **167** *Simpson's-in-the-Strand.*

Spectrum Colour Library **15** *Notting Hill Carnival,* **22** *Lord Mayor's Coach,* **84** *Kensington Palace,* **106** *Justice Scales Old Bailey,* **130** *Kew Gardens Palm House,* **131** *Kew Gardens Pagoda, Temperate House,* **164** *Haymarket Theatre.*

Tate Gallery **51** *Constable's* Flatford Mill, **51** *Dali's* Lobster Telephone.

The Bridgeman Art Library **12** *Regent St,* **17** *Henry VIII,* **24** *Westminster Bridge,* **33** *Thames Tunnel.*

The Corporation of London Records Office **10** *Charter of King John.*

The Mansell Collection **11** *Gin Lane,* **26** *Inigo Jones,* **27** *Christopher Wren, Sir J W Bazalgette,* **32** *Sewer Hunter,* **32/3** *Underground Mech. Railway.*

The Wallace Collection **89** *Frans Hals'* Laughing Cavalier.

World Pictures **6** *Horseguards,* **43** *Big Ben,* **169** *Tower of London.*

Zefa Picture Library UK Ltd **3** *Churchill Statue and Big Ben,* **54** *St James's Park Lake,* **90** *House Boats.*

All remaining photographs are held in the AA Photo Library with contributions from:

P Baker, R Day, D Forss, P Howard, S & O Mathews, B Smith, M Trelawny, R Victor, W Voysey, T Wiles, P Wilson, T Woodcock.